Advance Praise for

The Party of Death

"The power of this book is the force of its logic. Ramesh Ponnuru has given us the most significant statement on the need to protect human life in America since Ronald Reagan's *Abortion and the Conscience of a Nation*. Like Reagan, he is calling America to return to its best self. And there is reason to hope that the country is listening."

—PEGGY NOONAN

"Ramesh Ponnuru's book will be accepted almost immediately as the seminal statement on human life. *The Party of Death* is stunning as scholarship, ingenious in its construction, passionate—but never overbearing—in its convictions. It will be read for decades, and revered as the most complete and resourceful essay on great questions that divide America."

—WILLIAM F. BUCKLEY, JR.

"Ramesh Ponnuru was once, like Ronald Reagan, in favor of abortion. Then he watched its logic unfold, was slowly repulsed, and then went over into resistance. His book, *The Party of Death*, is an easily understandable account of the logic of death, from abortion to euthanasia and beyond. This book cries out for mass-market sales in the hundreds of thousands, as the tide turns."

—MICHAEL NOVAK

"Thorough, heart-breaking, infuriating—an indictment that is also a cry for action by the people who still believe that life is the ultimate value."

—BEN STEIN

The Party of Death

THE DEMOCRATS, THE MEDIA,
THE COURTS, AND THE
DISREGARD FOR HUMAN LIFE

Ramesh Ponnuru

Since 1947
REGNERY
PUBLISHING, INC.
An Eagle Publishing Company • Washington, DC

Cataloging-in-Publication data on file with the Library of Congress

ISBN 1-59698-004-4

Published in the United States by
Regnery Publishing, Inc.
One Massachusetts Avenue, NW
Washington, DC 20001

www.regnery.com

Distributed to the trade by
National Book Network
Lanham, MD 20706

Manufactured in the United States of America

10 9 8 7 6 5 4 3 2 1

For April, who makes everything better

Contents

Single Issues

THE PARTY OF DEATH started with abortion, but its sickle has gone from threatening the unborn, to the elderly, to the disabled; it has swept from the maternity ward to the cloning laboratory to a generalized disregard for "inconvenient" human life.

Legal abortion came to America because many Americans felt that in some cases it was the least bad response to tragedy. Only a small minority of Americans professed to have no qualms about abortion at all, to see it as no different from an appendectomy.

Many more people were persuaded that it was better for a woman to get a legal abortion than resort to the coat hanger. Advocates of legal abortion said that as many as one million illegal abortions were taking place every year, and five to ten thousand women were dying annually as a result.

Many people continue to support the legality of abortion for reasons like these. President Bill Clinton was politically astute in saying that abortion should be "safe, legal, and rare"—a slogan that pointed back to the back alley.

There was some self-deception in this resigned acceptance of abortion, and some plain old deception as well. American women weren't dying by the thousands in illegal abortions. And pro-abortion legislation seemed more modest than it was. In 1967, Ronald

Reagan, the new governor of California, reluctantly signed a law to allow "therapeutic abortions." Reagan soon discovered that some doctors were willing to call any abortion "therapeutic." A year later, he already regretted his decision.[1] The abortion license would not be confined to the hard cases.

Nor could the principles behind the license be confined to abortion. The Supreme Court ruled in 1973 that "emanations and penumbras" from the Constitution protected a right to abortion. The Constitution might not explicitly recognize the right, in other words, but it projected a shadow that protected abortion. Monstrous things can happen in the darkness. In time, it became clear that abortion had "emanations and penumbras" of its own in our law, politics, and culture.

In the late 1960s and early 1970s, abortion aroused misgivings more than it did organized opposition. Americans who put aside their misgivings about making some abortions legal never dreamt that they were weakening legal protections for all the unborn, or for the disabled, the elderly, the sick, and the depressed. Yet the logic of abortion, the dynamics of politics, and the habituation of the mind to yesterday's innovations have brought about these results.

The Democratic party has followed a more extreme version of the same trajectory America has. It reached its current state gradually, almost, it seems, accidentally. It did not make a conscious decision, some time in the late 1960s, to become the chief political vehicle for all those who think that the inviolability of human life is an outdated or oppressive concept. But it is today the party of abortion on demand and embryo-killing research, and is on its way to becoming the party of assisted suicide and euthanasia. And it is the party of those for whom abortion has become a kind of religion. (Gloria Steinem says that "reproductive freedom" is "a universal human right, at least as basic as freedom of speech or assembly."[2] At least?)

And we may not have reached the end of the line. Today, the country's leading newspaper considers the killing of sick infants—for their own good, you understand—a debatable proposition.

It is the linkage among these issues that makes it possible to speak of a "party of death." The phrase is meant to be descriptive, not (purely) pejorative. The party's core members are those who explicitly deny that all human beings are equal in having a right to life and who propose the creation of a category of "human non-persons" who can be treated as expendable. They are an influential minority in America, as in the developed world and the world generally. Their views can be defended with intelligence and sophistication, and are almost entirely coherent. The party of death has a vanguard, to borrow a term from another dismal chapter of the world's political history, made up of people who defend those views and all of their entailments—up to and including support for infanticide.

The party of death should not be confused with a conventional political party: It has members (and opponents) within both of America's major political parties, although it is much stronger today among Democrats than Republicans. The party of death has unwitting allies, too, just as it always has. Someone who reluctantly supports euthanasia to spare the dying from further suffering surely does not intend to advance a comprehensive agenda to undermine the protection of human life. Yet that is the effect, however modest, of her support.

We are sometimes told that polite conversation avoids the topics of sex, religion, and politics. Some would say that a book with this subject matter breaks all three rules. They might go on to worry that calling one side of the debate a "party of death" will raise the temperature still further.

We all have close friends and beloved relatives—I certainly do—who support legal abortion, or euthanasia, or both. Maybe we supported these things ourselves, once. I did. Maybe some readers still do. I hope that this book speaks to them with an honesty that does not seek to wound, but with a love that dares not refuse the truth. If the thought of belonging to a party of death disturbs them, perhaps they can be moved to leave it.

A note on terminology, which is a minefield when it comes to the issues this book considers. My own thinking about what words to use has evolved. For a long time, I resisted the labels "pro-life" and "pro-choice." "Pro-life" seemed less specific, and more propagandistic, than "anti-abortion." But as I came to see euthanasia and embryo-destructive research as assaults on the same principle that abortion violates, "pro-life" seemed as succinct a summary of my position as I could find. Pro-lifers, meanwhile, often object to the phrase "pro-choice" on the ground that many of the people who describe themselves that way in practice treat abortion as a public good (some of them, for example, want it subsidized). I have not attempted to impose a uniform style on the book in this respect. Usage varies by context, and I trust my readers will know what's what.

This book starts with *Roe* v. *Wade*—a decision that is more widely debated than it is understood—examining how it has corrupted the courts, politics, and even professional historians. It explores how *Roe* has given rise to a radical challenge to human rights (radical, because it denies the existence of human rights at their roots). It looks at new fronts in the party of death's war on human rights. And it concludes by looking at the evidence that Americans are turning away from the party of death.

Nobody could have predicted how *Roe* would play out in our history: how it would dominate Supreme Court confirmation hearings for decades to come, or how it would help reduce the Democrats to a minority party. The decision came down on January 22, 1973. The next day's *New York Times* carried a front-page story calling it "a historic resolution of a fiercely controversial issue."[3]

Part I

What *Roe* Wrought

CHAPTER 1

Overturning a Myth

I DO NOT OFTEN DREAM about Hillary Clinton. I did once, though, and I will try to clear away the haze and reconstruct it here.

She is at the podium, well into a campaign speech. The audience is more than sympathetic. NOW? The Democratic National Convention?

"Like so many of you in this room, I have been an advocate for women and children for years. And while we have more work to do, we should be proud of what we have accomplished. (Applause.)

"Because of our efforts, domestic violence is no longer hushed up, no longer seen as just a part of marriage. We treat it for what it is: a crime. We have raised awareness of rape, and made sure that the victims are no longer put on trial.

"You know, I'm old enough to remember when they called business a 'man's world.' Now almost everyone knows that a woman's place is in the boardroom. I know, we still have far to go. The pay gap has shrunk, but it hasn't disappeared. The lack of child care still keeps our society from realizing its full potential. And there are still some glass ceilings out there. I think we're going to break some of them soon! (Cheers, applause.)

"And we've fought for something else, too. No woman should ever find herself in jail because an unplanned pregnancy has left her desperate. We don't make criminals out of pregnant women in America. The Supreme Court guarantees that. If ideologues in the other party tries to change that, we will fight them every step of the way. ("HILL-A-RY! HILL-A-RY!")

"But that doesn't mean we're for abortion. Don't let anyone pretend that's what we stand for! Abortion is a tragic choice. We want to liberate women. Abortion is a sign that our society is pitting them against their children. (Scattered applause, murmurs.)

"We should all be able to agree that 1.3 million abortions a year is way too many, and we should work together to bring that number down. The most important thing we can do is to give women more options. We need to balance the federal budget. But let's do it by ending giveaways to big corporations that don't need the money— not by cutting programs that help women take care of their families.

"I'll admit that like many Americans, my thinking of this issue has changed over the years, and what I'm about to say may trouble some of my oldest friends and allies. I think maybe we've been so busy fighting the people who want to throw women in jail that we've somehow lost sight of the fact that abortion is a terrible act of violence against the young. If the law can discourage it—without, I want to repeat, making criminals out of women—then we ought to consider it. We ought to have laws that involve parents in their children's decisions, for example.

"I'm not saying that I have all the answers. I don't. But I think states ought to be able to try different approaches to protect women *and* children. And I think the Supreme Court ought to let them. Because America deserves better than abortion, and America deserves better than this fight we've been having for over a generation. And I'm willing to work with anyone, in either party, who wants to move past that fight."

The people in the audience had turned quiet by now, some in confusion, some in anger. People were looking at one another to see how to react.

Then I awoke. And I realized that if Hillary Clinton ever made that speech, she would be elected president of the United States.

○   ○   ○

Everything you think you know about Roe v. Wade is a lie.

Everyone "knows" that Roe legalized abortion in the first three months of pregnancy. Everyone knows, as well, that the Supreme Court's 1973 ruling was moderate and in line with public opinion, and that the public favors Roe to this day. And if anyone doesn't know, there is no shortage of reporters, legal commentators, and pollsters who will fill him in.

But saying that Roe v. Wade legalized abortion in the first three months of pregnancy is like saying that World War II pitted Germany against Britain: It's true in a narrow sense, but it's very far from being the whole story. The unvarnished truth is that the Supreme Court struck down the laws of all fifty states to mandate abortion-on-demand at any stage of pregnancy. No other country in the industrialized West imposes so few restrictions on abortion. Only a fraction of the American public supports such liberal abortion laws.

Roe held that states may not regulate abortion in the first trimester and may regulate it only in the interests of the mother's health in the second. Much of the confusion arises because Roe appears to allow state legislatures to ban abortion in the third trimester. But the Supreme Court took back this concession in the same breath it made it. Here is what Justice Harry Blackmun, writing for the Court in Roe, said about abortion late in pregnancy: "For the stage subsequent to viability, the State . . . may, if it chooses, regulate, and even proscribe, abortion *except where it is necessary, in appropriate medical judgment, for the preservation of the life or health of the mother*" (emphasis added).

Two sentences later, Blackmun referred to another case handed down the same day: *Doe v. Bolton*. Blackmun then said that the two opinions, both of which he wrote, "of course, are to be read together." In *Doe*, Blackmun wrote that "the medical judgment may be exercised in the light of all factors—physical, emotional, psychological, familial, and the woman's age—relevant to the well-being of the patient. All these factors may relate to health. This allows the attending physician the room he needs to make his best medical judgment. And it is room that operates for the benefit, not the disadvantage, of the pregnant woman."[1]

So: *Roe* required that any ban on late-term abortion include an exception allowing abortion to protect a woman's health; *Doe* defined that exception so broadly that it swallowed up any possibility of a ban. How could anyone ever be prosecuted for violating a ban on late-term abortions under this rule? The "attending physician"—in real life, very often an abortionist with a financial stake in the decision—can always say that in his medical judgment, the abortion was necessary to preserve the woman's emotional "health," especially considered in light of her "familial" situation. Any prosecution would have to be abandoned as unconstitutional. In other words: The Supreme Court has effectively forbidden any state from prohibiting abortion even in the final stages of pregnancy.[2]

Subsequent rulings by the Supreme Court have not altered this basic picture. The *Casey* decision, handed down in 1992, was widely described as a retreat from *Roe*. It allowed regulations of abortion so long as they do not impose an "undue burden" on the right to abortion. Applying that standard, the Court has allowed states to require parental notification before most minors can have abortions, and to require that women be informed about the facts of fetal development before having abortions. But the Court does not allow prohibitions on late-term abortions, even on types of abortion widely considered especially gruesome, unless they have broad health exceptions.

Large majorities of the American public oppose abortion after the first trimester. In January 2003, Gallup found that 68 percent of

Americans wanted abortion to be "generally illegal" in the second trimester. The figure for the third trimester was 84 percent.[3] Yet since *Roe* came down, almost nobody in America has been successfully prosecuted for performing a late-term abortion.[4]

The United States is alone among its peers in offering no legal protection to the unborn at any stage of development. The United Kingdom generally limits abortion to the first twenty-four weeks of pregnancy—and even then, generally requires two doctors to conclude that continued pregnancy would threaten the woman's mental or physical health. After that, abortion is permissible only in cases of fetal impairment, risks to the woman's life, or the risk of a grave, permanent injury to her health. In Sweden, the National Board of Health and Welfare has to sign off on abortions past the eighteenth week. After viability, it is allowed only in cases of severe fetal impairment or grave threats to the woman's health. In Denmark, a hospital committee must approve abortions past the twelfth week. France requires women seeking abortions within the first fourteen weeks to get counseling and observe a one-week waiting period. After fourteen weeks, two physicians have to determine that continued pregnancy poses a grave risk to a woman's health or that fetal impairment is very likely.[5] None of these countries has what pro-lifers would consider ideal abortion policies, but none of them is as extreme as what the Supreme Court has foisted on America.

The widespread notion that American states were moving toward liberal abortion laws and that *Roe* merely codified this trend is also a myth. Russell Hittinger has summarized the actual state of play in the years just before *Roe*:

In 1967, "reform" measures, usually concerning therapeutic exceptions, were turned aside in Arizona, Georgia, New York, Indiana, North Dakota, New Mexico, [and] Nebraska...In 1969, such bills failed to emerge from committee in Iowa and

Minnesota, and were defeated outright in Nevada and Illinois. In 1970, exceptions based on therapeutic reasons were defeated in Vermont and Massachusetts.

In 1971, on the eve of *Roe v. Wade*, repeal bills were voted down in Montana, New Mexico, Iowa, Minnesota, Maryland, Colorado, Massachusetts...Connecticut, Illinois, Maine, Ohio, and North Dakota. In 1972, even as *Roe* was under consideration by the Supreme Court, the Massachusetts House by a landslide vote of 178 to 46 passed a measure that would have bestowed the full legal rights of children on fetuses from the moment of conception. At the same time, the supreme courts of South Dakota and Missouri upheld their states' anti-abortion laws. It was surely telling that during the very month that Justice Blackmun finished the draft of his *Roe* opinion, 61 percent of the voters in Michigan and 77 percent in North Dakota by referenda voted down repeal.

To be sure, reformers and repealers won a few legislative victories prior to *Roe*. In 1967, Colorado liberalized its law. But it placed restrictions on abortion that were much more severe than anything permitted by post-*Roe* federal courts. Reform legislation also passed in North Carolina [1967], but with the rejection of mental health exceptions. California (1967), Georgia (1968), and South Carolina (1970) changed, but did not repeal, their abortion laws. The two most significant legislative victories for the repealers took place in 1970 in New York and Hawaii. These victories, however, were narrow and contentious, and did not approximate the percentages of pro-life victories in other states at the same time. At the time of *Roe*, there was evidence that the tide of opinion in New York had shifted back toward laws protecting the unborn.[6]

Hittinger may slightly overstate his case. He underplays how liberal California's "reformed" abortion law was in practice, and construes North Carolina's lack of an explicit mental-health exception as a rejection of that exception. But his account is much closer to the truth than the conventional narrative of inexorable liberalization. It is not at all clear that a majority of the public favored legal abortion even in the first months of pregnancy when *Roe* was handed down.[7]

In *Roe*, an old Texas statute against abortion was at issue. In *Doe*, the Court considered a recent, and considerably more liberal, Georgia law. The Court threw them both out and, in effect, threw out the abortion restrictions in place in every other state of the union.

The reasoning Justice Blackmun offered to justify this radical step was astonishingly flimsy. On its face, the Constitution says nothing to create a right to abortion. But the Constitution does protect aspects of privacy. The Fourth Amendment, for example, protects people's homes "against unreasonable searches and seizures." The Third Amendment restricts the government's ability to quarter troops in people's homes without their consent. In 1965, the Court decided that other types of privacy were protected by the "emanations and penumbras" of these specific privacy protections. It therefore struck down laws against contraception, even though the text of the Constitution says nothing about contraception, and even though it is inconceivable that the people who ratified the Constitution or its amendments meant to create a right to contraception (or to authorize the courts to create one later).

Blackmun, in *Roe*, decided that abortion was like contraception. The Fourteenth Amendment says that no state can "deprive any person of life, liberty, or property, without due process of law." On its face, the amendment appears to suggest that people cannot be fined, imprisoned, or executed except under validly enacted laws. But Blackmun ruled that abortion was part of "liberty" and, in effect, that it was such an important liberty that no restriction on it could represent "due process."

Even scholars who support legal abortion have admitted that Blackmun's work was shoddy. John Hart Ely, a prominent liberal legal scholar, was one of the earliest critics: "What is frightening about *Roe* is that this super-protected right [to abortion] is not

inferable from the language of the Constitution, the framers' thinking respecting the specific problem in issue, any general value deriv-
able from the provisions they included, or the nation's
governmental structure…At times the inferences the Court has
drawn from the values the Constitution marks for special protection
have been controversial, even shaky, but never before has its sense
of an obligation to draw one been so obviously lacking." "*Roe,*" he
wrote, "is bad because it is bad constitutional law, or rather because
it is not constitutional law and gives almost no sense of an obligation
to try to be."[8]

More recently, former Blackmun clerk Edward Lazarus has written that "[a]s a matter of constitutional interpretation and judicial
method, *Roe* borders on the indefensible…Justice Blackmun's
opinion provides essentially no reasoning in support of its holding.
And in the almost 30 years since *Roe*'s announcement, no one has
produced a convincing defense of *Roe* on its own terms. Instead…
the friends of *Roe* seek to find other constitutional bases to defend
its outcome."[9]

Coming up with those other constitutional bases for *Roe*'s holding has become something of a cottage industry within the legal
academy. It has been claimed that the Fourteenth Amendment's
guarantee of "equal protection of the laws" guarantees a right to
abortion. Or that the Thirteenth Amendment's prohibition on involuntary servitude does. Or the Ninth Amendment. It's in there somewhere! If nobody has advanced the theory that the Constitution's
strictures about letters of marque and reprisal are really about protecting abortion, it's only because the law reviews have not gotten
around to it yet.[10]

Another section of Blackmun's opinion has drawn less criticism,
but deserves plenty. Blackmun had analogized abortion to contraception. But of course the two cases differ profoundly in that the former involves the deliberate destruction of an existing human fetus.

After establishing to his satisfaction that the Constitution protects abortion, Blackmun turned to the unborn child. He pretended to leave unanswered "the difficult question of when life begins," although the sweeping right to abortion he declared plainly presupposed that it does not begin in the womb. Instead, he took up the question of whether the Fourteenth Amendment treats the fetus as a "person" deserving legal protection. He claimed that it does not. (Thus he ruled simultaneously that the Constitution is living, and the unborn child isn't.) It is not necessary to believe that the fetus *is* a "constitutional person" to think that Blackmun came nowhere near proving his point.

Blackmun made three arguments. Each attempted to show that the people who ratified the Fourteenth Amendment regarded the unborn as nonpersons. First, he noted that most of the Constitution's references to "persons" do not have "any possible pre-natal application." He mentioned the clause of the Constitution that commands states to extradite any "Person charged in any [other] State with Treason, Felony, or other Crime, who shall flee from Justice." Blackmun was right to say that this provision is not very likely to apply to fetuses. But it is unlikely to apply to infants or toddlers, either. Are they not persons? Blackmun's first example was the constitutional clause that stipulates that "No Person shall be a Representative who shall not have attained to the Age of twenty five Years..." So again, the Framers were not talking about fetuses. But they weren't talking about twenty-two-year-olds either. Are they not persons?

If the law wanted to recognize the personhood of the fetus, the chief way it could do so would be by protecting it from being killed. This brings us to Blackmun's second argument: that for much of the nineteenth century state laws did not prohibit abortions early in pregnancy. And it is true that measures to prohibit abortion at all stages of pregnancy had to await advances in scientific understanding that made it possible to know the facts of fetal development and to detect pregnancies early. But the laws were being tightened at the same time the country adopted the Fourteenth Amendment.

Third, Blackmun argued that some features of the anti-abortion laws were incompatible with a belief in the personhood of the unborn: notably, the exceptions they made for abortions to save a woman's life and their lack of penalties for the pregnant women. But it is plainly possible for a lawmaker to believe sincerely both that the unborn are persons who deserve protection and that abortion should be allowed to save the life of the mother. Lawmakers could also conclude that legal protection for unborn life could be accomplished without penalties for pregnant women—perhaps better accomplished. In at least five states, laws explicitly granted women immunity from prosecution in exchange for their testimony against abortionists or made their testimony inadmissible in court against her.[11]

In short: Evidence that the ratifiers of the Fourteenth Amendment considered the unborn to be "persons" worthy of protection under the law was literally staring Blackmun in the face. That evidence was the very laws he was overturning.[12]

Blackmun then reached his conclusion: "The decision vindicates the right of the physician to administer medical treatment according to his professional judgment... [T]he abortion decision in all its aspects is inherently, and primarily, a medical decision, and basic responsibility for it must rest with the physician." Note that this summary omits any mention of the woman seeking an abortion. Blackmun's focus was on the prerogatives of the medical profession, not feminism. Note also that Blackmun's premises once again assume the conclusion he is supposed to be trying to determine. Abortion is a "medical" procedure only if the fetus represents an illness or injury.

The press got the story on *Roe* wrong from the very beginning. The day after the ruling, the *New York Times* ran a front-page story reporting, "The Supreme Court overruled today all state laws that prohibit or restrict a woman's right to obtain an abortion during her first three months of pregnancy. The vote was 7–2 . . . [T]he Court drafted a new set of national guidelines that will result in broadly liberalized abortion laws in 46 states but will not abolish restrictions altogether." A *Times* editorial a day later said that the Court had recognized "a woman's right to obtain an abortion in the first three months of pregnancy . . . The majority opinion by Justice Blackmun stops short of the absolutist view that a woman is entitled to terminate her pregnancy whenever, however, and why ever she alone chooses."[13] (The *Times* was echoing the spin Chief Justice Warren Burger put in his concurring opinion: "Plainly, the Court today rejects any claim that the Constitution requires abortion on demand.")

The *Times*, the *Washington Post*, and the Associated Press have all had to correct the record occasionally. In 1982, Douglas Johnson, legislative director of the National Right to Life Committee, got the *Times* to declare that it would avoid using "the phrase 'in the first three months of pregnancy'" in connection with *Roe* because it "might be incorrectly interpreted to mean that abortions in the last six months of pregnancy remain illegal."[14] In 1996, David Brown wrote in the *Post* that "[c]ontrary to a widely held public impression, third-trimester abortion is not outlawed in the United States." Because of *Doe*'s definition of health, "life-threatening conditions need not exist in order for a woman to get a third-trimester abortion."[15]

Yet the mythology of *Roe* has proven impossible to kill. Notwithstanding Brown's article, the *Post* reverted to the first-trimester story in an article on *Roe*'s thirtieth anniversary[16] and in two articles a year later.[17] (To its credit, it ran corrections.) When the Republican governor of Massachusetts complained that the courts had not allowed states to make their own abortion policies, the *Boston Globe*

erroneously lectured him: "*Roe* v. *Wade*, the 1973 decision legalizing abortion, does not leave the states without say. Under *Roe*, states
may, and do, regulate abortion after the first trimester so long as the
life or health of the mother is not endangered."[18] Even more misleadingly, the same newspaper has reported that "the Supreme
Court ruled in *Roe* v. *Wade* that states could not restrict the right of
a woman to abort a fetus in the first trimester of pregnancy."[19] The
Atlanta Journal-Constitution, editorializing about George W. Bush's
alleged deception on abortion, referred to "the U.S. Supreme Court
decision legalizing early-term abortions."[20]

Very smart and otherwise well-informed people repeat this story.
Gregg Easterbrook is a well-respected journalist. Yet in October
2003, he wrote the following under the heading "What *Roe* Really
Said": "The key point is that *Roe* v. *Wade* itself considered third-
term abortions wrong . . . [B]anning most third-term abortions would
return the country to the original premise of *Roe*—one in which
women's choice is unrestricted in the first term, somewhat regulated
in the second term and proscribed in the third."[21]

By now, even conservatives who are skeptical of *Roe* have bought
the myth. Peter Berkowitz has been published widely in the conservative press, including *Policy Review*, a journal run by the conservative Hoover Institute. He writes:

> Public opinion appears to have stabilized in solid majorities not
> widely divergent from the principles articulated in the Court's key
> decisions. Early on in a pregnancy, the morally fraught choice
> whether to terminate her pregnancy is best left to the woman. Sub-
> sequently, as pregnancy advances, the choice is increasingly a mat-
> ter for state regulation in order to protect the life of the fetus or
> unborn child. Late in the pregnancy, in the interest of protecting
> developing human life, states may prohibit abortion.[22]

Occasionally the storyline is made a bit more sophisticated (and accurate), but still left very misleading. On *Roe's* thirtieth anniversary, *Chicago Tribune* reporter Leslie Goldman described its holding about each trimester accurately. But by omitting any reference to the broad definition of health, she left readers with the mistaken impression that the trimester scheme is important.[23] The Court itself had already said (in the 1992 *Casey* decision) that "[w]e reject the trimester framework, which we do not consider to be part of the essential holding of *Roe*." Describing *Roe* in his autobiography, former president Bill Clinton also leaves the health "exception" unexplained.[24]

Polls routinely find widespread public support for *Roe* v. *Wade* and opposition to its being overturned. The mistaken view of *Roe* as more limited than it actually is surely swells this support. So does the mistaken view, also spread by the media, that overturning *Roe* would criminalize all abortions.[25] The *New York Times*, editorializing against the Supreme Court nomination of Samuel Alito, said that he "might well" "vote to make abortion illegal."[26] Even if Alito joined four or more other justices to overturn *Roe*, however, it would be up to legislatures to set abortion policy; if the public did not want a ban, it would not get one.

Quite often pollsters compound the problem by themselves providing misinformation to the public. Before asking respondents what they think of *Roe*, an NBC News/*Wall Street Journal* poll taken in July 2005 gave them this bit of background information: "The Supreme Court's 1973 *Roe* versus *Wade* decision established a woman's constitutional right to an abortion, at least in the first three months of pregnancy." A survey by the Pew Research Center for the People & the Press, taken the month earlier, used the same language. Gallup uses the same language, too. FOX News's poll question has asked about "the Supreme Court decision called *Roe* v. *Wade* which made abortion in the first three months of pregnancy legal." The Associated Press, ABC News, the *Washington Post*, and CNN have all misdescribed *Roe* in their poll questions, too. A Harris poll in early 2006 asked whether voters would favor Alito's confirmation if they thought he "would vote to make abortions illegal."

When news organizations ask Americans what they think about this *Roe*-of-the-first-three-months, they are eliciting opinions about a judicial decision that does not exist. When they report on the results, they are compounding one falsehood with another.

The party of death has built a dual fortification around *Roe*. When legal scholars point out that it has no basis in the Constitution, *Roe*'s supporters say that it doesn't matter because the public has, supposedly, ratified *Roe* by agreeing with it. When pro-life activists demonstrate that the public opinion actually favors many restrictions on abortion, they are trumped by the majesty of the law. Constant deceit and misdirection are necessary to keep the defenses in working order.

Roe should be overturned as an offense against the Constitution, justice, and democracy. But before *Roe* can be overturned, it will be necessary to overturn the mythical version of the decision.

CHAPTER 2

Realignment

"I WAS BORN OUT of wedlock (and against the advice that my mother received from her doctor) and therefore abortion is a personal issue for me," wrote the minister. He went on to compare abortion to slavery. "If one accepts the position that life is private, and therefore you have the right to do with it as you please, one must also accept the conclusion of that logic. That was the premise of slavery. You could not protest the existence or treatment of slaves on the plantation because that was private and therefore outside of your right to be concerned." He asked, "What happens to the mind of a person, and the moral fabric of a nation, that accepts the aborting of the life of a baby without a pang of conscience?"[1]

Those words were written in 1977. Eleven years later, their author, the Reverend Jesse Jackson, was running for the Democratic nomination for president—and speaking very differently. "Women must have freedom of choice over what to do over their bodies," said the candidate.[2]

Jackson was part of a Democratic field that unimpressed pundits had labeled "the seven dwarfs." He wasn't the only former pro-lifer in the pack. Five of the dwarves had, earlier in their careers, opposed abortion. Delaware senator Joe Biden had voted to amend the

Constitution to reverse *Roe*. Illinois senator Paul Simon, the liberal lion, had been pro-life, too. In 1981, he introduced a resolution expressing the sense of the Congress that the states could generally ban abortion. In 1987 he answered yes when a pro-life group asked if he would "support the appointment of judges who will respect the sanctity of innocent human life."[3]

Missouri congressman Dick Gephardt, who would later become the leader of the House Democrats, had co-sponsored a constitutional amendment to ban abortion when he entered Congress in 1977. He called *Roe* "unjust." He switched positions in 1986, in preparation for his presidential run. In 2003, while preparing to run for president again, he addressed the issue in a speech to the annual dinner of the National Abortion and Reproductive Rights Action League. He blamed his pro-life past on the misfortune of having been "raised in a working class family of Baptist faith."[4]

Tennessee senator Al Gore voted with pro-lifers many times when he was in the House. He voted for an amendment to the Civil Rights Act of 1984 that would have protected "unborn children from the moment of conception." After Gore switched his position, he generally took the advice proffered by an aide: "deny, deny, deny" having ever been pro-life.[5]

Several of the Democrats' 1992 hopefuls had the same problem. As governor of Arkansas, Bill Clinton had written to the state's Right to Life organization in 1986: "I am opposed to abortion and to government funding of abortions."[6] Bob Kerrey, a Nebraska senator who ran against him, had also been pro-life.[7]

Even Ted Kennedy was once pro-life. He wrote to a constituent in 1971: "While the deep concern of a woman bearing an unwanted child merits consideration and sympathy, it is my personal feeling that the legalization of abortion on demand is not in accordance with the value which our civilization places on human life... When history looks back to this era it should recognize this generation as one which cared about human beings enough to halt the practice of war, to provide a decent living for every family and to fulfill its responsibility to its children from the very moment of conception."[8]

Richard Durbin of Illinois, who has the second-highest job in the leadership of the Senate Democrats, was one of the first voices to insist that John Roberts should not be confirmed to the Supreme Court unless he pledged his fealty to *Roe*. What Durbin was saying was that Roberts should be disqualified for the job if he took the exact same position that Durbin took in the 1980s. In a 1982 primary, Durbin boasted that he had served as master of ceremonies for annual pro-life rallies in Springfield, the state capitol, five times. He voted for constitutional amendments to overturn *Roe* and continued to express the wish that it be overturned as late as 1989. Six years later, he had done a complete 180, voting to keep even partial-birth abortion legal.[9]

The Democratic party, in short, was once home to quite a few pro-lifers. It was the party of Ed Muskie, Hubert Humphrey, and Tom Eagleton—all pro-life Democrats who had made it very near the top of American politics.[10] It was the party of the little guy. Yet somehow it turned its back on the littlest guy of all.

The shift appears to have been driven by Democratic elites, not rank-and-file Democratic voters. The party's nomination of George McGovern in 1972 represented the triumph of social liberals,[11] and of new forms of activism that displaced older party structures that arguably represented the voters better. These social liberals were much less likely than Democratic voters, or voters in general, to belong to a church. They tended to see legalized abortion as a step toward women's equality in the workplace and toward population control. (It is difficult for people today to comprehend how large a concern domestic population control was in the late 1960s and 1970s.)

McGovern himself was not very pro-abortion: He thought that states should set abortion policy, and he prevented the convention from adding a pro-abortion plank to the party platform.[12] As the years passed, however, the changes set in motion at that convention would transform both parties.

The new Democratic party would push some socially conservative Democrats into the Republican party. It would also cause some groups not previously engaged in American politics, such as evangelical and fundamentalist Christians, to become active Republicans. (It's instructive to note that two of the leaders of the National Right to Life Committee, Darla St. Martin and David O'Steen, began their careers active in the same Minnesota Democratic Farmer-Labor Party to which Humphrey and Eugene McCarthy belonged.) Socially liberal Republicans, meanwhile, would start to vote for the Democrats. In the process, the demographic profiles of the parties changed: The Republicans became more working-class, the Democrats more affluent.

The process took some time. Abortion was a much less partisan issue in the 1976 presidential race than it is now. A survey in September of that year showed that Democrat Jimmy Carter was getting 47 percent of the votes of supporters of a constitutional amendment to ban abortion—and 45 percent of the votes of its opponents.[13] In 1980, as well, knowing where a voter stood on abortion did not make it easy to predict for whom he would vote.

Carter and Ronald Reagan were key figures in redefining the parties. Carter's presidency coincided with rising evangelical opposition to abortion. Many evangelicals had supported Carter as one of their own in 1976. By 1980, many of them had concluded that he didn't speak for them politically, and abortion was one of the reasons. Reagan, meanwhile, symbolized the alliance among pro-lifers, conservatives, and the Republican party. He powerfully branded each group with the others' causes.

By the late 1980s, Democratic politicians had for years been voting for abortion rights at much higher rates than Republicans—and
at increasing rates. The Democratic platform committed the party
to *Roe* and to taxpayer subsidies for abortion; the Republican platform endorsed a constitutional amendment to ban abortion. Yet
Democratic voters were still more pro-life than Republican voters.[14]

By 1992, Americans' views of abortion had become a better pre-
dictor of their behavior in the voting booth than their views on affir-
mative action, defense spending, or the recently concluded Gulf
War. The economic issues that once divided the parties had ceased
to organize the political passions of activists. Surveys of delegates to
the Democratic convention found that they were more hostile
to pro-life groups and to Christian fundamentalists than they were
to conservatives, big business, the rich, or Republicans. Republican
delegates were warmer to union leaders, liberals, and Democrats
than to feminists and pro-choice groups. Yet even at this point, 61
percent of the pro-life Democrats who remained were unaware that
their party disagreed with them.[15]

Since that time, abortion and related issues have continued to
drive voters from one party to the other. The parties have become
more and more clearly defined as a pro-choice party and a pro-life
party—and, at the same time, as ideologically liberal and conservative parties. Democratic political theorists William Galston and
Elaine Kamarck have called it "the great sorting out." Republican
presidential candidates used to get more liberal votes, and Democratic candidates more conservative votes, than they do today. Now
voters who consider themselves conservative vote for the party that
presents itself as conservative.[16]

One effect of this sorting out has been the creation of the famous
division in American politics between "red" (Republican) states and
"blue" (Democratic) states that characterized both the 2000 and
2004 elections. What made that visual depiction of the state-by-state

election results so striking was that the country's political divisions
fell along the same lines as its cultural ones. The culturally conservative states voted for the Republicans, while the culturally liberal
ones voted the other. The states in which people tend to raise large
families voted Republican, and the states in which people tend to
raise smaller families voted Democratic.

There are fewer regional divisions in American politics than
ever. Southern Democrats and Northern Democrats no longer
seem, as they once did, to belong to two different parties. But the
geography of partisanship has gotten more stark. Republican states
are more Republican, Democratic states more Democratic, and the
in-between states fewer. The blue voters in red states tend to be clus-
tered together, and vice versa. People move to neighborhoods that
share their values. When a society and politics are divided over values, it stands to reason that people with the same politics will tend
to move to the same neighborhoods.

It would oversimplify matters to the point of obvious falseness to
say that people move to be near people who share their views of
abortion, just as it would oversimplify to say that tens of millions
of people have decided to switch to the party that reflects their views
of abortion. But abortion has been the biggest of the cultural issues
that have realigned American politics, and it has been their symbol.
It has been a fault line in our politics, most of the work taking place
below the surface.

The great sorting out has benefited the Republican party. A little
over a third of the public considers itself conservative, and a little
over a fifth liberal. If the Republicans get the conservatives and the
Democrats the liberals, the Democrats also have to get two-thirds of
the moderate vote to win a national majority. To put it another way:
Every two conservatives have to recruit one moderate to join them in
the voting booth; every two liberals have to recruit three moderates.

But it wasn't clear at every stage of the process which side would
benefit. In the late 1970s and early 1980s, Republicans thought that

they could expand their party by appealing to pro-life Catholics and evangelicals. A decade later, Democrats thought that they could use their support for abortion rights to win over suburban women. The effect of this strategic behavior was to deepen each party's association with its side of the abortion debate. In the late 1980s, for example, the Democrats became more monolithically for abortion rights in order to win votes. But the Republicans had already brought so many pro-lifers into its fold that it could not safely ditch them in order to compete for pro-choice women.

Mario Cuomo, the three-term governor of New York, played an important role in the Democratic party's redefinition as a nearly wholly owned subsidiary of the party of death. Cuomo was and is widely admired for his alleged intellectual ability and seriousness; he has been called "probably the nation's most gifted philosopher-politician."[17] His 1984 speech at Notre Dame sought to provide a sophisticated philosophical basis for political figures to claim to be "personally opposed" to abortion but in favor of its legality and even taxpayer support for it. He was effective at making that position respectable, especially for the many Catholic Democratic figures caught between the demands of their church and those of their party. (The Democratic vice presidential candidate that year, Geraldine Ferraro, was a Catholic supporter of abortion rights and had drawn criticism from Catholic bishops as a result.)

The "personally opposed" stance had suffered from an obvious flaw: The only defensible basis for judging abortion immoral—the conviction that it is usually the unjust taking of human life—also seemed to be a reason to enact a general legal prohibition on it. "Personally opposed" seemed to be nothing more than an incantation designed to keep incontrovertible premises from leading to inconvenient conclusions. Cuomo did not really solve this problem, but threw up numerous smokescreens to obscure it.

He argued that the view that human life begins at conception is religious. Banning abortion would violate religious freedom—the same religious freedom that made it possible for Catholics "to reject abortion." Cuomo has maintained this position for twenty years.[18] The religious argument fails because it ignores the rational justifications for opposing abortion.[19] Cuomo's argument that abortion rights have to be affirmed in order to affirm the right not to have an abortion is, meanwhile, transparently silly. Cuomo himself would reject it in any other case. He would never accept the idea that to ban machine guns is to open the door to making ownership of machine guns mandatory. He would never accept the idea that a right to infanticide has to be tolerated in order to prevent mandatory infanticide.

Perhaps sensing the inadequacy of these arguments, Cuomo offered others. Widespread disagreement with the pro-life position would make it impossible to ban abortion or to enforce a ban once enacted—so the attempt to enact it was futile. To overturn *Roe* so that states could set abortion policy would create "a checkerboard of permissive and restrictive jurisdictions." Women seeking abortions would just cross state lines to get them and nothing would be accomplished. Cutting off Medicaid funding of abortions would discriminate against the poor and constitute interference with medical decisions. Finally, Cuomo argued that people who shared opposition to abortion could reach different prudential judgments about how to act on that opposition—and in his judgment, it would be more effective for pro-life citizens to support government programs that make it easier for pregnant women to have babies, and to set a good example by not having abortions themselves, than it would be to push for legal bans on abortion.

Cuomo did not consider the possibility that a legal system that proclaims abortion as a right, indeed a constitutional right, reduces the effectiveness with which anyone can teach that abortion is immoral in the same way that illegal homicides are immoral. Not all sins should be crimes, as Cuomo insisted. But this sin is a sin because it is the unjust taking of human life, which ought to be illegal. Of course it is true that a national ban on abortion cannot be obtained now (partly because of the opposition of people such as Cuomo). But it is not futile to pursue an incremental strategy that improves the law and the culture bit by bit. This would result in a "checkerboard" of laws, but it should work to reduce the abortion rate and would reduce the law's injustice.[20] And if Cuomo really opposed abortion in any sense, he should have viewed a funding cut-off not as discrimination *against* poor women but as discrimination *in favor* of their children.

Cuomo was right to say that pro-life statesmanship includes an element of prudential judgment in addition to moral conviction. Should pro-lifers try to change the make-up of the Supreme Court, or to enact a constitutional amendment? If the latter, should the amendment seek to prohibit abortion or to return the issue to the states? These are just two of the many questions on which equally committed pro-lifers can disagree.

But no real pro-lifer disagrees with the goal of legal protection for the unborn. Here it may be instructive to take up an example that Cuomo raised: that of slavery. Cuomo argued that American Catholic bishops before the Civil War declined to raise their voices against it. They believed it to be evil, but they made a "practical political judgment" that "their opinion would not change people's minds" and might make the already-embattled position of Catholics in Protestant America even more perilous. "They weren't hypocrites; they were realists...The decision they made...was a measured attempt to balance moral truths against political realities. Their decision reflected their sense of complexity, not their diffidence. As history reveals, Lincoln behaved with similar discretion."

It is a mark of the strength of contemporary liberalism's commitment to abortion that one of its leading lights should have been willing to support temporizing on slavery in order to defend it. It is a further mark that liberals did not reject, or even take notice of, Cuomo's argument about slavery.

Cuomo's parallel fails at every level. Lincoln never accepted the existence of a right to own slaves. He never accepted that *Dred Scott* should remain the law of the land, or even that its principles should be binding on any branch of government. His goal was not only to put slavery on a path to extinction in practice, but also to end it as a legal possibility. He did not propose government programs to lure slave traders out of their business as a substitute for either goal. And he accepted an obligation to do what he could, under the political circumstances of the day, to advance his goals. His parallel in the abortion debate is the pro-life incrementalist. Cuomo's parallel in the slavery debate is not the bishop who failed to speak out for the abolition of slavery and of laws allowing it. It is the man who *opposed* any move in that direction.

Cuomo has never displayed any recognition of the dual nature of the injustice of abortion. Laws allowing slavery would have been an injustice even if nobody had held slaves, just as laws allowing the killing of Swedish-Americans with impunity would be unjust even if nobody actually killed Swedes. Pro-lifers have a slogan—"every child welcomed in life and protected in law"—that reflects this duality.

Robert P. George, a philosopher and professor of political science at Princeton, has aptly commented on Cuomo's position:

> Of course, it is possible for a person wielding public power to use
> that power to establish or preserve a legal right to abortion and
> even to provide public money for it while at the same time not
> wanting or willing anyone to exercise that right. But this does not
> get Cuomo off the hook. For someone who acts to protect legal
> abortion necessarily wills that abortion's unborn victims be denied
> the elementary legal protections against deliberate homicide that
> one favors for oneself and those whom one considers to be worthy

of the law's protection. Thus one violates the most basic precept of normative social and political theory, the Golden Rule. One divides humanity into two classes: those whom one is willing to admit to the community of the commonly protected and those whom one wills to be excluded from it. By exposing members of the disfavored class to lethal violence, one deeply implicates oneself in the injustice of killing them—even if one sincerely hopes that no woman will act on her right to choose abortion. The goodness of what one *hopes* for does not redeem the evil of what one *wills*.[21]

Cuomo's arguments, however weak, proved tragically influential. In 1992, Bill Clinton was achieving great success with his own version of the "personally opposed" line: He said that he wanted abortion to be "safe, legal, and rare."

By then, the pro-choice takeover of the Democratic party was complete. Ann Richards, the governor of Texas, served as chairperson for the Democratic convention that year. On the first day of the convention, she began her opening remarks with one of the abortion-rights slogans of the era: "My name is Ann Richards. And I am pro-choice and I vote."

There were still, to be sure, some holdouts. Governor Robert Casey of Pennsylvania was one of them. He had been a successful and, by most definitions, fairly progressive governor of one of our largest states. But he was also a Catholic who agreed with his church on the injustice of abortion. He wanted to speak to the convention and make the case for returning to the party's tradition of defending the weak—just as Republican conventions allowed pro-choice members of their party to defend their positions.

Neither Richards nor the party's chairman (Ron Brown) ever responded to Casey's letter expressing his desire to speak at the convention. "Eventually," Governor Casey later wrote, "I received a

carbon copy of a letter—not even addressed to me—from the par-
liamentarian of the convention to the general counsel for the
Democratic National Committee, denying my request because it
was out of order. The kind of letter they might have sent Lyndon
LaRouche, had he asked to address the convention."[22]

Other Democrats handed out buttons on the convention floor
depicting Casey as the pope. Pro-choice Pennsylvania *Republicans*
who had opposed Casey's election were seated on the platform.
Casey and his family watched from faraway seats.

The spin from the convention—and since then—has been that
Casey was not allowed to speak because he had not endorsed Clinton, the party's presidential nominee. The spinners can't get their
stories straight. Democratic operative Paul Begala said in 1996: "I
love Bob Casey, but my understanding was that the dispute was not
about his right-to-life views, it was about the Clinton-Gore ticket."[23]
In 2004, Begala was more definitive. Now he was certain that Casey
had been silenced based on his non-endorsement rather than his
outspoken advocacy for life, because he had "helped make that decision."[24]

Casey, in response to this spin, noted that Kathleen Brown, the
treasurer of California, had not endorsed Clinton—her brother Jerry
had been a rival candidate in the primaries—yet was allowed to
speak.[25] She supports abortion.

Mario Cuomo, that sincere and thoughtful opponent of abortion, did not speak a word in Casey's defense. He did, however,
speak at the convention, nominating Clinton. Among his arguments
for Clinton: "We need a leader who will stop the Republican
attempt, through laws and through the courts, to tell us what god to
believe in, and how to apply that god's judgment to our school-
rooms, our bedrooms and our bodies."[26]

CHAPTER 3

Safe, Legal, and Subsidized: Democratic Extremism in Defense of Abortion

GENERAL WESLEY CLARK, toward the end of 2003, decided to try his hand at being a Democratic presidential candidate. He wasn't very good at it, as an interview with the *Manchester Union Leader* a few weeks before the New Hampshire primary revealed. Clark told publisher Joe McQuaid, "I don't think you should get the law involved in abortion." McQuaid asked, "At all?" "Nope…" "Late-term abortions? No limits?" "Nope." "Anything up to delivery?" "Nope, nope." "Anything up to the head coming out of the womb?" "I say that it's up to the woman and her doctor, her conscience… You don't put the law in there." Reporter John DiStaso cut in: "So, life begins at delivery?" "Life begins with the mother's decision."[1]

The reaction to Clark's remarks was sufficiently negative that his campaign felt compelled to backtrack. He said that he supports a woman's right to choose abortion before viability, and supports her right to choose abortion after viability if her "doctor" thinks it is necessary. He did not want to go into the question of when viability occurs, but then why should he have? It makes no practical difference. He wants a woman to be able to get an abortion at any stage of pregnancy so long as an abortionist says she should have it. The government should not, then, be able to prohibit any abortion at any stage of pregnancy.[2]

It's an extreme position, to be sure, and one few Americans support when it is put that way. But Clark's position was no more extreme than that of most of his rivals for the Democratic nomination. It was no more extreme, indeed, than the law of the land. *Roe* v. *Wade* and *Doe* v. *Bolton* established a policy of abortion on demand at any stage of pregnancy. Clark's mistake was to speak too bluntly.

Yet it is possible to take an even more extreme position. The Supreme Court, after all, has not required states or the federal government to fund abortion. Yet the Democratic party doesn't just support *Roe*; it also supports taxpayer funding. The party's 2004 platform stated: "Because we believe in the privacy and equality of women, we stand proudly for a woman's right to choose, consistent with *Roe* v. *Wade*, and *regardless of her ability to pay.*"[3]

The Freedom of Choice Act is an attempt to make good on that promise. It has been rattling around the halls of Congress for years, and has not had much chance of getting enacted since the Republicans took control in 1995. But feminists have kept the bill alive in order to remind people of what they stand for.

Typically, the Freedom of Choice Act has been marketed as a "codification of *Roe*."[4] The law would put Congress behind the same policy the Supreme Court imposed in *Roe*. If the Court ever reversed *Roe*, then, the congressional statute would still be there to keep anything from changing. By giving *Roe* some democratic legitimacy, the law might also make it harder for pro-lifers to generate political support to overturn it.

But FOCA goes beyond *Roe*. Senator Barbara Boxer of California, its lead sponsor, puts it this way: "The Freedom of Choice Act also supersedes any law, regulation or local ordinance that impinges on a woman's right to choose. That means a poor woman cannot be denied the use of Medicaid if she chooses to have an abortion." The federal government and state governments would be required, in other words, to fund abortions. The bill also nullifies states' "informed consent" laws, which the Supreme Court has upheld but which Boxer regards as mandatory "anti-choice propaganda."[5] FOCA would "strike down a host of federal and state restrictions," exults the National Organization for Women.[6]

The Freedom of Choice Act, however far away it is from most voters' preferences, is well within the mainstream of the Democratic party. Its Senate co-sponsors include Hillary Clinton, Ted Kennedy, and Joe Lieberman (who is widely considered to be one of the most conservative Democrats).

Senator Boxer has been a co-sponsor of versions of FOCA since she was in the House fifteen years ago. Her website does not exaggerate when it calls her "[t]he Senate's leading defender of a woman's right to choose [abortion]."[7]

The present incarnation of FOCA bears Boxer's distinctive imprint: a note of hysteria. The opening section of the bill contains "findings" that she wants Congress to ratify, including these: "Prior to the *Roe* v. *Wade* decision, an estimated 1,200,000 women each year were forced to resort to illegal abortions...According to one estimate, prior to 1973, as many as 5,000 women died each year in the United States as a result of having an illegal abortion."

Boxer loves to make these points. After Justice Sandra Day O'Connor announced her retirement, Boxer threatened to filibuster whomever Bush nominated to replace her: "It means a minimum of 5,000 women a year will die. So all options are on the table."[8] The 5,000 figure is now a floor, not a ceiling. She came back to the 1.2-million figure when Bush nominated John Roberts for the seat.[9]

The 5,000 "estimate" dates back to 1936. That's "prior to 1973," all right, but it's also prior to the widespread use of penicillin. The man who made the 1936 estimate "apologize[d]" for it six years later, saying that 5,000 deaths was an absolute upper bound on the number of maternal deaths from abortion.[10] In 2004, Cecil Adams, author of the myth-debunking "Straight Dope" column, corrected journalist Ellen Goodman after she made a claim similar to Boxer's. He wrote, "It's not like this is a news flash, either. A reasonable approximation of the annual total [of maternal deaths from abortion] in the 60s has been public knowledge for 35 years."[11]

The 1.2-million figure is based on highly dubious studies as well.[12] It doesn't make any sense. There were 899,000 abortions in 1974 and 1 million in 1975, after *Roe*. To believe Boxer, you would have to believe that more women had abortions when they were illegal than had them when they were legal—that the legalization of abortion caused abortion rates to *fall*. Large estimates of the number of illegal abortions are also very hard to square with the relatively low abortion rates reported by the states that had liberalized their laws before *Roe*. California, for example, reported only 5,000 legal abortions in 1968.[13]

Every link in Boxer's chain of causation was broken. No nominee to replace O'Connor could possibly have overturned *Roe*, since there wouldn't be enough other votes on the Supreme Court; overturning *Roe* wouldn't prohibit abortion; and prohibiting abortion couldn't bring back a dystopian past that never existed. Boxer's threat to filibuster Bush's nominee to the Supreme Court—before she even knew whom he would nominate—proved empty. John Roberts's qualifications were too impressive for her to get enough Democratic support to mount a filibuster. But consider what Boxer was saying: She was so worried that the nominee would allow citizens and legislators to vote on abortion policy that she was willing to keep senators from voting on him. *Roe* keeps trumping democracy.

Boxer wouldn't even allow nominees who were suspected of hostility to *Roe* to get confirmed as federal appeals-court judges. She torpedoed Bush's nomination of Carolyn Kuhl to one such court because Kuhl, while serving in the Reagan administration and the first Bush administration, had worked on legal briefs that reflected those administrations' opposition to *Roe*. Kuhl, said Boxer, was "far outside the mainstream."[14]

Even if Kuhl did want to strike down *Roe*, she couldn't have done it as an appeals-court judge. The lower federal courts are bound to abide by Supreme Court precedents. So the true objection to Kuhl was that if she were confirmed, it might give her a leg up to get on the Supreme Court some day—where she might vote to let abortion policy be settled democratically.

Like Kuhl, Bush's nominee Priscilla Owen received the highest rating that the American Bar Association bestows. She, too, pledged to follow *Roe* as an appeals-court judge. But as a justice on the Texas supreme court, Owen had ruled on a parental-notification law. The law allowed judges, in some circumstances, to rule that the parents not be informed. (There was no requirement that parents consent, as most states demand before a minor can get a tattoo, or buy a lottery ticket.[15]) Democrats, including Boxer, complained that Owen used this "judicial bypass" too sparingly. That was the central accusation against her, and the motive for all the others. More than 70 percent of the public favors parental-consent laws.[16] Yet Boxer seemed to want judges who would frequently bypass such laws.

Boxer explained that Owen's nomination was putting the senator's feminism to the test: "[A]s someone who worked so hard to support qualified minorities and women, I have been praised by many in my State for doing just that. But I have to tell you, if you place on the bench a minority or a woman who has animosity toward the goals of minorities and women, you are dealing a great setback to both minorities and women...[T]his nominee is so far from the center that she is almost off, to the right. She is barely on that line at all. That differs from the mainstream values of my constituents and I believe of the majority of Americans."[17] Democrats held up a vote on Owen's nomination for four years.

Given her pro-abortion extremism and tendency toward the dire, it is no surprise that Senator Boxer reacts strongly even to mild restrictions on abortion. When the Senate voted to ban partial-birth abortion, she asked, "Don't we love our wives? Don't we love our daughters? Don't we love our aunts? Don't we love the women in our lives?"[18]

You don't have to propose an actual restriction on abortion, however minor, to get this kind of reaction from Boxer. Republican congressman David Weldon learned this when he proposed a federal law to prevent doctors and insurers from being forced to participate in abortions—either by performing them, paying for them, or making referrals for them. Boxer said that the proposal, which became law, "treats women worse than criminals."[19] The right to choose apparently does not apply to those who wish to be able to choose not to be complicit in abortion.

Abortion wasn't even directly at issue in the Unborn Victims of Violence Act. That act was designed for cases such as that of Laci Peterson and her unborn child, whom she had named Conner. When Scott Peterson killed both of them, California law treated it as a double homicide. The Unborn Victims of Violence Act— renamed Laci and Conner's Law after Laci's mother Sharon Rocha came out in strong support of it—established that attacks on pregnant women that fell within federal jurisdiction recognized two victims, too.

Pro-life groups had a straightforward reason to support Laci and Conner's Law: Criminals who assault the unborn in the womb violate their right to life just as surely as abortionists do. But why should pro-choice groups have gotten involved? Like Laci, these women *wanted* their babies. (In some cases, that's why the fathers assaulted them.)

But the mothers' view of their babies didn't matter this time to pro-choice groups. Wesley Clark had said that life began when the mother wanted it. For the party of death, it didn't even begin then.

"NOW Urges Immediate Action to Prevent Devastating 'Unborn Victims of Violence Act' from Passing in Senate" was the headline of a February 2004 press release. NOW president Kim Gandy called it "a direct threat to *Roe* v. *Wade*."[20] While debating the bill on a radio show, Gloria Feldt, the president of Planned Parenthood, was asked three times whether the Peterson crime had one victim or two. Feldt evaded the question twice, then pointedly said that Laci was "the victim."[21]

Senator Boxer sang in tune. "They want to undermine *Roe* v. *Wade* and a woman's right to choose," she said of the bill's sponsors. "It shocks me. I'm just at a loss for words, and that's hard for me to be."[22]

Boxer and California's other Democratic senator, Dianne Feinstein, backed an alternative bill that increased penalties for attacks on pregnant women but refused to recognize two victims. Rocha said that she was "dismayed" by their stand.[23] She was joined by less famous women, such as Shiwona Pace, who lost her daughter a day before her due date when her ex-boyfriend hired three men to beat her. "Your baby is dying tonight!" yelled one of her attackers, displaying more moral clarity than some senators.[24]

o   o   o

Tracy Marciniak was five days away from giving birth to a son, whom she had named Zachariah, on February 8, 1992. A prenatal visit the day before had shown him to be healthy. But her estranged husband came to her apartment and attacked her that night. He held her down and punched her hard, twice, in the stomach. He refused to let her call 911 for help.

After he finally relented and let her go to the hospital, Zachariah was delivered by emergency C-section. He had already bled to death. Marciniak had to spend three weeks in the hospital herself.

Marciniak lived in Milwaukee, and at the time Wisconsin law did not recognize that anybody had died in the assault. While she is pro-choice, she has become a strong advocate of laws to treat unborn children as victims of this type of crimes. Wisconsin Right to Life, she says, was the only group that would help her. Together, they helped get the state to change its laws. She testified to Congress, too, during the debate over the Unborn Victims of Violence Act.

She said at that time that she couldn't understand why pro-choice groups and lawmakers have fought her. "My son was five days from full-term, and for them to tell me my son was nothing, it's just wrong. Where were my child's rights when he was ripped from my womb and killed, and I was told he was nothing?"[25]

o   o   o

Pro-lifers may have hoped that Laci and Conner's Law would lead people to reflect on whether abortion is compatible, as a matter of logic, with the personhood of the unborn. But to say that the law was a "direct threat" to *Roe* was a stretch. Most states recognize that the unborn can be victims of crime. California is one of them, and abortion remains legal there. The Supreme Court has never ruled that states can't recognize fetal personhood in contexts other than abortion, or suggested that such recognition conflicts with *Roe*.

Boxer's pro-abortion extremism was too much for some congressional Democrats. About one-fourth of the Democrats in the House and the Senate voted for Laci's law in 2004. But three-fourths of the Democrats—including John Kerry and John Edwards, the party's presidential and vice-presidential candidates, and Hillary Clinton, its likely presidential nominee in 2008—stayed in lockstep with the abortion lobby.

When President Bush decided to use a health program for children to help pregnant women get coverage for their unborn children, the party of death had a similar, if more muted, reaction. Kate Michelman, then the leader of NARAL, the leading pro-choice group, said, "It is a legal pathway to making all abortions under all circumstances a crime."[26] Offering help to women who want their babies turned out, in the topsy-turvy world of the abortion lobby, to be "anti-choice."

Advocates of legal abortion, including most Democrats, also seek to subsidize the spread of abortion overseas. Pro-life administrations have stipulated that no international family-planning funds will go to organizations that perform abortions or advocate the legalization of abortion overseas. Pro-choice groups have protested bitterly. In December 2005, Democrats even held up a bill to combat the sexual trafficking of women and children in order to get the funds flowing to pro-abortion groups.

At home, Planned Parenthood's devotion to "privacy" has repeatedly hindered investigations into the rape (including the violent rape) of very young girls. In an Ohio case, for example, a twenty-one-year-old man drove the thirteen-year-old he had impregnated to a clinic for an abortion. The clinic made no attempt to notify the girl's parents and obtain their consent, as state law requires, and thus helped the man to evade the law. The state of Indiana suspects that Planned Parenthood has not complied with its legal duty to tell authorities about evidence of molestation. When the state sought medical records from the group as part of its investigation, Planned Parenthood sued to prevent disclosure—even though the state attorney general pointed out that such investigations had not resulted in any breach of confidentiality in decades. (Planned Parenthood lost.) A similar legal fight has taken place in Kansas. The Boxer Democrats have been silent about the abortion industry's stonewalling.[27]

To summarize the position of the Boxer Democrats, then: Abortion should be legal throughout pregnancy. Teenage girls should not have to inform their parents about it, much less get their consent. Nobody who would let the voters deviate from these positions should be allowed on a court. The Senate shouldn't even be allowed to hold a vote on such people. The law should not treat the murders of pregnant women as double homicides because it might lead people to look more negatively at abortion.

And taxpayers should pay for abortions, just in case there are some going undone. But federal funds should not be allotted to ensure the health of the unborn. Each of these positions is extreme by the standards of public opinion—but not by the standards of what the Democratic party has become.

Its radicalism would begin to come into the public's view only in 1995, when the Republicans took control of Congress and raised the issue of partial-birth abortion. That debate would make it clear that many Democrats didn't just support abortion at any point until birth: they supported it during birth, too.

CHAPTER 4

"Too Close to Infanticide"

"I think this is just too close to infanticide... [W]hat on earth is this procedure?" exclaimed Senator Daniel Patrick Moynihan.[1] The New York Democrat generally voted with his party, but this time he couldn't.

The "procedure" he was discussing had come to the attention of pro-life activists in 1992. Martin Haskell, an abortionist who owned clinics in Ohio, gave a presentation at a meeting of the National Abortion Federation on a method of abortion that he called "*Dilation and Extraction, or D&X.*"[2] He was using it "routinely" for abortions at twenty to twenty-four weeks, and sometimes through twenty-six weeks.

In a D&X, Haskell explained, the abortionist uses forceps and his fingers to pull the fetus feet-first from the uterus. Only the head of the fetus remains inside. "[T]he surgeon then forces [a pair of blunt curved Metzenbaum] scissors into the base of the skull... Having safely entered the skull, he spreads the scissors to enlarge the opening. The surgeon removes the scissors and introduces a suction catheter into this hole and evacuates the skull contents. With the catheter still in place, he applies traction to the fetus, removing it completely from the patient."

For Haskell, partial-birth abortion was superior to another possible method of abortion: Dilation and Evacuation, or D&E, which involves taking a fetus apart inside the womb and then removing the parts. The problem with D&E was that "most surgeons find dismemberment at twenty weeks and beyond to be difficult due to the toughness of fetal tissue at this stage of development." Another abortionist who used the same procedure as Haskell called it an "Intact Dilation and Evacuation," or "Intact D&E."

Pro-lifers found out about the presentation. Since D&X involved the partial delivery of the fetus, they quickly dubbed it "partial-birth abortion." In the summer of 1995, Florida Republican congressman Charles Canady introduced legislation to ban it. In a Democratic Congress, the bill would have gone nowhere. But the previous November, Republicans had won control of the House for the first time in forty years.

Kate Michelman was the head of NARAL, the abortion lobby, at the time. The group's vice president, James Wagoner, brought a copy of a congressional letter on the subject to her. "I remember sitting in my office," Michelman recalled years later, "and James saying to me: 'Kate. This is a disaster.'"[3]

For years, Michelman and company had been highly successful at putting a spotlight on the issues that divided pro-lifers from the public. Most pro-life activists wanted to ban abortion even in the cases of rape and incest; the public strongly disagreed. Most pro-lifers wanted to amend the Constitution to ban abortion; the public saw that as a radical step.

The partial-birth issue turned the tables on pro-choicers, putting their own extremism at the center of the debate. A ban on abortion in the case of rape was a theoretical possibility, if *Roe* fell and public opinion turned around. Partial-birth abortion was happening now. By attacking it, pro-lifers demonstrated how much *Roe* allowed, and how far pro-choicers would go. They brought attention to a horrifying reality that overwhelmed the abstraction of "choice."

It didn't take long for NARAL and its allies to devise responses. Partial-birth abortion, they said, was a propagandistic rather than a medical term. To this day, even some fair-minded observers echo this charge. Journalist William Saletan says that "the procedure in question is an abortion that sort of looks like a birth, not a birth interrupted by an abortion." It "doesn't take place anywhere near the appointed hour of birth," but rather around weeks twenty through twenty-four.[4] Yet a birth does not have to take place at an "appointed hour" to be a birth: Premature babies can be and are born late in the second trimester. Since the procedure involves a partial delivery, "partial birth" is as accurate as a succinct, easily comprehended label can be. The abortion lobby has preferred to speak of D&X or Intact D&E because these terms convey no information to most people.

The defenders' next point was that while the procedure may be grisly, so are all operations. Barbara Radford of the National Abortion Federation wrote: "Much of the negative reaction…is the same reaction that might be invoked if one were to listen to a surgeon describing step-by-step almost any other surgical procedure involving blood, human tissue, etc."[5] Well, sure: if that surgery involved puncturing someone's skull and then sucking out his brains.

These defenses didn't work too well, so more stress was placed on the notion that partial-birth abortions were done rarely and only for medical reasons. Planned Parenthood explained, "The procedure, dilation and extraction (D&X), is extremely rare and done only in cases when the woman's life is in danger or in cases of extreme fetal abnormality."[6] There were only five hundred to six hundred such cases a year.[7] Moreover, NARAL and Planned Parenthood claimed, the fetus felt no pain, since anesthesia given to the mother had already killed it.[8]

The press bought it. The *Los Angeles Times* reported that there were only two hundred such abortions a year. "Typically, it is used in late pregnancies to save a mother's life or after the detection of severe fetal abnormalities."[9] The *New York Times* also echoed the abortion lobby's talking points.[10] *USA Today*, the *New York Daily News*, and syndicated columnist Ellen Goodman all repeated the claim that anesthesia killed the fetus before the scissors made contact.[11]

Congressmen, mostly Democrats, repeated these lines. Congresswoman Sheila Jackson Lee and Senator Carol Moseley Braun said that anaesthesia killed the fetuses during floor debate over Canady's bill.[12] Barbara Boxer told *Nightline* viewers that partial-birth abortion was "an emergency medical procedure": "Is this going to be a country which outlaws a medical procedure that is used to save a woman's life? Are we going to put women to their deaths?"[13]

This defense failed to overcome congressional revulsion at the procedure. In November 1995, the House voted 288–139 to ban partial-birth abortion; while 123 Democrats voted against the ban, seventy-three defected from their party's position. A few weeks later the Senate also voted 54–44 for the ban, with nine Democrats crossing over.

But the worst was yet to come. In the following months, the defense of partial-birth abortion unraveled.

The claim about anaesthesia went first. Haskell had said in a 1993 interview that the fetus was not dead before the D&X began.[14] In March 1996, Dr. Norig Ellison, the president of the American Society of Anesthesiologists, testified before the House that the claim that anesthesia killed the fetus was "entirely inaccurate" and dangerous to spread, since it could cause mothers to turn down anesthesia to protect their unborn children.[15] (Dr. Ellison had made these points before, without receiving attention.) At this point, anesthesia dropped out of the debate.

Bill Clinton still had the other talking points to lean on. In April 1996, he vetoed the ban. He had explained his opposition earlier:

[T]here are a few hundred women every year who have personally agonizing situations where their children are...about to be born with terrible deformities which will cause them to die either just before, during, or just after childbirth. And these women, among other things, cannot preserve the ability to have further children unless the enormous size of the baby's head is reduced before being extracted from their bodies...I believe that people put in that situation ought not to have Congress tell them that they're never going to be able to have children again. Now, I know there are just a few hundred of them, and I know that all the votes were on the other side...But one of the things the President is supposed to do is to look out for the few hundred against the many millions when the facts are not consistent with the rhetoric. And I'm just telling you, you know, Hillary and I only—we only had one child. And I just cannot look at a woman who's in a situation where the baby she is bearing against all her wishes and prayers is going to die anyway and tell her that I am signing a law which will prevent her from ever having another child. I'm not going to do it.[16]

In September 1996, Ruth Padawer, a reporter for the Bergen County, New Jersey, *Record*, disclosed that a local clinic performed 1,500 partial-birth abortions per year—more than the abortion lobby and much of the media had claimed took place nationwide.[17] Within days, David Brown and Barbara Vobejda reported in the *Washington Post* that it was "possible—and maybe even likely—that the majority of these abortions are performed on normal fetuses."[18]

Their finding tracked with Haskell's remark that 80 percent of the partial-birth abortions he performed were "purely elective."[19]

Five months later, a bigger bombshell: Ron Fitzsimmons, executive director of the National Coalition of Abortion Providers, told *American Medical News* and the *New York Times* that he had "lied through [his] teeth" about partial-birth abortion. When *Nightline* interviewed him in November 1995, he had followed the party line: Partial-birth abortions were rare and performed only in extreme cases. In truth, he said, the vast majority were performed on healthy mothers with healthy babies. "The abortion rights folks know it, the anti-abortion folks know it, and so, probably, does everyone else."[20] He estimated that three to five thousand were performed each year.[21]

The Alan Guttmacher Institute, Planned Parenthood's research arm, maintained that there were "about 650" partial-birth abortions in 1996, or at any rate that the number fell between five hundred and one thousand.[22] It stuck to that line for several years. Later, it issued a new figure: There had been 2,200 partial-birth abortions in 2000. Either the number had tripled in four years, or one or both estimates were flawed. Since clinics' participation in the institute's survey is voluntary, both numbers are probably underestimates.[23]

Assume, however, that there are 2,200 partial-birth abortions annually. Is this a big number? Its defenders point out, accurately, that it is a small fraction of the total number of abortions each year in America. Yet it is also true that "[i]f a new virus [were] killing 2,200 premature babies annually in neonatal units, it would be on the TV evening news every week."[24]

Congressional Republicans reintroduced the bill against partial-birth abortion in 1997. The Fitzsimmons recantation hurt, but this time Democrats were prepared with an alternative. Tom Daschle, the leader of the Senate Democrats, introduced a bill to ban third-trimester abortions. This legislation was presented as a substantial concession to pro-lifers at the time, and has been since. In 2004, when John Kerry ran for president, some observers suggested that his vote for Daschle's legislation proved that he is not a pro-abortion extremist.[25]

But there was much less to the Daschle bill than met the eye. First: Since most partial-birth abortions take place before viability—in the second trimester, not the third—the bill would have left them untouched. Second: The bill, as supporters and opponents agreed,[26] left it to the abortionist to determine whether the pregnancy was pre- or post-viability.

Third: The bill would have allowed abortions after viability if "the continuation of the pregnancy would threaten the mother's life or risk grievous injury to her physical health." The words "grievous" and "physical health" made this restriction sound tight. It wasn't, because there were no adverbs attached to "threaten" and "risk": Any degree of risk would have nullified the law, and an abortionist would always be able to say that there was some risk. Warren Hern, a major practitioner of partial-birth abortion, said, "I will certify that any pregnancy is a threat to a woman's life and could cause 'grievous injury' to her 'physical health.'"[27]

Fourth: Daschle and most of the other supporters of the legislation favored *Roe* v. *Wade*. But if his legislation turned out somehow to have teeth, and to ban some abortions, any Supreme Court following *Roe* and *Doe* was likely to strike it down. Kerry, for example, pledged in 2004 that he would appoint to the Supreme Court only justices who would uphold *Roe*.[28] So, in effect, he was pledging both to support a law and to appoint justices who would overturn it.

Daschle's bill wasn't an alternative ban; it was an alternative to a ban. If one construes Daschle's motives charitably, his bill reflected naiveté about the way abortion law works in practice—the kind of naiveté that actual pro-lifers have had beaten out of them by the courts.

After Daschle's alternative failed, to his credit, he voted for the partial-birth ban. The majorities this time were a little larger:

295–136 in the House and 64–36 in the Senate. Clinton vetoed it again, "for exactly the same reasons I [vetoed] an earlier substantially identical version of this bill...last year."[29] He rested his case, that is, on the supposed medical necessity for partial-birth abortion in certain cases—enlarged heads and so forth—even though nobody had proven that such cases existed. The American Medical Association at one point supported the ban and then backed away from it on the grounds that doctors should not be subject to criminal penalties in the course of their work. But it has never backed away from its contention that partial-birth abortion "is not good medicine."[30]

The same drama played out again in 1999. By now, both sides knew the routine pretty well. The abortion lobby knew it could count on Clinton to veto any ban, and that the pro-lifers were likely to stay a few votes short of the two-thirds of Congress they needed to override the veto. Still, the debate continued to shed light on the extremism of the party of death.

During the debate, the chief Senate sponsor of the partial-birth abortion ban, Rick Santorum of Pennsylvania, asked Senator Boxer whether the two of them and the other senators had a right to life. She answered, "I support the *Roe* v. *Wade* decision." It was downhill from there for Boxer.

SANTORUM: Do you agree any child who is born has the right to life...?

BOXER: I agree with the *Roe* v. *Wade* decision, and what you are doing goes against it and will harm the women of this country...

SANTORUM: But I would like to ask you this question. You agree, once the child is born, separated from the mother, that that child is protected by the Constitution and cannot be killed? Do you agree with that?

BOXER: I think when you bring your baby home...the baby belongs to your family and has all the rights...

SANTORUM: You said "once the baby comes home." Obviously, you don't mean they have to take the baby out of the hospital for it to be protected by the Constitution. Once the baby is...completely separated from the mother, you would agree that baby is entitled to constitutional protection?

BOXER: I will tell you why I don't want to engage in this. You did the same conversation with a colleague of mine, and I never saw such a twisting of his remarks...[31]

SANTORUM: Let's say the baby is completely separated; in other words, no part of the baby is inside of the mother.

BOXER: You mean the baby has been birthed and is now in the mother's arms? It is a human being?...I would say when the baby is born, the baby is born and would then have every right of every other human being living in this country, and I don't know why this would even be a question.

SANTORUM: Because we are talking about a situation here where the baby is almost born. So I ask the question of the senator from California, if the baby was born except for the baby's foot, if the baby's foot was inside the mother but the rest of the baby was outside, could that baby be killed?

BOXER: The baby is born when the baby is born. That is the answer to the question...

SANTORUM: What you are suggesting is if the baby's foot is still inside of the mother, that baby can then still be killed.

BOXER: I am not suggesting that…

SANTORUM: But, again, what you are suggesting is if the baby's toe is inside the mother, you can, in fact, kill that baby.

BOXER: Absolutely not.

SANTORUM: OK. So if the baby's toe is in, you can't kill the baby. How about if the baby's foot is in?

BOXER: You are the one who is making these statements.

SANTORUM: We are trying to draw a line here.

BOXER: I am not answering these questions.[32]

These are the difficulties one takes on in defending the killing of a human being inches away from being born: You're forced either to defend infanticide openly, or to draw distinctions that amount to a deadly game of Hokey-Pokey.

Indeed, the party of death put up a little initial resistance to a bill that would protect those infants who were, so to speak, completely born. The Born-Alive Infants Protection Act was introduced in response to, among other things, a few court cases that had seemed to suggest that an infant who was fully delivered in the course of an attempted abortion had no legal protections. Congress also heard from nurses who testified that they had seen live-born babies left to die after attempted abortions.

The Associated Press, oddly enough, described the object of the bill's protection as a "fetus outside a woman's body."[33] NARAL attacked the bill as—guess what?—"an anti-choice assault" on *Roe v. Wade*. The bill, according to NARAL, would "inject Congress into what should be personal and private decisions about medical treatment in difficult and painful situations."[34] This time, however, most Democrats were unwilling to stand with NARAL. Only eighteen members of the House refused to vote for the bill. Jerrold Nadler, a staunchly pro-abortion Democratic congressman from New York, came up with a face-saving explanation for the retreat: The law was redundant, the babies were already protected, and nobody would ever dream of suggesting that they shouldn't be. He ignored the fact that NARAL had obviously suggested just that.[35] But the group got the message: The next time the bill came up, it did not oppose it.

CHAPTER 5

The Nullification Machine

AGAIN AND AGAIN IN federal judge Phyllis Hamilton's decision on partial-birth abortion, a curious phrase appeared: The fetus was said to be "disarticulated" during the procedure. It seemed, at first, as though Judge Hamilton were merely using another euphemism in an area that abounds in them. Thus Hamilton also referred to partial-birth abortion as an "intact dilation and evacuation," and we ran into our old friend, "termination of a pregnancy"—given the circumstances of an "Intact D&E," one almost expected to find the words "with extreme prejudice" added. Since the verb "articulate" has an anatomical sense ("to form a joint"), albeit one not often used in ordinary speech, the judge's usage was a euphemism for "dismembered" or, to be still more concrete, "torn apart."[1]

Abortion-on-demand has been made possible by the verbal redescription of human beings as though they were something else: "products of conception," "protoplasm," "a few cells," "potential life." The abortionist does not suck out the baby's brains; the abortion provider evacuates the cranial contents of the fetus or, even better, "reduce[s] the fetal calvarium." Disarticulation has been the prerequisite for disfranchisement, disposal, destruction.

Violence has also been done to the words of the Constitution. Its words about the proper allocation of responsibilities between legislatures and the judiciary have been unspoken, too.

By the year 2000, thirty states had prohibited partial-birth abortion. Public opinion condemned the procedure: Gallup finds that 68 percent of Americans favor a ban.[2] The abortion lobby had lost in the court of public opinion. So it did what it always does in such cases: It moved the issue to actual courts.

There are, of course, circumstances under which the courts may, indeed must, thwart the public's will by striking down popular laws. But on those occasions, what the courts do is place the temporary will of the public, as expressed in a law, below the public's permanent will, expressed in the Constitution. So if Congress, moved by a wave of hostility to criminal defendants, were to pass a law eliminating their right to confront their accusers, the courts would properly strike it down.

The public never ratified a right to partial-birth abortion, or any principle from which a right to partial-birth abortion can be reasonably derived. Yet court after court struck down the laws against partial-birth abortion. Back when Justice Sandra Day O'Connor was voting with the minority of *Roe* skeptics on the Supreme Court, she wrote that it was "painfully clear that no legal rule or doctrine is safe from *ad hoc* nullification by this Court when an occasion for its application arises in a case involving state regulation of abortion."[3] The nullification machine now went to work on laws against partial-birth abortion, with the eventual help of Justice O'Connor herself.

The courts that struck down laws against partial-birth abortion did so mainly on two grounds. First, the laws were held to be vague. While they prohibited D&X abortions, they could also, supposedly, be read to prohibit D&E abortions. To put it another way: The laws' intent was to prohibit the partial delivery of a baby followed by its killing and then complete removal from the womb. But the laws could (with strain[4]) be read to prohibit the dismemberment of a baby within the womb followed by the removal of its parts. The laws thus supposedly left abortionists in the dark about what was prohibited. They were unconstitutionally vague.

Judge Frank Easterbrook, in one of the few court decisions upholding the laws, explained what was wrong with this theory. For one thing, the minority of states that had been allowed to ban partial-birth abortion had seen no chilling effect on the use of D&E. Nor had there been any overzealous prosecutions. For another, courts could block overbroad applications of the law without striking down the law itself.

The second alleged defect of the laws was their failure to include a health exception. The AMA did not believe the practice to be medically necessary ever. Even the American College of Obstetricians and Gynecologists, which strongly opposed the bans, had to admit that a "select panel convened by ACOG could identify no circumstances under which this procedure…would be the only option to save the life or preserve the health of the woman."[5] But it insisted that each individual abortionist should be allowed to decide whether partial-birth abortion was the safest procedure. Not allowing him to make that decision would endanger the woman's health.

So: Partial-birth abortion could not be distinguished from other abortions, but at the same time there were (unspecified) cases in which it would be safer—*distinctly* safer?—than other abortions.

In the 2000 case of *Stenberg* v. *Carhart*, the Supreme Court voted 5–4 to strike down a Nebraska law against partial-birth abortion—and by extension, to strike down every state law—on both grounds.

Justice Kennedy had been in the majority in *Casey*, a 1992 case that modified *Roe* while maintaining its "essential holding." Kennedy thought that *Casey* represented a compromise on abortion. He dissented from the partial-birth ruling, arguing that the Court was turning its back on that compromise. He recognized that the demand for a health "exception" was really a demand for a loophole larger than any law could be. "Casting aside the views of distinguished physicians and the statements of leading medical organizations, the Court awards each physician a veto power over the State's judgment that the procedures should not be performed," wrote Kennedy. "Dr. Carhart has made the medical judgment to use the D&X procedure in every case...after 15 weeks gestation. Requiring Nebraska to defer to Dr. Carhart's judgment is no different than forbidding Nebraska from enacting a ban at all; for it is now Dr. Leroy Carhart who sets abortion policy for the State of Nebraska, not the legislature or the people."

In *Roe* and *Casey*, the Supreme Court had said that late-term abortion had to be available whenever continued pregnancy threatened a woman's health. Health had been broadly defined, as we have seen. The Court went still further in the partial-birth case: It no longer mattered whether the pregnancy itself posed any threat. The Court did not bother to pretend, as Clinton had, that there were pregnant women with health problems that could be solved only by partially delivering the babies, killing them, and completing the delivery. If a woman wants a late-term abortion, for any reason, legislatures may not close off one method of abortion and make her choose between a different method of abortion and no abortion at all. The Court asserts a right to a dead baby, at any stage of pregnancy, accomplished in any manner. In every important respect, the right to abortion is asserted as an absolute right.

Justice John Paul Stevens wrote a very short concurring opinion in the case, in which Ruth Bader Ginsburg, another member of the Court's liberal bloc, joined. The opinion had one paragraph and one point: "Although much ink is spilled today describing the gruesome nature of late-term abortion procedures, that rhetoric does not provide me a *reason* to believe that the procedure Nebraska here claims it seeks to ban is more brutal, more gruesome, or less respectful of 'potential life' than the equally gruesome procedure Nebraska claims it still allows... [T]he notion that either of these two equally gruesome procedures performed at this late stage of gestation is more akin to infanticide than the other, or that the State furthers any legitimate interest by banning one but not the other, is simply irrational" (emphasis in original).

Lower-court judges had sounded the same contemptuous note: It made no sense to distinguish between partial-birth abortions and D&Es. Judge Richard Posner, a Reagan appointee with some libertarian inclinations, called the laws against partial-birth abortion "irrational" and "peculiar": "[T]he statutes do not forbid the destruction of any class of fetuses, but merely criminalize a method of abortion... From the standpoint of the fetus, and, I should think, of any rational person, it makes no difference whether, when the skull is crushed, the fetus is entirely within the uterus or its feet are outside the uterus. Yet the position of the feet is the only difference between committing a felony and performing an act that the states concede is constitutionally privileged."[6]

Judge Maryanne Trump Barry felt so strongly about the issue that she issued an opinion striking down New Jersey's ban on partial-birth abortion even after the Supreme Court, by striking down all such bans, had rendered her decision superfluous. Attempts to distinguish partial-birth abortion from other abortions, she claimed, were "based on semantic machinations, irrational line-drawing, and an obvious attempt to inflame public opinion instead of logic or medical evidence. Positing an 'unborn' versus 'partially born' distinction, the Legislature would have us accept, and the public believe, that during a 'partial-birth abortion' the fetus is in the process of being 'born' at the time of its demise. It is not. A woman seeking an abortion is plainly not seeking to give birth."[7]

Right: "Semantic machinations" should be employed only when interpreting the words of the Constitution to protect partial-birth abortion. Judge Barry engaged in some creative pro-choice epistemology, if not in semantic machinations of her own, in redefining "birth." Whether a birth has occurred or is occurring depends, apparently, entirely on the mother's wishes.

But these judges did touch on a serious point. It is indeed hard to see any strong argument for regarding partial-birth abortions as more immoral or unjust than other abortions. But this hardly establishes that it is *irrational* to prohibit partial-birth abortions. A convict is just as dead whether he is killed by lethal injection or an electric chair, but it is not irrational for a state to adopt the least horrifying possible method of execution. Nor is it irrational for an opponent of the death penalty to highlight an especially terrible method of execution in order to draw attention to the case against capital punishment.

There is, however, a deeper problem with the judges' argument. They are saying that it is irrational to draw a moral distinction based on which parts of a fetus are within the womb. Location should not matter.

But it's not pro-lifers who made the right to life dependent on location. A pro-abortion Supreme Court did that. In the Court's jurisprudence, what distinguishes a baby entitled to legal protection from a fetus without such protection is precisely whether it is in the womb. A human being's stage of development does not matter: A premature baby born at seven months has more legal protections than an eight-month-old fetus inside the womb. Nor do the Court's rulings turn on what's done to this being: It's permissible to dismember a fetus within the womb, but not a baby outside it. Location is the key variable for the Court. Justice Stevens himself has suggested that a fetus—even a "9-month-gestated, fully sentient fetus on the eve of birth"—is not "a human being."[8] Birth is the event that transforms the fetus to a human being. And whatever else birth is, it is, as a matter of cold fact, a change of location.

It's Justice Stevens and his colleagues, in other words, who have created an irrational abortion policy. The legislators who tried to outlaw partial-birth abortion were trying to work around that fact. Conceding that the Court would not allow them to protect life within the womb, they tried to mark an outer boundary to the abortion right: to establish that they could protect human beings partway out of the womb. It is this attempt to draw a limit that the courts put down. In the process, they ascribed their own irrationality to others.

If Stevens and company now wish to say, "Womb, schwomb," then they ought either to abandon *Roe* and *Casey* or to declare a constitutional right to infanticide. Posner should issue an opinion stating that from the standpoint of the fetus/baby, it does not matter whether he is in the womb or a crib when he is killed. The judges could certainly find someone willing to make a plausible-sounding argument that it is sometimes safer for the woman if an abortionist extracts the baby completely before emptying its "intracranial contents."

Notwithstanding the evidence that the courts would find rationalizations for thwarting them, pro-life legislators tried again. In 2003, Congress passed, and President Bush signed, a ban on partial-birth abortion. The new law attempted to meet the Court's objections by defining the procedure as precisely as possible and by registering congressional findings that the procedure is never medically necessary—in the hope, which has so far turned out to be vain, that the courts would defer to the determinations of fact that Congress made in writing the law.

Lawsuits were immediately filed to block the enforcement of the law. Three federal courts considered the issue. Convenient euphemism was the order of the day in all of them. One abortionist testified that his goal was to "safely and efficiently empty the uterine cavity, rendering the woman unpregnant."[9]

Even before the cases were decided, it was clear on which side the weight of the judicial and academic establishments fell. In seeking to defend the law, lawyers for the Bush administration sought medical records that would shed light on whether partial-birth abortions really were medically necessary. The lawyers said that the hospitals could leave out any information that might make it possible to identify the women involved. But the courts responded by inventing what amounts to a special privacy right for records related to abortions—a right that doesn't apply to any other medical records, and that blocked the disclosure of even the non-patient-specific information the administration had asked for.

In the *Stenberg* litigation, defenders of the Nebraska ban had cited, as evidence for the claim that partial-birth abortion had little medical value, the fact that no medical schools taught it. Some major medical schools, in response, started teaching it in time to affect the next round of litigation. Faculty members from major institutions—Columbia, NYU, Northwestern—joined the lawsuits.[10]

The results of the litigation were thus not surprising. Judge Hamilton in San Francisco went first. She rather disdainfully waved aside those congressional findings. She also decided that medical experts who object to partial-birth abortion are biased, and that the most expert medical authorities of all are those who actually perform them. Given these assumptions, of course she ruled against the law. It is as though a judge were to decide whether capital punishment is fairly applied by listening only to executioners, and to exclude opponents of execution from the start.

The other courts reached the same result. The judge in New York, however, seemed notably reluctant to do so. Judge Richard Casey found that partial-birth abortion exposed fetuses to severe pain. He found that the claims that the procedure was sometimes necessary were "false," "incoherent," or "merely theoretical." In no case, he noted, could the National Abortion Federation or its witnesses "point to a specific patient or actual circumstance in which D&X was necessary to protect a woman's health." Casey considered partial-birth abortion "gruesome, brutal, barbaric and uncivilized." But he seemed to feel that the Supreme Court's decision had made it impossible for lower courts to affirm any law against partial-birth abortion, which may be correct.[11]

The question now is how the Supreme Court will rule when it next considers the issue. President Bush will have made at least two appointments to the Court by then. The new justices will have to decide if they want to maintain an abortion jurisprudence that is extreme in its distance from our founding law, from public sentiment, and from justice—or if they are prepared to articulate the Constitution.

CHAPTER 6

Is Abortion Good for You?

IT TURNS OUT THAT the death penalty reduces crime—at least when applied prenatally.

Such, at least, is the reasoning of some members of the party of death. In the early 1990s the iconoclastic liberal columnist Nicholas von Hoffman argued that

> [f]ree, cheap abortion is a policy of social defense. To save ourselves from being murdered in our beds and raped on the streets, we should do everything possible to encourage pregnant women who don't want the baby and will not take care of it to get rid of the thing before it turns into a monster... At their demonstrations, the anti-abortionists parade around with pictures of dead and dismembered fetuses. The pro-abortionists should meet these displays with some of their own: pictures of the victims of the unaborted—murder victims, rape victims, mutilation victims— pictures to remind us that the fight for abortion is but part of the larger struggle for safe homes and safe streets.[1]

Von Hoffman has little patience for arguments that abortion is not a form of killing: "Just snuff the little buggers and let's get on with it...The bumper sticker on the back of my car reads,

'CAUTION! THE FETUS YOU SAVE WILL GROW UP TO MUG YOU!'"[2]

If many people share von Hoffman's views, they have generally refrained from saying so during the course of our decades-long debate over abortion. But dress up those views with some regression analyses, and suddenly they become the conventional wisdom.

In 1999, University of Chicago economist Steven Levitt and Stanford law professor John Donohue wrote a paper arguing that abortion cuts crime. The legalization of abortion in the 1970s, they said, accounts for as much as half of the reduction in crime in the 1990s. Crime fell because criminals had been imprisoned, sure, but also because many had never been born.

When their paper was publicized that year, there were pro-lifers and pro-choicers who accused them of racism. But by 2005, their thesis seemed to have become uncontroversial in the mainstream media.

The most-hyped portion of *Freakonomics*, a 2005 bestseller that Levitt wrote with journalist Steven Dubner, is devoted to the abortion-cuts-crime theory.[3] The book presents Levitt as a "fearless," unconventional "rogue economist."[4] Yet he does not appear to have paid any substantial price for violating some alleged taboo against truth-telling. He has merely had to bask fearlessly in the media's praise. Reviewers in the *Washington Post*, the *Los Angeles Times*, and the *Wall Street Journal* accepted Levitt's theory without a word of criticism.[5] (The *Journal*'s reviewer wrote, "Criticizing *Freakonomics* would be like criticizing a hot fudge sundae." What could be more delightful than proof that abortion mows down the criminal class?) *Forbes* called the theory "entirely convincing," and *The Economist* claimed the book "moved methodically and persuasively through the statistical evidence" for it.[6] The *New York Times* stands out for having run three positive articles on the book. Some of them were gushing, and none of them questioned the abortion theory.[7]

Perhaps this uncritical reception reflected the surface plausibility of the theory. As Levitt and Dubner summarize it: "Legalized abortion led to less unwantedness; unwantedness leads to high crime; legalized abortion, therefore, led to less crime." They draw on another study to argue that "the typical child who went unborn in the earliest years of legalized abortion" would have been more likely than most children to be poor and to grow up with one parent—and thus to be criminals. "In other words, the very factors that drove millions of women to have an abortion also seemed to predict that their children, had they been born, would have led unhappy and possibly criminal lives."

It should be noted that all references to race in the 1999 paper have been studiously scrubbed from the book version of Levitt's argument. Levitt and Dubner are very careful not to say that the unborn children were disproportionately black, that blacks account for a disproportionate amount of crime, and that abortion therefore reduced crime by reducing the black population. Had this point been made explicit, the reviews might not have been quite so glowing.

If the abortion-cuts-crime theory is true, then its truth should be faced and its implications pondered. If it is true, then Levitt, Donohue, and Dubner deserve credit for advancing our understanding of some complicated social phenomena.

But is it true? For a long time, the only people who challenged it were a few researchers (notably Baruch College economist Ted Joyce) whose papers received rather less attention than Levitt's, and the journalist-blogger Steve Sailer. It is these critics, however unheralded, who appear to have the stronger case.

The most impressive evidence for the Levitt theory is that the states that legalized abortion a few years before *Roe* saw their crimes rates drop a few years earlier than the rest of the country. What *Freakonomics* ignores, however, is that crime had risen earlier in those same states. As Sailer writes, "[T]he two big urban areas that were the first to enjoy the purported crime-fighting benefits of legalized abortion in 1970, New York City and Los Angeles, were also the ground zeroes of the teen murder rampage that began, perhaps not coincidentally, about 16 years later."[8] (Levitt also ignores the facts that people move from state to state and that they cross state lines to get abortions, weakening the value of his correlations.)

If Levitt's theory were correct, one would expect murder rates to have dropped among younger teens before it dropped among older teens. The fourteen-year-olds of 1993 should have been more law-abiding than the fourteen-year-olds of 1983, since legalized abortion would have, supposedly, snuffed out many criminals in the later group. There should have been a much smaller drop in crime among the twenty-five-year-olds, all of whom in both years had been born before *Roe*.

As Sailer notes, this is the reverse of what happened. Between 1983 and 1993, murder rates went down among people older than twenty-five and went *up* among those younger. "[T]he first cohort to survive legalized abortion went on the worst youth murder spree in American history." The murder rate among the over-twenty-five set started falling in 1981. It started to go back up only when the set started including people born after *Roe*.[9]

Joyce notes that Levitt's theory also implies that crime should have fallen more among blacks than whites—since blacks would have reaped more of the supposed crime-fighting benefits of abortion. Didn't happen.[10]

In the fall of 2005, Christopher Foote and Christopher Goetz, an economist and researcher, broke through the media's wall of protection around *Freakonomics* with a study pointing out that some of Levitt's key evidence was based on a programming error and a faulty choice of statistics. Once those errors are corrected, that evidence "vanishes."[11]

The theory seems plausible to many people because of a common mistake. People naturally assume that if abortion had been prohibited (and the prohibition perfectly enforced) in America, the forty-five million unborn children aborted would have instead been born. But that is not the case. One effect of legalized abortion was to increase the rate of careless conceptions. Its availability made it easier for people to have casual sex and to dispense with contraceptives. Abortion is almost always "birth control" in the sense that it aims at preventing birth. The high repeat abortion rate—44 percent of abortions today are repeat abortions; 18 percent of abortions are performed on women who have already had two—suggests that it is sometimes the birth control of first resort.[12]

Further evidence of the effects of liberal abortion laws on sexual behavior comes from researchers Jonathan Klick and Thomas Stratmann. They have estimated that the legalization of abortion increased rates of syphilis and gonorrhea—accounting for a quarter of the incidence of these diseases.[13] *Freakonomics* got this much right: The legalization of abortion caused the number of conceptions to go up by 30 percent, while causing the number of births to go down by only 6 percent.[14]

Many of the unborn children who have been aborted since *Roe*, in other words, would never have been conceived in the first place without it. Every once in a while you will hear a pro-lifer arguing that without *Roe* and legal abortion, America would benefit from having forty-five million more workers and taxpayers. Whatever else may be said about this argument, it fails to reckon with abortion's full range of effects.

So *Roe* stimulated a lot of conceptions and a larger number of abortions. The next thing to remember is that it stands to reason that some of those extra conceptions made it through to birth. Some kids, paradoxically, would not have been born if not for legal abortion. Our intuitions guide us astray here: We cannot simply *assume* that abortion reduces the number of kids born in circumstances that are conducive to a life of crime.

We cannot even assume that abortion reduces the number of illegitimate kids. Many people, again, make an intuitive link: They think that because most pregnant single women face a choice between abortion and single motherhood, society therefore faces the same choice at the macro level. But that's not necessarily so.

In 1996, two liberal social scientists wrote a paper noting that the availability of abortion and contraception had raised out-of-wedlock birth rates:

> Women who were willing to get an abortion or who reliably used contraception no longer found it necessary to condition sexual relations on a promise of marriage in the event of pregnancy. But women who wanted children, who did not want an abortion for moral or religious reasons, or who were unreliable in their use of contraception found themselves pressured to participate in premarital sexual relations without being able to exact a promise of marriage in case of pregnancy. These women feared, correctly, that if they refused sexual relations, they would risk losing their partners. Sexual activity without commitment was increasingly expected in premarital relationships.
>
> Advances in reproductive technology eroded the custom of shotgun marriage in another way. Before the sexual revolution, women had less freedom, but men were expected to assume responsibility for their welfare. Today women are more free to choose, but men have afforded themselves the comparable option. "If she is not willing to have an abortion or use contraception," the man can reason, "why should I sacrifice myself to get married?" By making the birth of the child the physical choice of the mother, the sexual revolution has made marriage and child support a social choice of the father.

Many men have changed their attitudes regarding the responsibility for uplanned pregnancies. As one contributor to the Internet wrote recently to the Dads' Rights Newsgroup, "Since the decision to have the child is solely up to the mother, I don't see how both parents have responsibility to that child." That attitude, of course, makes it far less likely that the man will offer marriage as a solution to a couple's pregnancy quandary...[15]

Abortion may not lead to fewer unwanted children; it may lead to the birth of *more* children who aren't wanted by their fathers. While this result may sound counterintuitive—and some research supports the opposite view[16]—it is worth noting that abortion and illegitimacy rates rose in tandem during the 1970s and have fallen in tandem since the 1990s.

The trends on infanticide are one place to look to check the thesis that abortion reduced "unwantedness." But the infanticide rate increased steadily during the three decades after 1970—from a rate of 4.3 per 100,000 infants to a rate of 9.2. "Infanticide fell dramatically" because abortion was legalized, claims *Freakonomics*. It cites one study. Here's what the abstract of that study says: "The legalization of abortion was not associated with a sudden change in child homicide trends. It was, however, associated with a steady decrease in the homicides of toddlers (i.e., one- to four-year-olds) in subsequent years. Although in the predicted direction, the decrease in homicides of children under 1 year of age was not statistically significant."[17]

Joyce has said that the drop in crime that Levitt attributes to abortion has much more to do with the end of the crack wars.[18] The crack wars caused a massive increase in murder starting in the mid-1980s, and then petered out in the mid-1990s. That raises the question of what effect abortion had on the crack wars. The truth is that we have no idea. Levitt assumes that abortion had nothing to do with its beginning but everything to do with its end.[19]

In what may be the strangest passage of *Freakonomics*, Levitt and Dubner invoke the example of Romania. The Communist regime banned abortion in 1966 on the ground that the fetus was the collective property of the nation. The result, according to our freakonomists, was an increase in crime and, eventually—they leave the chain of causation obscure, perhaps out of necessity—the violent end of the regime. Communist Romania may not make for good analogies with the U.S. for a variety of reasons. One stands out: The ban led to a 100 percent increase in Romanian fertility rates. American fertility rates, remember, dropped only 6 percent when abortion was legalized here. The magnitudes aren't remotely similar.[20]

Even if Levitt were right that abortion cuts crime, what would follow from this conclusion? Levitt and Dubner note that their theory implies that it takes hundreds of abortions to reduce the homicide total by one.[21] As a crime-control strategy, abortion is "terribly inefficient."

Even if it were more "efficient," it would raise obvious moral objections. Let's say that we could apply a kind of prenatal profiling to figure out which unborn children were the most likely to grow up to become criminals. Would we be justified in eliminating them for that reason? What if we could pinpoint with complete accuracy which five-year-olds were budding criminals? Obviously we would not think it permissible to eliminate them. Whether it is morally permissible to eliminate unborn children is what the abortion debate is about. Anyone who thinks abortion should be tolerated as a way of reducing crime probably already favors tolerating abortion for other reasons. People who think that abortion should itself be considered a crime will not be swayed.

Pro-lifers thus need not fear that their case will be weakened should research ever prove that abortion really does reduce crime. At present, the balance of evidence suggests that it does not. The eagerness with which many people greeted claims that it does shows how much some people want to find social benefits from abortion and its legalization.

Chief among those alleged benefits has been a reduction in the number of "unwanted children." The argument that abortion reduces illegitimacy is a sub-species of that claim, and the argument that it reduces crime is a corollary of it. The second great benefit of legal abortion is supposed to be that it brought an end to the tragic death of women in back-alley and coat hanger abortions. Legalization thus improved the health of women.

But the benefits for women's health are hard to see. It is, of course, impossible to get precise figures on the number of illegal abortions performed before *Roe* or the number of women who died as a result of them. Activists seeking "reform" and then "repeal" of anti-abortion laws exaggerated those numbers, claiming that as many as one million illegal abortions took place every year in America. They claimed that five to ten thousand women died in these abortions. Bernard Nathanson, one of the founders of the National Association for the Repeal of Abortion Laws (NARAL), would admit years later, after changing his mind about abortion, that these numbers had been made up.[22]

As we have seen, some politicians and journalists still stand behind these claims. The official numbers tell a different story. The National Center for Health Statistics attributes 1,313 women's deaths to illegal abortions for the year 1940. That number had declined to 159 by 1966, and to forty-one by 1972. The Centers for Disease Control report similar numbers: They attribute thirty-nine women's deaths in 1972 to illegal abortions—but also attribute twenty-four women's deaths that year to legal abortions. They attribute eleven women's deaths in 2000 to legal abortions.[23]

It is quite possible that the official figures undercount the number of maternal deaths from illegal abortion in 1972. But there is no reason to doubt the sharply downward trend. The development of antibiotics seems to have done more to lower the maternal death rate from abortion than any legal change.[24] Mary Calderone, medical director of Planned Parenthood, estimated in 1960 that 90 percent of illegal abortions were performed by physicians and concluded that most were safe for the mothers.[25]

If *Roe* saved women from deaths in illegal abortions, the effect was too small to have any noticeable effect on the death rate for women: "Centers for Disease Control statistics show no decline in the years after *Roe* in the death rate of women aged fifteen to thirty-four, the group of women who account for ninety-four percent of all abortions."[26]

The Alan Guttmacher Institute, the research arm of Planned Parenthood, comes close to conceding these points. In a 2003 paper, the institute noted the dramatic decline in maternal deaths from abortion that resulted from antibiotics. The article's author, Rachel Benson Gold, tries to stick to the party line: "By making abortion legal nationwide, *Roe v. Wade* has had a dramatic impact on the health and well-being of American women. Deaths from abortion have plummeted, and are now a rarity." She refers to a graph that carries the caption *"The number of deaths from abortion has declined dramatically since* Roe v.Wade." The graph itself, however, shows no such thing. Even though the graph starts with 1965—thus missing the truly dramatic decline starting in the 1940s—the graph clearly demonstrates that the number of maternal deaths from abortion fell far more (and fell faster) from 1965 to 1973 than it has since then.[27]

In judging the impact of *Roe* on health, any small gains that the end of illegal abortions may have yielded have to be set against some disadvantages, such as the spread of STDs mentioned earlier. (There is also the much-disputed question of whether abortion contributes to the risk for breast cancer.[28]) Are those questionable gains worth ending the lives of more than one million unborn children every year? How you judge that question will turn on how you regard abortion. For anyone who takes the view that it is as wrong to kill a human being in the womb as to kill any other human being, the back-alley argument cannot have much weight. Prohibiting abortion might lead to a few tragic cases in which women die in the course of obtaining illegal abortions; and a conscientious pro-life policy would do what it rightly could to prevent such cases. But it would not license the killing of hundreds of thousands of human beings in order to prevent those tragedies.

In other words, the contending arguments about the practical effects of abortion are something of a sideshow. Very few people support legal abortion simply because they think it reduces crime. Very few people who support abortion would change their minds if they came to believe that it does not reduce crime. The same principle applies to the other side. The abortion debate is, for the most part, about things that social science can't measure.

CHAPTER 7

The Politics of Personhood

"ABORTION ... AND EUTHANASIA ... are both choices for death." The words are not those of a right-to-lifer. They come from the opening sentence of a book in *defense* of a constitutional right to abortion and euthanasia by the eminent liberal legal theorist Ronald Dworkin.[1]

Dworkin was not saying that the choice to have an abortion or to euthanize someone is necessarily made out of a sick love of death for its own sake. His point—which also applies to embryo research, which became a hot topic a few years after he wrote—was that these choices, whatever motivates them, are always, and necessarily, choices to kill a living organism. While his sentence did not make the point explicitly, they are also always choices to kill living *human* organisms.

We have developed ways of talking that enable us to pretend that this point can be blinked away. In the case of abortion and embryo research, the main technique is to suggest that there is some great mystery about "when life begins," and that this alleged question is a religious or philosophical one. Yet science has long since solved the mystery. From conception onward, what exists is a distinct organism of the human species. The philosophical question is what we make of that fact. To jumble these issues together—the essentially scientific issue of categorizing an embryo as human and living, and the moral question of whether it follows from that categorization that it has a right to life—is a logical error. Justice Blackmun, of course, proceeded in just this erroneous fashion in *Roe*. And if we are not careful, talking in terms of "meaningful life," or, as Dworkin does, of "life in earnest,"[2] can lead us into this error as well.

All of us who read this page were once human embryos. The history of our bodies began with the formation of an embryo. We *were* those embryos, just as we were once fetuses, infants, children, and adolescents. But we were never a sperm cell and an egg cell. (Those cells were genetically and functionally parts of other human beings.) The formation of the embryo marks the beginning of a new human life: a new and complete organism that belongs to the human species. Embryology textbooks say so, with no glimmer of uncertainty or ambiguity.[3]

That new organism is alive rather than dead or inanimate. It is human rather than a member of some other species. It is an organism distinct from all others. It is not a functional part of a larger organism (the way a kidney is part of a larger organism). It maintains its own organic unity over time. It directs its own development, according to its genetic template, through the embryonic, fetal, and subsequent stages. Such terms as "blastocyst," "newborn," and "adolescent" denote different stages of development in a being of the same type, not different types of beings. At each of our earlier stages of life, we have been, as we are now, whole living members of the species Homo sapiens.

Honest and clear-eyed supporters of Dworkin's "choices for death" do not deny the biological facts. Rather, they argue that making choices to kill human beings, and allowing people to make these choices, can be justified. This is why I have adapted Dworkin's phrase to speak of a "party of death."

And here we come to the fundamental question in dispute. That question can be described in different ways: whether all human beings have a right not to be killed; whether membership in the human species is enough to confer rights; whether we accept the existence of a category of human non-persons. Opponents of abortion, embryo-destructive research, euthanasia, and infanticide believe that all human beings should be protected from being killed. They believe, further, that to the extent America fails to provide this protection it betrays its own founding principles. The party of death, on the other hand, believes that some human beings deserve that protection and some do not.

It is because abortion, euthanasia, and embryo-destructive research all raise this question that they are so deeply linked to one another. Two qualifications must, however, be made to this linkage. First: It is obviously true that not everyone who supports one of these things supports them all. Not everyone who opposes one of them opposes them all, either. But the correlations, just as obviously, are strong.

Second: Each issue raises some special questions of its own. Some people defend one type of embryo-destructive research, for example, on the ground that embryos taken for research from fertility clinics "would be discarded anyway." That isn't an argument that applies to abortion, euthanasia, or even other types of embryo-destructive research. The argument about discardedness, like other such specific questions, deserves to be considered on the merits.

Yet it isn't really what the debate is about. For one thing, most of the people who make the argument also support research on embryos that haven't been "discarded," such as embryos that have been created specifically for research purposes. For another, the argument about discardedness tacitly assumes that human embryos have little moral weight. Nobody in the U.S. supports taking living death-row prisoners' hearts from them to be transplanted into sick

people—even if this were done painlessly.[4] The fact that these prisoners are about to be "discarded" does not affect our judgment. Our
use of the word "discarded" in relation to embryos is evidence of a
prior decision to treat them as less than human. And that decision *is*
what the debate is about.

Similarly, if most supporters of abortion believe that embryo
research should go forward, then it's unlikely that their views really
turn on their view of women and their "rights over their bodies."
They are willing to support the destruction of human embryos even
when those embryos are *not* within a woman's body.

Once we see that the central issue in the debate over the sanctity
of life is whether all human beings have basic rights, it becomes easier to see what the central issue is not. The debate sometimes seems
to be about everything under the sun. Sometimes it appears to be a
struggle between religious Americans and the more secular-minded.
Or between those who would impose their morality on others and
those who would keep government out of private decisions. The
debate is also, supposedly, a prism through which people's attitudes
about the changing roles of women are refracted. It's about sex. It's
about party politics. Or all of the above.

The Supreme Court, in a passage from the *Casey* decision of
1992 usually attributed to Justice Anthony Kennedy, defended abortion rights by invoking "the right to define one's own concept of existence, of the universe, and of the mystery of human life" (all of this,
naturally, to be found in the Constitution). So the debate over abortion is really about competing concepts of existence, the universe,
and the mystery of human life. That pretty much covers everything,
doesn't it?

The political commentator Morton Kondracke has written that
at least some opponents of abortion and embryo research "are as
much about punishing illicit sexual activity as they are about saving
'life.'"[5] It is certainly true that opponents of abortion and embryo

research tend to view sex outside marriage as immoral, while supporters of abortion and embryo research do not. But this fact does not establish much about motives. First of all, the reference to embryo research already suggests that Kondracke has gone off track. How does restricting embryo research punish illicit sexual activity? People are debating research on embryos that were created either through in vitro fertilization or through cloning. Sex, licit or illicit, has nothing to do with it.

Second, to the extent that attitudes toward sex are a factor, there is no reason to assume that it affects only one side of the debate. Surely it is possible that some people support abortion because it enables sexual activity that they might otherwise have to forego—or, to put it more abstractly, because it helps to underwrite the sexual revolution. Pro-lifers tend to adhere to larger ethical systems, especially of a religious nature, that also condemn sex outside of marriage. But these systems almost always condemn abortion more severely than they do sexual immorality, as do almost all opponents of abortion. Indeed, one reason opponents of abortion are concerned about sexual misconduct is that it can lead to abortion.

Is the debate a clash over these larger worldviews? Is it really a religious war? Americans who go to church (or temple or mosque) regularly are much more likely to oppose abortion than other Americans. But the opposition includes people who belong to a variety of faith traditions. It includes Catholics, evangelicals, Mormons, Muslims, some Jews, and the occasional agnostic or atheist. There is nothing sectarian, in the classic sense, about the pro-life movement.

Is it, then, a struggle between religious believers generally and the irreligious? To say that is to slander the many people who support legal abortion and consider themselves religious.[6] In addition, the basic pro-life argument—the one made in this book is an example—does not depend on any theological assertions. The argument does not rest on the teaching authority of any church, any special revelation from God, or any biblical passage or interpretation thereof. The Bible is silent on embryo research.[7]

The pro-life argument on abortion is that eight-week-old fetuses do not differ from ten-day-old babies in any way that would justify killing the former. A lot of people believe that God forbids the killing of ten-day-old babies, and many of them would be unable, if pressed, to give a persuasive account of non-theological reasons for holding such killing to be wrong. We do not take opposition to killing babies to be therefore an essentially theological view.

o   o   o

George McKenna has also written against the notion that the moral rule against taking innocent human life is peculiarly religious. McKenna cited the case of Nat Hentoff, a contemporary atheist who is also a pro-lifer (among many other things he is). He cited, as well, an atheist from the past.

His name was Whittaker Chambers. He was a figure of great controversy in the late 1940s because he exposed Alger Hiss, a former State Department official, as a long-time Communist spy. Chambers knew about Hiss's secret Communist activities, because he had participated in the same activities during the 1930s; he had received stolen State Department documents from Hiss and passed photocopies of them along to Moscow.

Chambers came from a nominally Protestant home, but he lost whatever scraps of religion he had during college, and of course was a staunch atheist during his thirteen years as a Communist. (He became a Quaker some time after he left the party in 1938.) In 1952 he published *Witness*, a memoir of his Communist years. In it he recalls that in the mid-1930s his wife (who also held no religious belief) told him that she thought she was pregnant. Since this was one of the most intense periods in his career as a Soviet agent, they planned an abortion. His wife went to a doctor to verify her pregnancy, and when she returned, he asked what the doctor said. "She said that I was in good physical shape to have a baby," his wife replied. Then there was silence. Finally, it dawned on him: he asked if she wanted to have the child:

My wife ran over to me, took my hands, and burst into tears. "Dear heart," she said in a pleading voice, "we couldn't do that awful thing to a little baby, not to a little baby, dear heart." A wild joy swept me. Reason, the agony of my family, the Communist Party and its theories, the wars and revolutions of the twentieth century, crumbled at the touch of the child.

So it happened [McKenna continues] that Whittaker and Esther Chambers, having no religious law at the time, joyously went ahead to bring their first child into the world. Their consciences bore them witness…

It is not religious doctrine [that unites pro-lifers], precious as that doctrine is to most of them. It is a law written in their hearts telling them that we may not kill people just because their birth will be inconvenient or their death will be greeted with relief.[8]

McKenna's comment about "a law written in their hearts" alludes to a Biblical passage (Romans 2:15) that asserts that people without knowledge of the Lord may nonetheless have moral knowledge. Here faith and reason need not be in conflict.

o   o   o

Maybe the most tempting misconception is that what divides people on the sanctity of life is the value they place on individual liberty. Supporters of legal abortion typically frame the issue this way: They believe that the government should not override the liberty of women to make personal decisions, while opponents of abortion do not respect a woman's right to make personal decisions free of government interference.

But this framing of the issue is tendentious. When the meaning of "personal decision" is specified, it quickly becomes clear that the dividing line is not belief in liberty vs. unbelief. Everyone believes that there are some decisions that individuals may properly make free of governmental coercion, and others that they may not. Supporters of legal abortion do not believe that a mother has the liberty, which the government must respect, to kill a five-year-old in her care; opponents do not believe that government should prevent a woman from getting her ears pierced.

The disagreement concerns whether abortion really is a "personal" decision. Opponents consider it a decision to do something unjust to another person. Liberty does not protect the unjust killing of another person. Even staunch libertarians believe that the basic function of government is to protect us from having our rights violated by unjust aggression. If abortion is such an unjust killing of another person, the government should prohibit it. A preference for liberty cannot tell us whether abortion (or euthanasia, or embryo research) is rightly characterized as such.

The party of death often tries to make another argument about liberty. There are many competing views about whether a fetus is a person with a right not to be killed, it says, and government should leave people free to adopt whatever view they reach. But this view replicates Justice Blackmun's error. The law will either treat the fetus as a human being with a right to be protected from unjust killing or it will not. It cannot be neutral in the matter. It will have to follow one of those competing views. People are, of course, free to adopt any view they want; they can take the view that five-year-olds do not have a right to life. But almost all of us would rightly reject the idea that anyone has the right to *act* on that understanding. And we would reject it even if we lived in a society where large numbers, or a majority, of people held that understanding.

The point can be made another way. This is a pluralistic country in which people have different religions, different moral beliefs, different folkways, and different conceptions of the good life, and people committed to particular views and lifestyles must therefore tolerate people who disagree with them. Our pluralism and tolerance are, in the main, valuable. But pluralism cannot be pluralistic about its own ground rules, especially the rule against killing one another. The classic expression of tolerance is the saying, "Live and let live." The party of death seeks to appropriate the value of tolerance as though it owned it, but it refuses to "let live."

Nor does Justice Kennedy's decision to define liberty in cosmic terms advance the discussion. Anyone who thinks that he can refuse to pay his taxes based on his own "concept of existence" is in for a rude awakening.

The argument for the sanctity of life is straightforward. If human beings have intrinsic dignity and worth, then they have this dignity and worth simply because they are human beings. It follows that all human beings have this dignity and worth. They are equal in the fundamental rights that attach to being human. These rights—and to have any rights at all must be to have the right not to be killed—cannot depend on particular qualities that some human beings have and others do not. They cannot depend on race, or age, or sex; nor can they depend on stage of development or condition of dependency.

Most people believe these things, although they may not accept all their implications. But there is a contrary view. The party of death holds that there are no "human rights" in the sense of rights that come simply from being human. Rather, some human organisms have basic rights because of qualities that they, in particular, happen to have; and those human beings who do not have these qualities are not persons with rights.

So, for example, some people take the view that human beings become "persons," and acquire rights, only when they acquire the capacity for abstract mental functioning, and cease to be persons with rights when they lose this capacity. If "capacity" is taken to mean immediately exercisable capacity (as it usually is on this view), then it is possible to allow abortion, research that destroys human embryos, and euthanasia of the permanently comatose and persistently vegetative.

There are, however, difficulties with this view.

First: By treating human organisms and "persons" as separate, though mostly overlapping, categories, it assumes that a distinction can be made between a person and the body that person merely "inhabits." The "person" is an aware, conscious "self" that floats above the body, as a sort of ghost in the machine. An embryonic (and fetal, and infant) body comes into existence before this person does, and the person can die before the body does. But this dualism is untenable. It contradicts everyday experience: We sense and perceive, which are clearly bodily actions, but also engage in conceptual thinking, which cannot be reduced to bodily actions; and it is clearly the same subject who does both types of things. The dualist who utters his idea refutes it in the act of voicing it. We *are* (among other things) our bodies.

Second: The capacity for abstract mental functioning varies continuously. But it is impossible to identify, without arbitrariness, the minimum level one must have to enjoy rights. It is also impossible to explain why people who have more of the quality should not be regarded as greater in worth, dignity, and rights than people who have less of it. (This is true, and necessarily true, of any of the qualities generally proposed as the conditions of worth: self-awareness, rich interactions with others, the ability to experience pain and pleasure, etc.) The notion that all human beings are created equal becomes a self-evident lie.

Roe v. *Wade* is undemocratic in a procedural sense: It circumvented the normal processes of democratic policy making. But it is also undemocratic in a deeper sense: It violates the principle of human equality that is the moral basis for democratic self-government, and specifically for American democracy.

That may, incidentally, help explain why the pro-life movement has persisted in this country when it has largely vanished from Europe. Other countries have grounded freedom and equality in the requirements of social peace; America has grounded them in those of moral truth ("We hold these truths...").

Third: This arbitrariness makes it impossible to confine the category of lives deemed unworthy of protection to the unborn and the persistently vegetative. Newborns, for example, do not have the ability to perform abstract mental functions, either. (See Chapter 15 for a look at the ghoulish implications some have drawn from this fact.)

Fourth: Treating a difference of quantity as morally decisive requires treating a difference of kind as irrelevant. There is a radical difference that separates both an adult human being and a human embryo from both a kitten and a sperm cell. The first two are complete, living human organisms and the second two are not. Yet the party of death ignores that basic difference while making a difference of degree—the adult's greater age and development of his capacities—the basis of a radical difference in treatment. To draw distinctions in this way is to violate the most basic canons of justice.

It is sometimes objected that the argument just sketched, for the equality of all human beings in having a right not to be killed, clashes with our everyday intuitions and should therefore fall. Thus the liberal columnist Jonathan Alter calls the pope "perverse" for wanting to protect the life of "a tiny clump of cells no bigger than the period at the end of this sentence."[9] Anna Quindlen calls the embryo "a cluster of undifferentiated cells."[10] The liberal columnist Michael Kinsley says that embryos are "microscopic clumps of cells" that have less in common with you or me than a mosquito. He writes, as well, that it makes little sense to object to the killing of embryos when miscarriages occur routinely in nature.[11] The liberal philosopher Michael Sandel notes that we do not typically bury or have mourning rites for miscarried embryos.[12] Ellen Goodman asks whom you would save in a burning IVF clinic: the embryos or a child who happened to be there?[13] Jeffrey Hart, arguing in favor of embryo research, says that early-stage embryos "do not look like human beings."[14]

But of course the embryo looks exactly like a human being: It looks like a human being in the embryonic stage of development. Each of us looked like that at that age. Science has opened up whole worlds of knowledge and possibility to us. Among the knowledge that we have gained is that human beings at their beginnings look like nothing we have ever before seen. Embryos are composed of cells, it is true; but it is also true that Kinsley, Quindlen, and Alter are clumps of cells. Alter is correct to suggest that they are larger clumps of cells. But it's hard to see why size should be the difference between having a right to life and lacking one. And unlike mosquitos, but like you or me, human embryos are complete human organisms.

The analogy between miscarriages and the deliberate destruction of embryos fails utterly. To start with the less important flaw: Many miscarriages result from incomplete or defective fertilizations, and therefore do not represent the death of a human organism; rather, no such being existed in the first place. More to the point: It's simply an error to suppose that the occurrence of an event in nature justifies the deliberate mimicking of that event. There have been many societies in human history where infant mortality rates were quite high, but those high rates do not establish that infanticide would have been morally justified in those societies. The high natural death rate among ninety-year-olds does not make it all right to burn down nursing homes. The tsunami that occurred in December 2004 does not mean that it's okay to slaughter Asians.

Nor can the point about burials hold much weight. As a matter of fact, many mothers *do* grieve intensely over miscarriages. But there are many factors that affect our emotional responses to deaths without affecting the right to life. We may, for example, grieve more over the death of a middle-aged man than an elderly one, or of a healthy man than one who had suffered a long illness, without thinking any less of the latter's right not to be killed.

Goodman's question about the burning building doesn't prove the point she thinks it does. Think about another hypothetical situation: You're in a burning building. You can either rescue a research scientist who is making great strides toward a cure for Alzheimer's disease, or rescue four heroin-addicted fifty-eight-year-old men who have spent their lives rotating through the penal system and are likely to continue to do so. Whom do you save?

Let's say you save the scientist. Are you therefore saying that it's permissible to kill hopeless old addicts? Are you saying that such people do not have the same right not to be killed that the scientist does? Of course not. Neither Goodman's question nor mine asks you to contemplate killing anyone. The moral question posed by the burning-building scenarios is the extent to which you can show favoritism without being unjust. That's an interesting question. But in answering it we might reasonably take account of all kinds of things—family ties, the life prospects of potential rescuees, the suffering they would undergo if not rescued, etc.—that aren't relevant to the question: Can we kill them?

To put it another way: In affirming that all human beings have an equal right not to be killed, we need not affirm that all human beings have equal claims on us in all respects.[15]

Finally, moral intuitions are far from an unfailing guide to moral truth. Human history offers ample precedent for denying rights to groups of human beings because they do not look like us, where "us" includes all the people who have the power to deny those rights—especially when supposing that "they" have no rights makes it easier for us to pursue our goals. It is easy to discount the rights of beings who cannot tell their stories. Our history should teach us, however, that our natural sentiments, instincts, and intuitions can go badly awry and have to be examined in the light of reason. Our duty is to form our sensibilities around our convictions, not the other way around.

As I mentioned earlier, one occasionally runs into defenses of abortion that are not based on the denial of the embryo's humanity or personhood. One such defense is Judith Jarvis Thomson's famous argument that the fetus does not have a just claim on the use of its mother's body and time, and can rightly be evicted from the womb.[16] But in abortion, the death of the fetus is often the goal of the procedure, and always the means to the end. It is a deliberate killing that usually rips apart the fetus or does some other violence to him in the womb. Trespassers, even those more blameworthy than the fetus, are generally dealt with less harshly.

The structure of the intent matters. Many pro-lifers have argued that "emergency contraception," the so-called "morning-after" pill, is not just contraceptive but abortifacient: It acts not only by preventing conception, but also by blocking the development of a newly conceived embryo. (Indeed, the Pill sometimes has this effect.) There may be an argument against playing Russian roulette in this way—taking this pill may cause a death or not. But the argument would be one of fairness, rather than the stronger argument against deliberate killing.

Now is as good a time as any to note that belief in the right to life of all human beings does not commit anyone to pacifism. In just wars, enemy soldiers are killed in self-defense or in the defense of others against unjust aggression. They are not killed on the theory that they are not persons and have no basic right to life. In embryo research, euthanasia, or the vast majority of abortions, no such justification based on defense is available.

Supporters of the death penalty, meanwhile, generally claim either that murderers forfeit their own right to life by taking the life of another or that execution is an extension of a community's right to self-defense. I do not, myself, accept either argument or support the death penalty. Again, however, the arguments for it do not apply to the killing of innocent human beings who are not threatening the lives of others. That evil is in a class by itself.

CHAPTER 8

Silencing Dissent

THE SUPREME COURT WAS widely expected to overrule *Roe* v. *Wade* in 1992. Republican presidents opposed to *Roe* had appointed the last five justices. A case involving regulations on abortion in Pennsylvania, *Planned Parenthood* v. *Casey*, offered the Court an opportunity to toss *Roe* onto the scrap heap. Instead, three of those justices—Sandra Day O'Connor, Anthony Kennedy, and David Souter—joined a majority in favor of "the essential holding of *Roe*."

The Court did not re-affirm *Roe* on the theory that the Constitution really does protect abortion. Nor did it say that it had gotten the Constitution wrong in *Roe*, but had to stick with its decision to keep the law stable. It took a stab at both arguments. The *Casey* Court rejected a "literal reading" of the Constitution and ventured instead on a vision quest that allowed it to embrace "the right to define one's own concept of existence, of meaning, of the universe, and of the mystery of human life." Turning to the question of stability, the Court noted—surely correctly—that "for two decades of economic and social developments, people have organized intimate relationships and made choices that define their views of themselves and their places in society, in reliance on the availability of abortion in the event that contraception should fail."

But the Court did not seem to think that these arguments were sufficient to rescue *Roe* (as they plainly are not).[1] Instead, what appears to have clinched the Court's decision was that reversing *Roe* would undermine the Court's own standing.

The *Casey* Court spoke as though the mere existence of disagreement with it is scandalous. The decision began thus:

> Liberty finds no refuge in a jurisprudence of doubt. Yet, 19 years after our holding that the Constitution protects a woman's right to terminate her pregnancy in its early stages, *Roe* v. *Wade*, 410 U.S. 113 (1973), that definition of liberty is still questioned. Joining the respondents as amicus curiae, the United States, as it has done in five other cases in the last decade, again asks us to overrule *Roe*.
>
> Soon the Court started to thump the table.
>
> Where, in the performance of its judicial duties, the Court decides a case in such a way as to resolve the sort of intensely divisive controversy reflected in *Roe* and those rare, comparable cases, its decision has a dimension that the resolution of the normal case does not carry. It is the dimension present whenever the Court's interpretation of the Constitution calls the contending sides of a national controversy to end their national division by accepting a common mandate rooted in the Constitution.

The Court went on to say that there will be "inevitable efforts to overturn" such decisions and "to thwart [their] implementation." But it would take a very "compelling reason" to get the Court to overturn its decisions, because the Court does not want to appear to be guilty of "a surrender to political pressure and an unjustified repudiation of the principle on which the Court staked its authority." Without a compelling reason, "to overrule under fire . . . would subvert the Court's legitimacy."

The Court would also undermine its legitimacy by breaking its promise to supporters of *Roe*. These supporters may have faced "criticism," "ostracism," or "violence." They may have "struggle[d] to accept" the ruling even though they oppose abortion. These people have been "tested by following." By overruling its decision, the Court would have "broke[n] its faith with the people":

> Like the character of an individual, the legitimacy of the Court must be earned over time. So, indeed, must be the character of a Nation of people who aspire to live according to the rule of law. Their belief in themselves as such a people is not readily separable from their understanding of the Court invested with the authority to decide their constitutional cases and speak before all others for their constitutional ideals. If the Court's legitimacy should be undermined, then, so would the country be in its very ability to see itself through its constitutional ideals. The Court's concern with legitimacy is not for the sake of the Court, but for the sake of the Nation to which it is responsible.

So the Court "speak[s] before all others" for our constitutional ideals. But nobody else is allowed to speak afterwards (at least, nobody who disagrees). The Court may not have spoken with the authority of the Constitution, exactly. But it spoke with the authority of the country, which "sees itself"—sees its own reflection?—when it looks at the Court. So there was no need, really, for anyone else to speak.[2]

The Court, in *Roe*, had already said that no state legislature anywhere could depart from its favored abortion policy. No matter how deeply the public of Minnesota or Mississippi opposed third-trimester abortions, they could not prohibit them. *Casey* re-affirmed that conclusion. The justices professed their reluctance to "mandate our own moral code," but that comment was either disingenuous or self-deceptive: If they really didn't want to take sides in the underlying moral argument about the justice of abortion, they would have let legislatures set abortion policy.[3]

But *Casey* went further. In defending "abortion rights," the Court made a broad assertion of its own supremacy and displayed a marked intolerance for conflicting views. The plain meaning of its words about "end[ing] national division" is that the pro-life movement should cease to exist. Its members are to put down their placards and go away. The Court has spoken; the issue is settled.

Worse: The Court is saying that the more a decision it has made is criticized, the less likely it is to reconsider that decision. Probably everyone has felt this way at some point: You've made a mistake, someone is criticizing you, but you don't want to lose face by admitting it. But when we are aware of this psychological response, we tend to try to correct it—not to defend it openly. (We may even realize that persisting in error to spite our critics tarnishes our reputation all the more.) The Court is not just stubborn. It is intolerant.

And it is fearful: To allow the critics to succeed in swaying the Court—to allow this issue to be handled democratically, as it had been handled before 1973—would tear the country apart.[4] This fear is the point of its reference to anti-abortion violence, and related to its wish that pro-lifers would disappear. Never mind that the Court's own decision to short-circuit democratic debate has, more than any other factor, made abortion such a neuralgic issue.

There is a certain futility to the Court's impatient demand that the abortion debate be recognized as settled. No matter how many times the justices, and various other worthies, proclaim the debate to be over, it just keeps continuing. (When *Roe* came down, the *New York Times* editorialized: "The Court's verdict on abortions provides a sound foundation for final and reasonable resolution of a debate that has divided America too long."[5]) The Court lacks not only the constitutional authority to shut down debate; it lacks the power. But its evident desire to do so is shared by the abortion lobby as a whole.

Abortion clinics have sought, and won, statutes and judicial injunctions limiting the free-speech rights of pro-lifers. To regulate demonstrations outside abortion clinics so as to reduce the risk of violence is one thing. But restrictions on peaceful protest have also been imposed. Colorado enacted a law creating a hundred-foot "bubble" around entrances to medical facilities (defined to include abortion clinics). Within the bubble, it is illegal to come within eight feet of someone to pass her a leaflet, to show her a sign or picture, or to give advice, or to say something in protest, unless she first consents. The statute was obviously designed to impede pro-life expression, and pro-life expression alone. The restrictions do not apply to any form of speech other than speech intended to educate, protest, or counsel.

(The distinctions the law makes, incidentally, wouldn't make sense even if they were compatible with the First Amendment. What possible purpose is served by saying that pro-lifers cannot approach a woman to try to counsel her against abortion but can shout at her from eight feet away through a bullhorn?)

The Supreme Court upheld the Colorado law in 2000. To do so, it had to mangle its own precedents and invent another new right: a right not to be subjected to unwanted communications, which is hard to reconcile with free speech traditionally defined. Not to worry: The Court has no intention of applying this principle to other areas of the law.

As Justice Antonin Scalia wrote in dissent, "Having deprived abortion opponents of the political right to persuade the electorate that abortion should be restricted by law, the Court today continues and expands its assault upon their individual right to persuade women contemplating abortion that what they are doing is wrong...

[L]ike the rest of our abortion jurisprudence, today's decision is in stark contradiction of the constitutional principles we apply in all other contexts."[6] Justice Kennedy, one of the justices responsible for *Casey*, to his credit dissented. He took the view that *Casey*, by making it impossible to prohibit abortion, made it all the more important to allow opponents of abortion to try to persuade women of its immorality. But the Court is not guided by a principle of governmental non-interference in abortion decisions. The government may interfere quite a bit so long as it is trying to keep pro-lifers from influencing those decisions.[7]

The party of death seems to have a kind of censoring impulse. It is striking how many of the arguments associated with it do not attempt to make the case for abortion or its legality so much as they attempt to rule arguments against it out of bounds. Or to challenge its opponents' standing or right to say anything at all.

We are all familiar, for example, with the refrain that men should not be talking about abortion. To see the emptiness of this tactic it is necessary only to ask why it is never, ever directed at pro-choice men. The truth is that polls about attitudes toward abortion do not uncover substantial differences between men and women.[8] (Marriage is one of several demographic characteristics that matter more than sex. Married men are more pro-life than single men, and married women more pro-life than single women.)[9]

When President Bush nominated John Roberts to the Supreme Court, Democratic senator Dianne Feinstein of California said that she would be "representing the views and concerns of 145 million American women" in his confirmation hearings. She went on to say that she would therefore find it "very difficult... to vote to confirm someone to the Supreme Court whom I knew would overturn *Roe*."[10]

But of course there are women—tens of millions of them—who think abortion should be restricted. There are even women who

believe that abortion should be illegal, or legal only when the life of
the mother is at stake or the pregnancy results from rape or incest.
How many such women are there? According to the Center for the
Advancement of Women, a group that supports abortion, a majority
of American women (51 percent) take this pro-life position.[11] So
Feinstein is off by at least 74 million women.

Even more commonly, supporters of the abortion license — and
of euthanasia and embryo-destructive research — claim that pro-lifers and their arguments have no place in democratic debate because
they are religious. In the aftermath of the Terri Schiavo controversy,
Howard Dean, chairman of the Democratic National Committee,
said, "The issue is: Are we going to live in a theocracy where the
highest powers tell us what to do?"[12] At the Democratic convention
the previous year, Ron Reagan Jr. had spoken in favor of federal
funding for research involving the cloning and killing of human
embryos. He said that the opponents of the funding believed in the
moral worth of embryos as "an article of faith," but should not be
allowed to impose "the theology of a few" on the rest of us.[13]

Mario Cuomo, the former governor of New York, who functions
as the Democratic party's elder statesman-philosopher, says (in defi-
ance of the plain facts of human embryology and developmental
biology) that the conviction that "life begins at conception" is a "not
a scientific conclusion" but "a religious conclusion." He chastises
President Bush for making a "faith-based judgment on stem cells"
and abortion and attempting to impose it on the country.[14]

Whether or not they know it, these Democrats are echoing the
late John Rawls, the most influential liberal political philosopher
(which is of course to say the most influential political philosopher)
of the last thirty years. Rawls argued that in a modern democracy,
policies must be based on what he called "public reasons," rather
than on personal interests, secret rationales, or sectarian religious
dogmas.[15] Peter Beinart, the editor of the liberal *New Republic*,

wrote in a Rawlsian vein when he scolded pro-lifers after the 2004 elections for neglecting the duty to make arguments that are, in principle, "accessible to people of different religions, or no religion at all."[16]

Rawls's concept of "public reason" sounds fine in bare outline. While there is no constitutional requirement that people make political arguments in terms that can be understood by fellow citizens with different religious views, it is a reasonable request. Because an appeal to a religious belief, authority, or text will be unpersuasive to people who do not accept them, it will often be counterproductive for advocates of any political cause to make such an appeal. (Often, but not always. The contention that blacks, like whites, were made in the image of God and thus deserve fair treatment was probably "accessible" to more people when it counted than were purely secular arguments. Most Americans do not find such religious rhetoric alienating, and in a democracy that ought to count for something.)

But the party of death uses public reason to stack the deck against pro-lifers by placing them outside the realm of acceptable debate. The Mario Cuomos and Ron Reagans of the world—and even their academic equivalents—don't look very hard for conservatives' reasons. Cuomo is simply incorrect to say that the proposition that conception marks the beginning of a new human life is religious in nature; it is biological fact. The argument that it is immoral to set aside one class of human lives as expendable, meanwhile, is philosophical and rational. At no point does the argument developed in this book, for example, rely on the authority of the Bible, or the Vatican. It does not rely on the assertion that the newly conceived embryo, or the fetus, has a soul, or was made in the image of God.

Justice John Paul Stevens dismisses the notion "that a fetus is a 'person'" as a "religious view," writing patronizingly that "a powerful theological argument can be made for that position"—the implication being that no other kind of argument can.[17] He does not attempt to offer any support for these claims.

In truth, it is no more "religious" to claim that six-month-old fetuses should not be killed than it is to claim that teenagers should not be killed. A government that acts on the claim about fetuses is no more "theocratic," by virtue of its having done so, than a government that acts on the second claim. A government that generally bans abortion does not thereby take a position on whether the fetus has a soul, any more than it takes a position on whether thirty-five-year-olds have souls by banning their killing.

Some religious institutions would applaud a ban on abortion or euthanasia. But this fact hardly establishes that these policies lack a rational foundation. Religious teachings can reflect reason. The most influential religious opposition to the party of death is that of the Catholic Church. Even people who do not accept the correctness of its teaching on those issues ought to be able to see that it is based on premises that are in principle rational and accessible to non-Catholics and, indeed, to non-Christians: the (undeniable) premise that human embryos are members of the human species, for example.

The Catholic Church has never definitively stated whether it believes that human embryos have souls. Nor does it believe that Scripture yields a definitive view of the ethics of embryo research. The religious component of the church's teaching is the view that God wants us to do justice. Ascertaining what justice is in particular cases, such as the case of embryo research, is the work of reason. The opponents of embryo-killing research, however religious they may be, do not generally believe that God has told us in some direct way what the government's policy toward the research should be. They understand themselves to be making reasoned arguments.

It may be objected that apparently reasoned arguments against embryo destruction are really rationalizations for religious views.

The opponents are often evangelicals and Catholics. It is certainly possible that their reasoning goes wrong because they are influenced by extra-rational, unacknowledged factors. But the reasoning of people from different religious traditions or none can go wrong, too. Atheists and agnostics may have their own forms of rationalization. Self-consciously secular thinkers can generate their own orthodoxies. Liberals tend to assume, without realizing it, that the rational view of any controversial moral issue is likely to be the one that most non-religious people take. The idea that a religious tradition could strengthen people's reason—could help them reach rationally sound conclusions they might not otherwise reach, and stick to them when there may be reasons of emotion or self-interest not to do so—rarely occurs to them.

During the presidential campaign of 2004, Joseph Bottum of the *Weekly Standard* quipped that John Kerry apparently believed that the fact that his church opposed abortion was a reason he had to support it. The mental tic Bottum neatly identified is a special case of liberalism's general tendency to identify reason with irreligion.[18]

It may also be objected that while some people may decide to oppose abortion for rational reasons, many others oppose it because a priest, minister, or televangelist told them to. But even if it were the case that 95 percent of pro-lifers formed their views in that fashion, establishing the point would do nothing to weaken the reasonableness of their position. (Nor would it demonstrate the unreasonableness of a position if 95 percent of the people who hold it were found to do so simply because they slavishly follow the direction of the *New York Times* editorial page and allied opinion-setters.)

Here is another blind spot of Rawlsian public reason. If large numbers of people prefer pro-life policies but are unable to articulate suitable "public reasons" for them, their views are held to be sub-rational and therefore can't prevail. If philosophers can articulate rational reasons for these policies but the average Joe can't understand their reasoning, those reasons are deemed insufficiently accessible to the public. What is ignored here, as such critics of Rawlsian public reason as Robert P. George and Christopher Wolfe have observed, is the possibility that people can have inarticulate but genuine knowledge. They note that most people could not, if pressed, make an airtight case that murder is wrong. Yet their belief that it is wrong is perfectly rational and amounts to genuine knowledge.[19]

The party of death's hymns to reason end up truncating reason. They are pleas for open debate designed to rule things out of debate. John Rawls himself notoriously ruled that arguments against abortion could not meet the test of his "public reason."[20] To a pro-lifer, it begins to look like a kind of trick. Let us imagine a pro-lifer who says that abortion should be illegal because it kills human beings. His pro-choice friend responds that this sort of theological talk is inadmissible in a democracy because it violates the rules of open debate. We can see that this pro-choicer has misrepresented his friend's views and shut down the discussion — all in the name of reasoned argument. Yet that conversation happens all the time in our politics, and somehow we don't see it.

Rawls himself, an honest and thoughtful man, eventually did see it and backed down from his claim about abortion.[21] Howard Dean and company haven't yet.

CHAPTER 9

The Corruption of History

OUR LAW SCHOOLS HAVE tried for years to devise rationales for treating abortion as a constitutional right. In 1989, academic historians took a turn at the job. This time, the effort wasn't just unconvincing. It was fradulent. What follows is a case study in the academic betrayal of truth.

The Supreme Court was at the time considering the case of *Webster* v. *Reproductive Health Services*. On behalf of 281 historians, a team of lawyers submitted a legal brief urging the Court to re-affirm *Roe*. "Never before," the brief begins, "have so many professional historians sought to address this Honorable Court in this way." [1]

Later signatures would bring the total number of historians above four hundred. The brief was modified and resubmitted again three years later, when the Supreme Court again considered abortion in *Planned Parenthood* v. *Casey*. [2]

The historians claimed that Americans had recognized the right to choose abortion at the time of the Republic's founding. Further, they argued, nineteenth-century legislators restricted that right for four reasons that either no longer apply or are no longer constitutionally permissible: to protect women from unsafe abortions, to help physicians to constitute themselves as a profession, to enforce gender roles, and to prevent Catholic immigrants from increasing their proportion of the population. A concern for the life of the fetus "became a central issue in American culture only in the late twentieth century." Since restrictions on abortion impose severe costs on women and since the historic rationales for those restrictions are discredited or obsolete, the historians concluded, the Court should reaffirm *Roe* v. *Wade*.

In *Roe*, Justice Blackmun had asserted both that it was "doubtful" that the common law had ever prohibited abortion and that nineteenth-century statutes did not reflect a belief in the personhood of fetuses. The brief bolstered his argument. It also served the party of death by portraying anti-abortion laws as an aberration from an American tradition, *Roe* as the restoration of that tradition.

The brief has been influential. But it is an utter fraud, riddled with scholarly abuses and inaccurate conclusions. Its key claims are simply indefensible.

The common law always restricted abortion, and the campaign against abortion did seek to protect fetal life. Moreover, the published work of the historians who signed this brief disproved its historical arguments, and the very sources on which the brief relied contradicted its thesis. Its shoddiness was too pervasive and tendentious for mere incompetence to explain it.

The brief's history of abortion begins with the following paragraph:

As the Court demonstrated in *Roe* v. *Wade*, abortion was not illegal at common law. Through the nineteenth century American common-law decisions uniformly reaffirmed that women committed no offense in seeking abortions. Both common law and popular culture drew distinctions depending upon whether the fetus was "quick," i.e. whether the *woman* perceived signs of independent life. There was some dispute whether a common-law misdemeanor occurred when a third party destroyed a fetus, after quickening, without the woman's consent. But early recognition of this particular crime against pregnant women did not diminish the liberty of the woman herself to end a pregnancy in its early stages (emphasis in original).

Almost every statement in this paragraph is false or misleading.

The paragraph strongly implies that abortion was legal even after quickening, except possibly when women did not consent. The historians' first source for their contention that "abortion was not illegal at common law" was Justice Blackmun, who in turn based his more tentative version of this claim on a 1971 article by Cyril C. Means Jr.[3] Means acknowledged that many authorities on the common law held abortion to be illegal. He argued, however, that two fourteenth-century cases held abortion at any stage of pregnancy to be neither a felony nor even a serious misdemeanor, and that great legal writers from the thirteenth through the seventeenth century had misunderstood and even deliberately misrepresented the common law.

Research since 1971 has thoroughly discredited Means's article. Full records of the cases at issue show that only procedural and evidentiary problems prevented the imposition of penalties, thus vindicating the legal writers from the charges of scholarly error and misconduct.[4] Indictments or appeals of felony for abortions dating as far back as 1200 demonstrate that neither a woman's consent nor the absence of quickening rendered abortion legal. Nor were women who sought abortion immune from prosecution, in England or the colonies.[5]

The brief's second citation on abortion's status as a "common-law liberty" is of pages 3–19 of James C. Mohr's *Abortion in America*. The brief elsewhere praises this book ("widely regarded as accurate and comprehensive") and highlights Mohr's signing of the brief. Most of the cited pages do not examine the issue at hand, but on page 3 Mohr writes, "After quickening, the expulsion and destruction of a fetus without due cause was considered a crime."[6] Whoops. The historians next cite Means, repeating his slander against the common-law writers.

Last, they cite pages 119–121 of Angus McLaren's *Reproductive Rituals* to claim, "Even in cases involving brutal beatings of women in the late stages of pregnancy, common-law courts refused to recognize abortion as a crime, independent of assault upon the woman, or in one case 'witchcraft.'" Neither the cited pages nor any other pages of McLaren's book contain anything to support this proposition. On page 121, McLaren notes that "it is necessary to turn to the writings of the common-law advocates" to understand the legal status of abortion between 1650 and 1800; after examining a few of these writings, he summarizes, "Seventeenth-century jurists thus recognized that a woman could be charged with procuring her own abortion, but only after the foetus had quickened."[7]

As that McLaren quote suggests, the brief didn't have to make up sources to find support for the claim that abortion *before* quickening was legal at common law. Mohr's book, for example, actually supports that claim.[8] Blackmun, in *Roe*, even claimed that this point was "undisputed." That's an overstatement. Courts in America disagreed over the legality of pre-quickening abortion at common law.[9] The two leading nineteenth-century American treatises on the common law both treated abortion before quickening as an offense.[10]

The more interesting question is *why* the law took note of quickening. It appears that it entered the common law because of two gaps in scientific knowledge. First, embryology was not well enough understood for "medical men" to agree on "the time when the foetus may be stated . . . to have a distinct existence," as a British court put it in 1811.[11] Later in the century, Francis Wharton, one of the treatise writers, wrote: "The notion that a man is not accountable for destroying the child before it quickens, arose from the hypothesis that quickening was the commencement of vitality with it," but that theory "is now exploded in medicine, the fact being considered indisputable, that 'quickening' is the incident, not the inception of vitality."[12]

Second, prosecuting abortion before quickening presented an evidentiary problem. As Mohr explains: "Practically, because no reliable tests for pregnancy existed in the early nineteenth century, quickening alone could confirm with absolute certainty that a woman really was pregnant. Prior to quickening, each of the telltale signs of pregnancy could, at least in theory, be explained in alternative ways by the physicians of the day."[13]

Robert Byrn provides a useful summary of the common law's stance toward abortion:

> (a) even the earliest common law cases do not support the proposition that abortion was regarded as a "liberty" or "freedom" or "right" of the pregnant woman or anyone else; (b) "quickening" was utilized in the later common law as a practical evidentiary test to determine whether the abortion had been an assault upon a live human being in the womb and whether the abortional act had caused the child's death; this evidentiary test was never intended as a judgment that before quickening the child was not a live human being; and, (c) at all times, the common law disapproved of abortion as [wrong in itself] and sought to protect the child in the womb from the moment his living biological existence could be proved.[14]

The moment "existence could be proved," of course, depended on contemporary scientific knowledge.

After claiming that abortion was legal, the historians next turn to claiming that it "was not uncommon in colonial America." They cite McLaren as the sole support for this astonishing statement. But his book deals with England, not America. The cited chapter contains just one quote on the prevalence of abortion—by an Englishman, in 1824, referring to the impressions that led Parliament to pass an anti-abortion law in 1803.[15]

The extremely high birthrates of the time and the danger and ineffectiveness of contemporary methods of abortion suggest that it was uncommon. So does the high proportion of brides who were pregnant on their wedding day, a datum the brief oddly adduces in support of its contention. In *Intimate Matters*, John D'Emilio and brief signatory Estelle B. Freedman list coitus interruptus, prolonged nursing, and abstinence as methods used to limit family size in colonial America, adding that "other means to impede conception or terminate pregnancy were rarely employed."[16] Mohr writes that abortion was "a fundamentally marginal practice."[17]

In order to show that "working class married women . . . resorted to abortion as the most effective available means of 'conscious fertility control,'" the brief refers to Rosalind Pollack Petchesky's *Abortion and Woman's Choice*. A glance at the relevant page of that book reveals that the quote comes from a theoretical generalization—"As a popular method of conscious fertility control, abortion among poor and working-class women never abates but increases with time"—and one of dubious validity.[18]

A page later, the brief asserts, "To limit the number of children they bore, women adopted a range of strategies, including abortion." Puzzlingly, it illustrates this contention in a footnote thus: "One physician wrote that 'abortion is not always associated with crime and disgrace; it may arise from causes perfectly natural and altogether beyond the control of the female.'"[19] But the physician in question was clearly talking about spontaneous abortions, i.e., miscarriages.[20]

The brief then turns to the claim that the abortion laws between 1820 and 1860 were aimed at maternal safety. According to the

brief, New York lawmakers sought to protect women from dangerous medical treatment when they passed abortion regulations in
1828—a claim first made in another influential article by Means.
His argument hinged on a proposed, but never passed, section of the
bill that would have outlawed any surgery not necessary for the
preservation of a patient's life. The sections regulating abortion contained similarly worded exceptions allowing abortions to save a pregnant woman's life; hence, he reasoned, they too were intended to
prevent unnecessary operations from endangering lives.[21]

Mohr's book explicitly refutes these arguments. If lawmakers had
wished to regulate abortion merely as a dangerous form of surgery,
they would neither have treated it separately nor have passed abortion regulations while defeating the proposed regulations on all surgery. The brief also reports that the "act finally adopted applied only
to surgical abortion"; but a glance at the text of the law, quoted by
Mohr, reveals that it applied to abortions by "any medicine, drug,
substance or thing whatever... any instrument or other means whatever."[22]

The historians next examine the alleged motives for the laws
enacted from the mid-nineteenth century onward, starting with the
desire of the "regular" physicians associated with the new American
Medical Association to raise their status and incomes through regulation. The brief, relying on Mohr, describes the physicians' movement against abortion as "one chapter in a campaign by doctors that
reflected a professional conflict between 'regulars' (those who ultimately became the practitioners and proponents of scientific medicine) and 'irregulars,' who were often willing to perform abortions."
Mohr lists three professional motives for the regulars' support for anti-
abortion laws: such laws enlisted the power of the state to penalize, and
to remove a competitive advantage of, the irregulars; they enforced
standards on wayward regulars, thus "promoting a sense of profession-
alism"; and they let doctors "recapture what they considered to be

their ancient and rightful place among society's policymakers and savants."[23]

Neither the brief nor Mohr presents any evidence that anti-abortion legislators understood themselves to be acting primarily in these interests—or that the voting public understood the laws in that light. Whatever the physicians' motives, they succeeded by persuading others of the justice of their cause. Many AMA members in the 1860s and 1870s also supported the legalization and regulation of prostitution as a public-health measure, but failed to convince their contemporaries.[24]

Mohr's book makes clear that physicians opposed abortion in large part because of a concern for fetal life. He writes, "The regulars' opposition to abortion was partly ideological, partly scientific, partly moral, and partly practical." He explains the "moral" component of their opposition thus: "The nation's regular doctors... defended the value of human life per se as an absolute."

Opposition to abortion as a species of killing forms the basis of each of the other three components. The doctors' "ideological" opposition to abortion consisted of their belief in the Hippocratic Oath, which states: "I will neither give a deadly drug to anybody if asked for it, nor will I make a suggestion to this effect. Similarly I will not give to a woman an abortive remedy." The "scientific" component of the physicians' stance was their realization "that conception inaugurated a more or less continuous process of development... From this scientific reasoning stemmed the regulars' moral opposition to abortion at any stage of gestation."[25]

By the "practical" reasons, Mohr means the professional motives already mentioned: eliminating competition, enforcing standards, and gaining the status of policymakers. The last two goals imply a prior determination on other grounds of a standard to enforce and a policy to make. Nor can the goal of eliminating competition be understood without reference to the physicians' abhorrence of abortion; otherwise, they could have performed abortions themselves.[26]

The campaign against abortion did *not* play a substantial role in professionalizing American medicine. Books on medical professionalization written by signatories to the brief do not even mention the campaign. Signatory Paul Starr's well-regarded *The Social Transformation of American Medicine* mentions the campaign once, in a footnote on the involvement of physicians in projects of moral reform.[27] *For Her Own Good*, written by signatory Barbara Ehrenreich and Deirdre English, discusses professionalization as it relates to female patients without once mentioning the campaign.[28] Signatory Judith Walzer Leavitt's *Brought to Bed* focuses on how childbirth moved from the home to the hospital; although the brief cites the book to show the centrality of "the medical profession's gradual consolidation of authority" to that shift in location, the book nowhere discusses the physicians' campaign against abortion as a part of that shift.[29] The brief cites all three books in its section on professionalization without mentioning these inconvenient silences.

Because the historians want to argue that anti-abortion laws were in part a response to anxieties about nineteenth-century feminism, they have to get around the fact that nineteenth-century feminists opposed abortion. So the brief does what it can to imply the reverse:

> The women's movement of the nineteenth century affirmed that women should always have the right to decide whether to bear a child and sought to enhance women's control of reproduction through "voluntary motherhood," ideally to be achieved through periodic abstinence. Anxieties about changing family functions and gender roles were critical factors motivating the all-male legislatures that adopted restrictions on abortion.

The brief cites Linda Gordon's *Woman's Body, Woman's Right* on "voluntary motherhood." But Professor Gordon also writes, "It is important to stress the fact that neither free lovers nor suffragists"—the advocates of voluntary motherhood—"approved of contraceptive devices," let alone abortion.[30] Most feminists, she recognizes, opposed abortion.[31] She signed the brief anyway. So did Carl N. Degler, whose book *At Odds* notes that "during the Nineteenth century feminists and free lovers alike condemned abortion because it destroyed a human being."[32] So, of course, did Mohr, whose book also reported the truth about early feminists' views of abortion.[33]

This section of the brief was altered when it was resubmitted to the Supreme Court in *Planned Parenthood* v. *Casey* (1992). The *Casey* brief acknowledges that "some feminists" (a curiously dismissive phrase, considering that the group included such luminaries as Elizabeth Cady Stanton, Susan B. Anthony, and Victoria Woodhull) opposed abortion, but asserts that they did so "not on moral grounds, but as an object example of women's victimization at the hands of men."

While it is true that feminists viewed abortion as a result of "women's victimization," compassion for women who considered abortion did not preclude moral opposition to it. *The Revolution*, a feminist journal, argued that

> [T]he woman is awfully guilty who commits the deed. It will burden her conscience in life; it will burden her soul in death; but oh! thrice guilty is he who, for selfish gratification, heedless of her prayers, indifferent to her fate, drove her to the desperation which impelled her to the crime.[34]

An 1874 editorial in another feminist publication, *Woodhull and Claflin's Weekly*, dubbed abortion "the Slaughter of the Innocents." It observed that abortion was often a reaction to "the slavery that child-bearing almost necessarily entails in our society as at present organized," but also declared that abortion "stamps the brand of Cain upon every woman who attempts or is accessory to it." Those who performed abortions did not get off lightly, either: "Let those who see any difference regarding the time when life, once begun, is taken, console themselves that they are not murderers having been abortionists."[35]

At this point, the brief makes, for once, a largely accurate point: that many anti-abortion physicians were concerned by the declining birth rates of white Protestants in comparison to those of immigrants, particularly Catholic immigrants.[36] They viewed abortion as a contributing factor to "race suicide." It is worth noting, however, that these nativist fears did not lead the physicians to wish that contraceptive and abortion use among Catholics and immigrants would increase. Nor did they lead anyone to advocate the employment of state subsidies, charity, and proselytization for that purpose. These solutions would have been as logical a response to fears of "race suicide" as prohibitions on abortion, yet they were unthinkable, in large part because of the moral opposition of anti-abortionists to what they saw as murder. Horatio Robinson Storer, a leading anti-abortion physician whose oft-expressed nativism the brief mentions, "went out of his way to praise" a Catholic bishop who declared his opposition to abortion.[37] Nor does nativism explain why abortion was opposed more vigorously than contraception.[38]

Physicians and feminists were not alone in attacking abortion as "infanticide" and "murder." A *New York Times* article on abortion declared, "Thousands of human beings are thus murdered before they have seen the light of this world." It described the abortionist's trade as "a systematic business in wholesale murder."[39] An 1880 *National Police Gazette* article began, "The civilization of today is opposed to babies, and its basest product is the abortionist... He lives upon the crushed and mangled bodies of tender, breathless infants."[40] The authors of *Light on Dark Corners*, a book of advice on the sexual instruction of youth, alluded to "the hecatombs of infants that are annually sacrificed to Moloch" as a result of "this monstrous crime."[41]

These anti-abortionists made arguments based both on "the right to life" and on the slippery slope to "post-natal child-murder." And contrary to the brief's assertions, both statutes[42] and judicial opinions interpreting them[43] recognized fetal personhood. That recognition was implicit in legislators' decisions to increase the punishment for attempted abortion when it could be proven that the attempt had killed a fetus, and to group abortion with offenses against children in the criminal code.

The brief then nastily concludes that since nineteenth-century anti-abortion laws were (supposedly) motivated more by racism and sexism than by concern for the unborn, so the modern pro-life movement can be assumed to be merely feigning that concern as a cover for its own racism and sexism.

The brief was an elaborate lie (I've only summarized its failings in this chapter).[44] In truth, abortion was always a serious indictable offense at common law when it could be proven that the fetus was alive and moving, both in colonial America and in England for centuries before that. Abortion was a rare occurrence among colonial Americans. And the most important reason why nineteenth and early twentieth century state legislators tightened their restrictions on abortion was their belief, reinforced by recent scientific advances, that abortion unjustifiably took human life.

The historians reached their false conclusions by mischaracterizing sources, misreporting facts, and supporting claims with citations that have no relevance to those claims. They ripped quotations out of context. They relied on discredited sources—even on sources that signatories to the brief had themselves discredited. They contradicted books on which they relied heavily, even when they had written those books themselves. The historians have never offered an honest word of explanation or retraction. Sylvia Law, one of the lawyers who submitted the brief, later declared in a forum that "there is tension between truth-telling and advocacy."[45] It's obvious how that tension was resolved.

By signing the brief, historians specializing in subjects covered by it endorsed beliefs they do not hold. Mohr's case was particularly egregious, though he at least declined to sign the *Casey* version of the brief. Other historians were simply ignorant.[46] Signatories included authorities on the history of architecture, early modern France, and North China. Luminaries like Arthur Schlesinger Jr. and Sean Wilentz, for instance, each signed briefs but were hardly experts in the field. Yet signatories asked the Supreme Court to pay attention to their claims about the history of abortion law because of their professional credentials.

And the brief has had great influence. Press coverage in 1989 tended to assume its accuracy.[47] Legal scholar Walter Dellinger, who was soon to become an assistant attorney general in the Clinton administration, devoted most of an article in *The New Republic* to an uncritical summary of it.[48] Even George Will, an opponent of *Roe*, wrote a column that largely accepted the brief's factual account (while questioning its legal conclusions).[49]

In *The New York Review of Books*, legal philosopher Ronald Dworkin wrote, "The best historical evidence shows" that "anti-abortion laws, which were not prevalent in the United States before the middle of the nineteenth century, were adopted to protect the health of the mother and the privileges of the medical profession, not out of any recognition of a fetus's rights." A footnote revealed that by "best historical evidence" Dworkin meant the historians' brief.[50] He used its argument to support his contention that fetuses have never had the status of "constitutional persons." Dworkin repeated this argument, again citing the brief, in his 1993 book *Life's Dominion.*[51]

Laurence Tribe, like Dworkin one of the most prominent constitutional theorists of his generation, consulted the brief extensively for his book *Abortion: The Clash of Absolutes.* One chapter concerned "Two Centuries of Abortion in America." Tribe described the brief as "the point of departure for much of this chapter."[52]

When historian Joseph Ellis was caught making up stories about his past to impress his students, he was suspended by his university and faced calls for his dismissal. It was treated as a major scandal. Yet what the historians who signed the brief—and especially those who knew it was false—did was far worse. They put their scholarly authority behind lies. They attempted to corrupt a judicial proceeding of great importance. Yet there have been no calls for firings or even reprimands of these historians. Nobody has asked for the bare minimum: a retraction by the historians and those, such as Tribe and Dworkin, who parroted their falsehoods.

When the brief was first publicized in 1989, an article in *The Nation*, the left-wing weekly, exulted, "The signatures on this amicus brief, many those of eminent mainstream scholars, signal a coming of age for the historians who have entered the field since the 1960s."[53] They certainly do.

Part II

Bioethics of Death

CHAPTER 10

The Doctor Will Kill You Now: Euthanasia Advances

IT WAS EASY TO FORGET, during the weeks in March 2005 when the controversy over Terri Schiavo filled the airwaves, that assisted suicide is illegal in Florida—as it is in every state but Oregon (where it is legal for the terminally ill). The debate on television, on op-ed pages, and in the Congress often seemed to center on whether Florida law was wise to give her husband Michael Schiavo the right to make the life-or-death decision.

But Florida law does not recognize Mrs. Schiavo's right to kill herself, let alone her husband's right to make that choice for her. If, having (miraculously) recovered sufficient faculties to do it, she had begged a physician to give her a lethal injection, her wish could not legally have been granted. If she had recovered her faculties and then refused to eat or drink, the response of her caregivers would almost certainly have been to try to talk her into changing her mind.

What the state of Florida allows patients to do is to turn down medical treatments and, when they cannot make medical decisions, to designate others to decide for them. Turning down treatment can, of course, cause the patient's death. The decision to turn down treatment may even be made with the precise intention of causing death, as was the case with Michael Schiavo's decision.

Yet Florida does not allow assisted suicide. Why does the state allow patients to die the potentially agonizing death of starvation but not to receive a quick, painless lethal injection? That question was frequently asked during the Schiavo controversy, both by people who favored the syringe and people who opposed starvation.

The answer begins with the fact that a patient can have many reasons to decline certain medical treatments, or a husband can have to decline treatments for his incapacitated wife. Perhaps the treatment would involve pain. Perhaps the patient would rather spend her final days at home among loved ones, even if she could live longer in a hospital. Nobody believes that these are illegitimate choices or that the law should prevent them from being made. Nobody believes that there is any moral imperative to do everything possible to extend a person's lifespan—although such was the heat of the Schiavo debate that pro-lifers were sometimes wrongly accused of holding something like that view.

Two people with the same strong belief in the sanctity of life may come to different conclusions about what course of treatment to pursue for a stricken relative. The progress of medical technology has increased the number of dilemmas that we face: It seems likely that more and more of us will grapple with agonizing choices and familial conflict by the sickbed. (In earlier generations, Mrs. Schiavo would have died rather than been revived after her heart stopped.) There may be ways to make these tragedies less painful. Federal anti-drug laws may have caused doctors to be too wary of prescribing pain medication that could ease patients' suffering, and those laws and the attitudes they reflect should be adjusted. But the problem can only be ameliorated, never solved: which is another way of saying that it is less a problem than a condition.

If the law allows a patient to decline treatment, it will have to allow it even when he is declining it solely for the purpose of hastening or causing his own death. If the law allows a surrogate to decline treatment for an incapacitated patient, it will have to allow it even when the surrogate's intent is to bring about the patient's death. The legislature, in allowing such scenarios to take place legally, is not blessing these "choices for death" (to invoke, once again, Ronald Dworkin's approving phrase). Otherwise, it would repeal or relax the laws against suicide and assisted suicide. It is, rather, viewing these choices as abuses that must be tolerated in order to achieve the good of allowing people to make medical decisions for themselves and their families.

The law tries, in its imperfect way, to recognize the moral distinction between acts based on the desire to bring about death and acts based on other desires. There are other, less precise ways of capturing that distinction. For example, sometimes people will say that it is permissible to "let someone die" but not to "kill him." Or they will say that it is all right to withhold "extraordinary" but not "ordinary" medical treatments. There is wisdom in both thoughts, so long as they point us toward the question of intent. What constitutes an "extraordinary" medical treatment, for example, should not be thought of as a technical question to be settled by doctors and bioethicists. Rather, we should consider "ordinary" treatment to consist of treatments that couldn't be withheld or turned down except for improper reasons (such as the desire to see the patient die).

The difference between letting someone die and killing him, meanwhile, shouldn't come down to a word game about whether death results from an "act" or an "omission." The question, rather, should be if death is a predictable but unintended consequence of a decision—whether that decision is to administer a painkiller or to withhold a treatment—or if it is the goal (or the means to a goal).

The Supreme Court, in a series of cases from the 1990s, has struggled to defend a right to refuse medical treatment without endorsing (or definitively rejecting) a right to suicide. But there's a catch, and it's not just, as Justice Scalia noted from the start, that it isn't clear that the Constitution really contains either right. In the 1990 *Cruzan* case, the Court seemed—the language was offhand— to say that food and water constitute a medical treatment and that the Constitution required all states to allow patients to turn down this treatment. Further, it seemed to say that all states had to let their surrogates turn down basic sustenance for them. The law in Florida, adopted post-*Cruzan*, accepts this obligation.

Yet in most cases, the only reason to disconnect an incapacitated patient from a feeding and hydration tube is to cause death. The Court seems to have taken the nation a half-step toward assisted suicide without anyone, even pro-lifers, quite realizing it. Apart from rare cases in which food or fluid would hasten death or cause physical damage, it's hard to see any reason for allowing patients to be denied food and water but not given a lethal injection.

That was the confused legal backdrop against which the Schiavo drama played out. Michael Schiavo wanted Terri Schiavo's feeding and hydration tube to be removed so that she would die. He claimed that this action would be in keeping with her wishes. His evidence for this claim consisted of two statements. Michael Schiavo's brother, Scott, said that she had told him that she did not want to be on life support the way Michael and Scott's grandmother had been. "If I ever go like that, just let me go," she had supposedly said. Terri's sister-in-law Joan Schiavo said that the two had watched a TV movie about a man on a feeding tube and that Terri had said, "No tubes for me."

Terri's siblings and parents, the Schindlers, did not believe that she would have had those wishes. They thought it suspicious that Michael Schiavo and his relatives remembered these alleged wishes only in 1997, seven years after her incapacitation. They had not mentioned them in 1992, when Michael Schiavo sued doctors for negligence in Schiavo's treatment and, in the course of his suit, promised to spend the rest of his life taking care of her with the proceeds of the suit. (He won a $1.1 million settlement.) Nor did they mention them in 1994, when Schiavo and the Schindlers clashed in court over whether Terri should be treated for an infection.

The Schindlers considered Michael to have abandoned Terri upon having children with and becoming engaged to another woman. They also contested the diagnosis, crucial to the case for withdrawing the tube under Florida law, that Terri was in a "persistent vegetative state." Their lawyers produced experts who said that she was actually "minimally conscious."

Florida courts sided with Michael Schiavo.[1] For years, as appeals were filed, the case became a low-profile cause for pro-lifers. The (Republican) state legislature in Florida had tried to intervene in favor of the Schindlers but were rebuffed by the courts. In the spring of 2005, when the Schindlers' appeals began to run out and permanent withdrawal of the tube looked imminent, the dispute began to draw national attention. Congress tried in various ways to force federal courts to consider the issue anew.

At first, congressional support for intervention was bipartisan and, indeed, nearly unanimous. Many congressmen had misgivings about whether Terri's wishes were really being respected. Calling for a new hearing seemed like a modest step to many. And, perhaps most important, the only voters really paying attention to the case in the beginning were pro-lifers and disability-rights activists who opposed the killing of Terri Schiavo. There seemed to be no political downside to stepping in.

That changed within days. The public reacted strongly against the intervention. Many people favored the removal of the tube. Others thought that Congress should stay out of the dispute. Even some pro-life conservatives, perhaps unaware that the Supreme Court had already gotten the federal government deeply involved in the issue, wondered whether it was appropriate for the feds to undo the judgments of Florida courts. Still others recoiled from the whole awful tragedy and its exploitation by the media and politicians. They wanted it off their screens.

The liberal intelligentsia, seeing that a majority was with them, expressed a kind of gleeful fury about the case. They were pushing on an open door, since pro-lifers barely made the principled argument against euthanasia. For understandable political and legal reasons, those who wanted to keep feeding Terri emphasized that it was not clear that she was in a "persistent vegetative state." But in so doing, they let the notion that it is acceptable for people who are in that state to be starved to death slide right by. It made tactical sense to question whether Mrs. Schiavo really would have wanted to die this way. But in asking it, pro-lifers failed to challenge the notion that it is acceptable to kill those who wish to be killed.

The concept of the "sanctity of life" was a spectral presence in the debate, never given a rational form. So it was easy for people to fall into the assumption that it was an essentially religious concept. Proponents of feeding Mrs. Schiavo were, by and large, Christians, and Christian conservatives at that.[2] They often claimed, or implied, that they were doing God's will. Resisting euthanasia thus came to be seen as somehow theocratic, and irrational. Pro-lifers were "emot[ing] with bug-eyed religiosity," the *Financial Times* calmly opined. Hendrik Hertzberg called them "Christianists" in *The New Yorker*, a label that implicitly (and with malice aforethought) compared them to bin Laden and his followers.[3]

It cannot be denied that pro-lifers were guilty of some excesses. Some of them, on the basis of very little evidence, accused Michael Schiavo of having caused his wife's collapse through abuse. They should have refrained from that kind of charge (which ended up backfiring anyway). Yet one need not excuse such conduct to see that the portrayal of pro-lifers as categorically irrational turned matters upside down. There is a perfectly rational case against euthanasia. The case *for* it, on the other hand, almost inescapably rests on what might be described as a kind of irrational spirituality.

The case against starts, once again, with the idea that human beings have inherent worth and dignity, and therefore are equal in fundamental rights, simply by virtue of being human. The right to life has to be among these rights, which means that it cannot depend on race, or age, or health, or sex. It cannot depend even on whether the person who has it wants it: He doesn't cease to be a human being with the full complement of rights simply because he wants to die. (It is because the right is intrinsic to human beings that it is also inalienable, as our Founders, who were not theocrats, put it.)

The alternative view is that some human beings have the right not to be killed on the basis of qualities that they, in particular, have: for example, the immediately exercisable capacity for conceptual thinking or other types of mental activity. If that quality is what confers the right to life, then abortion, embryo-destructive research, and the euthanasia of the permanently comatose or persistently vegetative are all acceptable. But since human mental capacity varies continuously, we will have to identify a non-arbitrary minimum level necessary to possess rights, and then explain why people who have more of that quality should not be regarded as greater in worth and dignity than people who have less of it. It is impossible to do either.

Thus it ends up being impossible to confine the category of lives deemed unworthy of protection to the unborn and the persistently vegetative—impossible not just practically, but in principle. We have seen how this works at the beginning of life: Whether our criterion is the ability to reason, self-awareness, or the capacity to experience pain, newborn infants do not differ from late-term fetuses. Pro-choicers who find Peter Singer's advocacy of infanticide repulsive cannot come up with a persuasive argument for why he is wrong. He differs from them only in his willingness to embrace the logical consequences of the premises he joins them in affirming.

For the law to allow people to take innocent human lives—even their own—is necessarily for it to join the party of death in regarding some lives as not worth living. This is perhaps especially true when the law restricts the "right" to commit suicide to specific categories of people, such as the severely disabled and ill. As bioethics writer Eric Cohen noted in *The Weekly Standard*, at least one Florida appeals court that considered the Schiavo case made this move without even realizing it. It simply assumed that the only reason anyone—including Mrs. Schiavo herself, or rather the Mrs. Schiavo of the past looking at the situation—could want to keep the tube connected was the possibility that "a miracle would somehow recreate" her cerebrum. It assumed, that is, that Mrs. Schiavo would not have wanted to continue living indefinitely in a persistent vegetative state, because no one would. It was all right to end her life, that is, because it was, objectively, not a life worth living.[4]

Mrs. Schiavo was commonly described as "brain dead." Christopher Hitchens used the Schiavo controversy as the occasion for another of his denunciations of "religious fanatics": "The end of the brain, or the replacement of the brain by a liquefied and shrunken void, is . . . if not the absolute end of 'life,' the unarguable conclusion of human life. It disqualifies the victim from any further say in human affairs." Mrs. Schiavo, he writes, was already Michael Schiavo's "ex-wife" before the tube was pulled.[5]

Hitchens's statement, taken literally, is truer than he appears to realize. Most people accept brain-death as the criterion for death. But the prevailing standard has required the death of the whole brain, not just the cerebrum. The person must not only lack higher mental functions, that is, but have ceased to exist as an organism. Hitchens was moving the goalposts: treating people without higher mental functions as expendable by redefining them as already dead.

The argument that allowing euthanasia violates a basic human right, denies the ground of human equality, and would also in principle require acceptance of evils that almost everyone can recognize as such corresponds, in its conclusions, with the Judeo-Christian tradition. But it does not at any point rely on the premise that God is a Trinity, or that He even exists, or that the pope or the church can teach infallibly in moral matters.

The argument *for* euthanasia, however, often seems to depend on a kind of superstition: on a dualism that separates a person from his body. This dualism holds a person, understood as a consciousness, to be important and worth protecting, but does not so hold the physical organism that this person merely "inhabits." The person is the "ghost in the machine" or, to use Anna Quindlen's more recent metaphor, the tune in the music box. Libertarian commentator Glenn Reynolds took this valorization of the willing, desiring self pretty far: "If Terri Schiavo's desire is to die, then in fact, you're making her into a non-person by not following it." *Not* to kill her was to destroy her personhood because it was to disregard her will.[6]

This dualism facilitates the denial of a right to life in cases where there is no reasoning, conscious self—as in abortion and the euthanasia of the "vegetative." As such, it is open to the same egalitarian objections mentioned earlier. But the party of death's dualism is also, as we saw in Chapter 7, untenable.

During Terri Schiavo's last days, we heard, perhaps, too much about God, and not enough about justice. As Kant said: "[S]uicide is not abominable because God has forbidden it; on the contrary, God has forbidden it because it is abominable."[7] The commentariat seized on religious objections to killing Mrs. Schiavo, and were all too eager to engage in hyperbolic arguments about theocracy, rather than deal directly with the ethical issues involved in the Schiavo case.

The party of death even adopted a holier than thou stance, arguing that Christian conservatives were behaving faithlessly by striving to keep Mrs. Schiavo from attaining her eternal reward. If they really believed in the next life, went the argument, they would not have gone to such lengths to prolong this one. They were guilty of theological hypocrisy.[8]

This was an extremely careless argument. To begin with, plenty of conservative Christians do not believe that anyone is *guaranteed* admission into Heaven. Worse, the argument wholly ignores the distinction between not prolonging someone's life and deliberately ending it. Nobody involved in the Schiavo case argued that heroic measures must always be taken to prolong the lives of dying patients (which, incidentally, Mrs. Schiavo was not until the tube was disconnected). Everyone, if asked, would have to concede that it could sometimes be permissible to take someone off life support, even when death was a predictable consequence of that action—if, for example, the patient preferred to die at home rather than in a treatment center. Nobody, with the possible exception of the DEA, opposes the use of pain medication to relieve suffering in every case where its use risks causing the patient's death. The claim that pro-lifers are "absolutists" on life cannot survive even cursory examination.

What pro-lifers opposed was an action—the removal of a feeding and hydration tube. This action didn't coincidentally result in death—*the entire point was to cause death*. The party of death pretended this distinction did not exist. If one followed this logic, churches should fund death squads to usher even more people into paradise (apparently, Jim Jones had the right idea).

It was in the middle of the Schiavo controversy that the Democratic party, already the party of abortion and of embryo-destructive research, started also to become the party of euthanasia. Many Democrats had voted to intervene in the case. But once the intervention turned out to be unpopular, they opted to pin the blame for it on the Republicans and, in particular, the "religious Right." There had never before been a national controversy about euthanasia that required the Democrats to plant their flag firmly in one camp.

Liberalism had once stood above all for the protection of the vulnerable. Hubert Humphrey said that liberals looked to the wellbeing of "those who are in the dawn of life, the children; those who are in the twilight of life, the elderly; and those who are in the shadows of life, the sick, the needy and the handicapped." After a generation of supporting abortion, liberals are no longer so inclined. Cohen concluded: "Instead of sympathizing with Terri Schiavo—a disabled woman, abandoned by her husband, seen by many as a burden on society—modern liberalism now sympathizes with Michael Schiavo, a healthy man seeking freedom from the burden of his disabled wife and self-fulfillment in the arms of another."[9]

Howard Dean, the head of the Democratic party, vowed that Republicans would pay for trying to save Schiavo's life. Half a month after her death, he said, "We're going to use Terri Schiavo later on...This is going to be an issue in 2006, and it's going to be an issue in 2008."[10] He may be overestimating the political potency of euthanasia as a cause. Those Americans who disapproved of Congress because they thought Republicans were politicizing a tragedy, or because they simply wanted it off their television screens, are unlikely to respond positively to Democratic attempts to pick the scab. In the months since Schiavo's death, no state has been moved to join Oregon in formally approving assisted suicide. (Schiavo, not being terminally ill, would not have been eligible for assisted suicide even in Oregon.)

Schiavo's death was surrounded by euphemisms, the need to resort to which also suggests a limit to the public's enthusiasm for euthanasia. Those who defended the withdrawal of the tube scrupulously avoided the words "starvation" and "dehydration." While the press was not allowed to witness her deteriorating condition, it was told that her "dying process" unfolded with soothing music in the background and a stuffed animal by her side.

But what the country tolerated was bad enough. If anyone on death row were ever starved to death, it would rightly be considered cruel and unusual punishment. Nobody would bother debating whether the federal government should step in.

People die every day, and people are killed every day. It's not every day, however, that most Americans support the deliberate killing of an innocent woman. Pro-lifers have always said that mercy killing is wrong, and also warned that once it started the mercy killers would cease to be fastidious about whether they were really following a patient's will. It's not just that the slope is slippery, but that we have already slid too far down it.

CHAPTER 11

Parts Is Parts:
Bioethics at the Cutting Edge

MILLIONS OF AMERICANS THOUGHT that it was right to disconnect Terri Schiavo's feeding and hydration tube so that she would starve to death. Would they have approved if, before removing the tube, doctors had removed her usable organs?

If it's true, as Christopher Hitchens wrote, that Mrs. Schiavo was already dead, then taking her organs would have been no different than taking them from a cadaver. The law does not allow people to donate their severely disabled spouses' organs. But if it is permissible to kill someone in Schiavo's situation—or, rather, if there is nothing left to "kill"—then the law is just forcing organs to go to waste.

If you follow the reasoning of some bioethicists, this waste was the real tragedy of Schiavo's final days.

Wesley Smith, an attorney for the International Anti-Euthanasia Task Force, has done more than anyone else to bring the troubling direction of contemporary bioethics to public attention. In a series of books, in articles, and a weblog, he has told a story that is, as horror writer Dean Koontz has put it, "more hair-raising than any novel you've ever read."[1]

Part of that story concerns the attempt to redefine death. If severely disabled or ill patients can be classified as dead, it becomes possible to harvest more usable organs. In a grimly utilitarian world-view, that's a good thing.

Psychiatrist Stuart Youngner told Smith that he does not see how it harms a patient to take his organs when his heart has stopped but before his brain has. He thinks it important for the patient, or his family, to agree in advance to donate organs under those circumstances. But if consent has been obtained, why not? "[T]he donor is not feeling anything. You are about dead, you are probably dead, you are as good as dead, although you might not be exactly dead. It is an ambiguous state but the donors themselves are beyond harm."[2]

Several members of the International Forum for Transplant Ethics argued for a redefinition of death in the medical journal *The Lancet* in 1997:

> If the legal definition of death were to be changed to include comprehensive irreversible loss of higher brain function, it would be possible to take the life of a patient (or more accurately to stop the heart, since the patient would be defined as dead) by a lethal injection, and then to remove the organs needed for transplantation subject to the usual criteria for consent. Another approach would be not to declare such individuals legally dead, but rather to exempt them from the normal legal prohibitions against "killing" in the way that was considered for anencephalic infants. Arguments in favor of these steps would be humanitarian, to obviate the futile use of resources needed to keep alive an individual with no hope of recovery, and to make available organs suitable for transplantation.[3]

The authors referred to "anencephalic infants": children born missing most of their brains. Allowing the harvesting of organs from them has been more than "considered."

Smith tells the story. In 1988, Loma Linda University briefly ran a program in which physicians from all over the country were encouraged to send anencephalic infants, with parental permission, for use as organ donors. "The program lasted only eight months before it had to be suspended... [T]he primary reason for shutting down the initiative was that physicians referred *non-anencephalic*, disabled babies to Loma Linda for organ procurement." The referring physicians thought the restriction was pointless. "I have grown up in the last nine months," said the chief of neonatology at Loma Linda. "The slippery slope is real."[4]

Even the proposition that Terri Schiavo's organs should have been fair game has found some takers among bioethicists. Bill Allen, the director of the bioethics program at the University of Florida College of Medicine, asserted that she was not a person and that Michael Schiavo should have been allowed to authorize the removal of her organs.[5]

Attempts to subvert the rule that organ donors have to be dead—and not just "as good as dead" or kinda-sorta dead—are utilitarian attempts to increase the supply of donated organs. But they might backfire even in narrowly utilitarian terms. People might be less likely to list themselves as organ donors if they fear that doing so might lead them to be killed for their organs. They might be less likely to volunteer their organs if they worry that it will tempt a hospital to view them as potential sources of organs rather than as patients.

Jack Kevorkian, also known as "Doctor Death," found a way around that problem: Take the organs of suicidally depressed people. In the 1990s Kevorkian became famous for performing assisted suicides. Juries wouldn't convict him. "Polls show a majority of Americans support Kevorkian's efforts to help the terminally ill end lives of suffering," Stone Phillips told NBC viewers. In fact, most of his (usually female) victims were not terminally ill. Some weren't even in physical pain. Some were having trouble adjusting to new disabilities; some were depressed after abuse by their husbands.[6]

Kevorkian got his nickname early in his medical career because of his habit of trying to photograph patients' eyes at the moment of their deaths. Also early in his career, he campaigned to legalize experimentation on death-row inmates. (Nazi concentration-camp experimenters, he once explained, "did the right thing," except for the lack of anesthesia and consent forms.) His goal was to create a new field of medicine called "obitiatry."[7]

It was to further that goal that he sought to make assisted suicide legal and routine—and then to normalize the practice of taking his victims' organs in the process of killing them. With the help of his good press, he was able to start putting this plan into practice. He participated, for example, in the killing of Joseph Tushkowski, a quadriplegic. Tushkowski's kidneys were removed. ("They didn't remove his sweater. They just pulled it up, then cut the belly," said the coroner. "This is not a situation to be compared with the highly skilled act of organ procurement surgery…We're talking about a chopped-up body.") Kevorkian and his lawyer held a press conference announcing that the dead man's kidneys were available on a first-come first-served basis. Smith notes that "the organ transplant community mostly raised mere procedural objections to the plan."[8]

(It was Kevorkian's good press that ultimately interrupted his project. He provided 60 Minutes with footage of one of his killings for a fawning profile of him, and the footage made it possible to convict him. He is now in jail.)

When we pay attention to euthanasia, it is during episodes such as the prosecution of Kevorkian or the Schiavo case. We are not very aware of the slow, creeping advance of euthanasia; and we don't pay careful attention even during those high-profile episodes.

Many people think that euthanasia is confined to the cases of the terminally ill. Both the Kevorkian and Schiavo cases should have exploded that myth. The same myth persists with regard to euthanasia in the Netherlands. The Associated Press ran two stories in 2005 suggesting that euthanasia there is confined to the terminally ill.[9] In fact, Dutch euthanasia has never been thus limited as a matter of law or practice. A Dutch documentary depicted the case of a woman who was so upset about the possibility that she would slip back into anorexia that she requested (and obtained) an assisted suicide.[10]

So far, the only overt assisted-suicide law in America is Oregon's, and it *is* restricted to people with terminal illnesses. Even if we expected that limit to hold over time, it would not make the law justifiable. Some advocates for the disabled, such as the dedicated and aggressive critics of assisted suicide at Not Dead Yet, regard this restriction as a kind of discrimination against the severely disabled: "By assuming that it is irrational for a non-disabled person to end his or her life, but rational for a disabled person to do so, the law assumes that the non-disabled person's life is intrinsically more valuable and worthwhile than that of a disabled person."[11]

But the limit won't hold, and that prospect alarms many disabled people.[12] After Oregon's law took effect, a pro-euthanasia group in the neighboring state of Washington explained in a fundraising letter that it had "expanded [its] mission to include not only terminally ill individuals, but also persons with incurable illnesses which will eventually lead to a terminal diagnosis." The Hemlock Society, which may be the leading pro-euthanasia organization nationally, started calling for the legalization of assisted suicide for people with "incurable conditions." It also uses the phrase "irreversibly ill adult" to describe the object of its lethal solicitude. If you take them at their word, they want people with arthritis to be able to have themselves killed.[13]

Any assisted-suicide law practically presupposes that it can be rational for some people to commit suicide. "Rational suicide" is indeed one of the key concepts of the new bioethics, and it is used to counsel mental-health workers not to fight all of their patients' suicidal impulses. If it is rational for someone to choose suicide, then it might be irrational *not* to choose it.

The Dutch have followed this thought almost to the end of the chain. Involuntary euthanasia remains illegal there, but it is lightly punished and widely practiced. It is estimated that in 1990, Dutch doctors committed euthanasia without request almost six thousand times. That's almost 5 percent of the country's total deaths that year.[14]

In the United States, involuntary euthanasia is committed under the cover of laws that allow surrogates to decline "medical treatment" for patients. Consider the case of Marjorie Nighbert, a businesswoman who suffered a stroke. She needed a feeding tube, but was not terminally ill. She had once told her brother, however, that she didn't want a tube in the case of terminal illness, and he interpreted her remark to mean that she wouldn't want a tube if she required one to stay alive. He had her tube removed. She was still capable of asking for food and water, however, and did.

The issue went to court. A judge appointed a lawyer to conduct a twenty-four-hour investigation, during which feeding resumed, into whether Nighbert was competent to make her own "medical" decisions. The lawyer reported that while she may have been competent when the dehydration started, she was not competent after several weeks of it. That was enough for the judge to rule that she had not been competent to request food and water. The dehydration and starvation resumed, and Nighbert died. Wesley Smith has many more horror stories in this vein. (Koontz was right.)[15]

In the future, more involuntary euthanasias will be committed under the aegis of "Futile Care Theory." This is another case of a reasonable idea pursued to the point of madness. Assisted suicide in America took off, as we have seen, from an overly broad interpretation of the right to decline medical treatment. The reasonable point with which the "futilitarian" bioethicists begin is that doctors are not obligated to do everything their patients demand. In particular, they are obligated not to provide treatments that have no realistic chance of curing an illness. The doctor is not, for example, the servant of a patient's insanity. If he asks to have his arm cut off because he has frequent headaches, the doctor should refuse him.

The futilitarians go way beyond this point. They think that doctors should be able to refuse wanted medical treatments based on judgments of the patient's quality of life. So, for example, a premature baby named Ryan Nguyen was taken off dialysis because the hospital decided that there was no point to keeping him under permanent care. His parents sought an injunction, and were accused of child abuse for doing so. They were eventually able to transfer him to another hospital, which treated him. Eventually he came off dialysis and, although he died at age four, is reported to have been generally happy during a life that was much longer than it would have been had the original hospital had its way.[16]

Dr. Marcia Angell, when she was executive editor of the *New England Journal of Medicine,* sided with the futilitarians. Care of the permanently unconscious, she wrote, wasted resources and demoralized caregivers. She pondered redefining death to include the diagnosis of permanent unconsciousness, or establishing mandatory time limits on care. Her ultimate policy advice was that the legal presumption in favor of life be changed for such patients. If their families took the "idiosyncratic view" that they should have medical care, they would have to prove it in court.[17]

The American Thoracic Society has come out against medical interventions that are "highly unlikely to result in a meaningful survival for the patient." It also takes the position that health-care providers have a "right to limit a life-sustaining intervention without consent of a patient or surrogate."[18]

A generation ago, patients and their families had to struggle against doctors who gave them treatments they didn't want. The medical profession has overcorrected for that fault, and is still doing so. The rise of Futile Care Theory is a stark demonstration that the trend toward assisted suicide has less to do with the increased respect for the autonomy of patients than with the decreased respect for life (and equal rights). The new bioethics values autonomy much more when patients want to die than when they want to live.

For some time now, bioethicists have been in the business of "professionally guid[ing] the unthinkable on its passage through the debatable on the way to becoming the justifiable until it is finally established as unexceptionable."[19] Dr. Youngner and Dr. Robert Arnold have speculated about a future in which assisted suicide and organ harvesting have been combined, much as Jack Kevorkian has long wanted:

> Machine dependent patients could give consent for organ removal before they are dead. For example, a ventilator-dependent ALS patient could request that life support be removed at 5:00 P.M, but that at 9:00 A.M. the same day he be taken to the operating room, put under general anesthesia, and his kidneys, liver and pancreas removed...The patient's heart would not be removed and would continue to beat throughout surgery, perfusing the other organs with warm, oxygen- and-nutrient-rich blood until they were removed. The heart would stop, and the patient would be pronounced dead only after the ventilator was removed at 5:00 P.M., according to plan, and long before the patient could die from renal, hepatic, or pancreatic failure.
>
> If active euthanasia—e.g., lethal injection—and physician-assisted suicide are legally sanctioned, even more patients could

couple organ donation with their planned deaths; we would not have to depend only upon persons attached to life support. This practice would yield not only more donors, but more types of organs as well, since the heart could now be removed from dying, not just dead, patients...

If a look into such a future hurts our eyes (or turns our stomachs), is our discomfort any different from what we would have experienced 30 years ago by looking into the future that is today?...Given the difficulties our society is likely to experience in trying to openly adjudicate these disparate views, why not simply go along with the quieter strategy of policy creep? It seems to be getting us where we seem to want to go, albeit slowly. Besides, total candor is not always compatible with the moral compromises that inevitably accompany the formulation of public policy.[20]

CHAPTER 12

Stem Sell:
The Trouble with Ron Reagan

JUST WEEKS AFTER THE death of Ronald Reagan, his son addressed a national political convention. Reagan was the first president allied with the pro-life movement, and he did more than any other person to establish the right to life as a Republican cause. Reagan wrote a book against abortion as a sitting president.[1] He proclaimed a national "sanctity of life" day declaring "the unalienable personhood of every American, from the moment of conception until natural death." He blocked federal funding of research on human embryos.[2]

But Ron Reagan Jr. was speaking to the Democrats, not the Republicans, and his message was very different from his father's.

The former president had spent years suffering from Alzheimer's disease. His death was taken, in some quarters, as an argument for government-funded stem-cell research that would use cells taken from human embryos.[3] The research could, the argument ran, yield a cure for Alzheimer's disease, among many others, and thus spare other families the heartache the Reagans had endured. The research is controversial, however, because the process involves killing the human embryo used to produce the stem cells.

In August 2001, President George W. Bush had authorized funding for research using embryonic stem cells, with one condition:
The cell lines eligible for federally funded research had to have
been produced before the date on which he announced the funding. He did not want to encourage the destruction of more embryos
by providing funding for embryos destroyed after that date. Many
congressmen—most Democrats, and a significant number of
Republicans—want to lift that restriction on funding. Democrats
believe that their support for increased funding will win them votes.
Reagan's death increased the pressure on Bush to relax his policy.
Ron Reagan Jr.'s speech to the Democratic convention was a way of
turning up the heat.

Ron Reagan began by saying he was "not here to make a political speech." (He just wandered into the convention hall and found
himself in front of a TelePrompTer.) He was here, rather, to talk
about "what may be the greatest medical breakthrough in our or in
any lifetime: the use of embryonic stem cells—cells created using
the material of our own bodies—to cure a wide range of fatal and
debilitating illnesses: Parkinson's disease, multiple sclerosis, diabetes, lymphoma, spinal cord injuries, and much more. Millions are
afflicted . . . Now, we may be able to put an end to this suffering. We
only need to try."

He asked listeners to imagine being diagnosed with Parkinson's
disease in ten years' time. He asked them, further, to imagine a doctor's offering a therapy by taking "a few skin cells from your arm."
The doctor would take the nucleus of one of your cells, insert it
into an egg cell, and use the resulting embryo to produce stem
cells. Those stem cells could then be made "to become the very
neural cells that are defective in Parkinson's patients." Those
healthy neural cells would then be "injected into your brain"—
with no risk of tissue rejection, since the stem cells would match
you genetically.

"In other words," he continued, "you're cured." But wait—there's more. The stem cells "can be induced to recreate virtually any tissue in your body. How'd you like to have your own personal biological repair kit standing by at the hospital? Sound like magic? Welcome to the future of medicine."

Reagan then turned to the moral debate.

By the way, no fetal tissue is involved in this process. No fetuses are created, none destroyed. This all happens in the laboratory at the cellular level.

Now, there are those who would stand in the way of this remarkable future, who would deny the federal funding so crucial to basic research. They argue that interfering with the development of even the earliest stage embryo, even one that will never be implanted in a womb and will never develop into an actual fetus, is tantamount to murder.

Many of these opponents, he allowed, are well-meaning and sincere. Their belief is just that, an article of faith, and they are entitled to it. But it does not follow that the theology of a few should be allowed to forestall the health and well-being of the many...

It is a hallmark of human intelligence that we are able to make distinctions. Yes, these cells could theoretically have the potential, under very different circumstances, to develop into human beings—that potential is where their magic lies. But they are not, in and of themselves, human beings. They have no fingers and toes, no brain or spinal cord. They have no thoughts, no fears. They feel no pain. Surely we can distinguish between these undifferentiated cells multiplying in a tissue culture and a living, breathing person—a parent, a spouse, a child.

Reagan was confident that the country would side with him. "The tide of history is with us." In the upcoming election, he said, "[w]e can choose between the future and the past, between reason and ignorance, between true compassion and mere ideology."[4]

The speech was the most widely viewed discussion of stem-cell research in 2004, or any presidential-election year. It also manifested most of the troubling features of that discussion.

Hype. The research could provide "the greatest medical breakthrough in our or any lifetime," presumably putting to shame the mere development of modern antibiotics. "We only need to try." "[Y]ou're cured." "Like magic." In truth, neither Ron Reagan nor anyone else knows for sure what "the future of medicine" holds, and the biological repair kit he envisions is highly speculative.

But Reagan is hardly alone in exaggerating the promise of embryo-destructive research. He was introduced by Democratic congressman Jim Langevin, who has been paralyzed since a shooting accident during his teen years and who suggested that federal funding for the research would help him walk again. The Democrats' vice-presidential candidate, John Edwards, promised that if John Kerry and he were elected, "people like Christopher Reeve are going to walk, get up out of that wheelchair and walk again."[5]

The Democratic platform claimed that "[s]tem-cell therapy offers hope to more than 100 million Americans who have serious illnesses—from Alzheimer's to heart disease to juvenile diabetes to Parkinson's." A letter from 264 congressmen to Bush, pleading for increased funding, made the same claim, throwing in cancer for good measure.

Serious and responsible advocates of the research don't claim that it is likely to yield a cure for Alzheimer's. Rick Weiss reported in the *Washington Post* that "given the lack of any serious suggestion that stem cells themselves have practical potential to treat Alzheimer's, the Reagan-inspired tidal wave of enthusiasm stands as an example of how easily a modest line of scientific inquiry can grow in the public mind to mythological proportions." One stem-cell researcher explained the misconception thus: "People need a fairy tale." Even after Weiss's article appeared, John Kerry peddled the fairly tale in a national radio address.[6]

Heart disease and cancer are also pretty far down the list of illnesses that might respond to treatments based on stem-cell research. But they, like Alzheimer's disease, are indispensable to generating the figure of "more than 100 million Americans." (The figure assumes that everyone with high blood pressure, a heart disease, needs embryonic stem-cell therapy.) Polls on embryonic stem-cell research usually find strong public support—in part because the pollsters prep respondents by telling them, misleadingly, that the research may yield cures for Alzheimer's and the rest. Reporters then claim that people are more likely to support funding the more "informed" they are.[7]

Slipperiness. In the course of a short speech, Ron Reagan keeps changing his tune about the embryo that is created and then destroyed in the course of the research he is advocating. First, he refers to embryonic stem cells as "cells created using the material of our own bodies." Only a very alert listener would catch the contradiction a few sentences later. There, he explains that the "material of our own bodies" would have to be combined with "a donor egg cell" and stimulated to produce what he calls "new cells."

The new cells are, in truth, a new human embryo. Reagan doesn't get around to explaining that until—well, actually, he never does. He denies that the new biological entity created is a fetus, which is a bit of misdirection. Then he says that an early-stage embryo has no moral worth and that it's okay to "interfere with [its] development," which is a rather delicate way of saying "tear it apart." If you were coming to this topic cold, as most Americans are, you would have no clear idea what happened in the research.

Again, Reagan's tactic is a familiar one. Pollsters who find strong public support for embryonic stem-cell research rarely point out that a human embryo is destroyed in the course of that research.

You might also miss something else: What Ron Reagan was talking about wasn't just embryonic stem-cell research. He was advocating cloning. In his scenario, the treatment of patients would involve the creation of embryonic human beings who shared their genes. Cloning is the best-known term for what he was talking about.

It's also the term that advocates themselves formerly employed. Because the word caused most people to recoil, they started talking instead about "therapeutic cloning" or "research cloning." They claimed that this type of cloning had nothing to do with "reproductive cloning." Senators Dianne Feinstein and Orrin Hatch introduced a bill to ban "reproductive cloning" and allow the "therapeutic" kind. Sometimes the bill's supporters just say it "bans cloning." It's an attempt to head off a bill, backed by President Bush, that *actually* bans cloning.

The pro-cloners' terminology was pure propaganda. The cloning of an organism always amounts to reproduction (albeit asexual reproduction). The cloning procedure in both the "reproductive" and "therapeutic" cases is identical. The only difference is that in "therapeutic" cloning, the cloned embryo is destroyed in the course of research (which is hardly therapeutic for it), while in reproductive cloning the embryo is implanted in a woman's womb so that it can progress to the next stage of development and ultimately to infancy. Under the Hatch-Feinstein bill, it would effectively be a crime under federal law *not* to kill a category of human beings. It would, thankfully, be impossible to enforce. If a cloned embryo were found to have been implanted, would the federal government really order a woman to abort it?

Most people still opposed cloning even when positive adjectives were placed in front of it. The next tactic, still often used, was to drop the word altogether in favor of "somatic cell nuclear transfer" or "nuclear transplantation." They are both accurate terms, and they have the advantage that most people have no idea what they mean.

(They are the "D&X" of the cloning debate.) Most people certainly would not be able to tell that those terms denote the creation of new living human beings for research purposes. John Kerry, characteristically, tried to have it both ways during his 2004 presidential run. His campaign said both that he favored "creating cloned human embryos for research" and that he opposed it.[8]

Ron Reagan (or his speechwriter) hit on the most elegant solution of all to cloning's p.r. problem: Don't call it anything.

Temporary ethics. In 2001, President Bush was urged to fund research using the "leftover" embryos at fertility clinics. The research was justified on the ground that the embryos were going to be "discarded" anyway. Advocates swore up and down that they would draw the line at creating embryos for the sole purpose of research. "Private companies are creating embryos specifically for stem cells, and I think that's a very bad idea...which gets on the path of cloning," Senator Arlen Specter told FOX News in June 2001. Senators Tom Daschle, Chris Dodd, Tom Harkin, and Orrin Hatch all said similar things.[9]

One year later, each of those senators were in favor of a bill to allow the creation, through cloning, of embryos that would be killed to produce stem cells. In 2004, the Democrats gave Ron Reagan a platform to promote blowing through the ethical limits that had been so important in 2001.

Not to worry: Advocates claimed that there were ethical limits they still respected. They had no intention of letting clones develop to the fetal stage and taking their stem cells, or organs, then. The Hatch-Feinstein bill included a limit: No destructive experimentation on embryos older than fourteen days.

Then came Ron Reagan, arguing that cloning should not only be allowed, but subsidized. Biotech interests and their allies persuaded the voters of California to hand them $3 billion of borrowed money for stem-cell research, including cloning.

And what do you know? The Hatch-Feinstein bill was reintroduced, but this time without the time limit. All the same senators
still support it. The biotech industry, meanwhile, has gotten the
state of New Jersey to pass a law authorizing human cloning for,
among other purposes, the harvesting of "cadaveric fetal tissue"—in
other words, the corpses of cloned fetuses.

If the goal is to generate healthy tissues that match a patient's
genetic profile, it seems circuitous to clone him, produce stem cells
from an embryo, and then get them to generate the tissue. It would
be much simpler to let the embryo grow to the point that it produced the tissues itself, and then take it apart.[10]

Once scientists find it promising, or businesses find it profitable,
to bust through the new limits, they will—unless laws are put in
place to stop them. After all, they will insist, we have to side with
"reason" over "ignorance." Most of the other arguments for embryo-
killing research will apply with equal force to killing fetuses. If it's
wrong to ban, or even to refuse to subsidize, embryonic stem cell
research because such actions would amount to "political interference with science," as countless congressmen suggest—well, then,
it would be wrong to refrain from subsidizing the creation of fetuses
for research purposes, too. (For that matter, it would be wrong to
continue to maintain any legal restrictions on human experimentation to the extent they impede scientific progress.) The party of
death will keep pushing its principles further.

I don't mean to suggest that arguments for embryonic stem-cell
research are usually as bad as Ron Reagan's. Quite often, they're worse.

Reagan didn't say anything as uninformed as Senator Feinstein,
the co-sponsor of a cloning ban, did when she assured Tim Russert
that her bill would "clearly make it illegal to inject one of these stem
cells into a woman's uterus" to create a pregnancy.[11] Nobody besides
Feinstein has ever maintained that injecting a stem cell into a uterus

would result in pregnancy. A cloned embryo could be destroyed to produce stem cells, or it could be implanted to start a pregnancy.

Ron Reagan didn't say anything as nutty as what congressman Joe Barton, a Texas Republican, said in explaining why he was voting to lift Bush's restrictions on funding. He didn't deny that "leftover" embryos at fertility clinics are living human beings. He notes that we allow adults, such as soldiers, to sacrifice their lives for the greater good. He argues that if the embryos were capable of voluntarily deciding to sacrifice themselves for the good of science, some of them would; and since parents have custody of their children, they can make this choice for them. If he buys his own logic, any parents out there who want to sacrifice their children for science have a green light from the chairman of the House Energy and Commerce Committee. Perhaps we can also set up an army of child soldiers.[12]

Ron Reagan never even attempted to explain why it was so important for the federal government to fund embryonic stem-cell research when the private sector and some state governments are already funding it. But at least Reagan didn't claim, as John Kerry did, that Bush had imposed a "ban" on stem-cell research: a lie Kerry and his running mate John Edwards often repeated.[13]

Other lowlights of the debate include Senator Hatch's remark that "it would be terrible to say because of an ethical concept that we can't do anything for" patients, and Senator Specter's response, upon being asked when he believed life began: "I have not found it helpful to get into the details."[14]

Ron Reagan is, by comparison, a giant of moral reasoning. Which is not to say that his attempted justifications for killing human beings in the embryonic stage of life are at all persuasive. He begins with the familiar canard that the belief that all human beings have a general right not to be killed is "theology." He then argues that it is permissible to kill embryos because they lack fingers and toes. So much for quadriplegics, who lack the use of fingers and toes and even arms and legs. This is the old argument that embryos aren't human because they don't look like us.[15]

Finally, he argues that embryos have no moral standing because they cannot develop on their own; they would have to be implanted in a womb to develop. But this argument proves too much. It is equally true that a six-week-old infant, denied a suitable environment for survival and growth, will fail to thrive and, indeed, die. We do not therefore conclude that the six-week-old is something other than a human being with rights.

Here, too, incidentally, Reagan is on firmer ground than, say, Orrin Hatch. The Republican senator suggested that a clone could never become a human being because it was "never fertilized" and would never be implanted: "I do not believe that life begins in a Petri dish." Senator Feinstein has said the same thing about fertilization. So has Anna Eshoo, a cloning advocate in the House of Representatives. Consider the implications of this theory if reproductive cloning should ever take place among humans. If a thirty-five-year-old cloned human being walked up to Hatch, would Hatch deny he was looking at a human being with rights? No fertilization would have taken place. (Implantation may not have happened, either: Some researchers are trying to develop artificial wombs.) To emphasize that clones aren't fertilized is to play games with words. The whole *point* of cloning is to create a human being using a process that mimics, though it is not identical to, fertilization.[16]

Some advocates of cloning have gone so far as to deny that an embryo would be created at all. Since there's no fertilization, they say, there's no embryo.[17] The replacement term "nuclear-transfer construct" appears to be enjoying a vogue.

We're not killing you: You never existed.

CHAPTER 13

Cell Division

IT'S NOT QUITE RIGHT to say that Americans are "debating stem-cell research," as we are often told.[1] Research using stem cells taken from adults' cells is not controversial. Neither is research on stem cells taken from umbilical cord blood or placental tissue.

It's misleading even to say that we've been debating "embryonic stem-cell research." As Robert P. George and Patrick Lee have observed, if we were debating killing five-year-olds to get their organs, nobody would say that the controversy was "about organ transplantation."[2] What is precisely at issue is the killing of human embryos.

The embryo, alas, has even fewer defenders in Washington than the fetus. The fight against abortion has been able to draw on long-standing traditions of opposition, on horrifyingly accurate images of dismemberment, and on the joy often felt at news of a pregnancy. In contrast, most people hadn't heard of embryo-destructive research until a few years ago, only dimly understand it now, and visualize nothing in particular when they think of it.

A thick fog of obfuscation has made it hard for many people to get a clear view of the issue. While most pro-lifers have nonetheless been resolute in opposing embryo-destructive research, there have been some prominent defections. As a result of those defections, majorities in both houses of Congress want more funding for research involving so-called "spare" embryos—which involves killing those embryos left over from in vitro fertilization attempts. Most of the presidential candidates for 2008, even on the Republican side, agree. A majority of the House would ban the production of human embryos by cloning, but the Senate does not have the supermajority that would be necessary to enact a ban, and may not even have a majority. There are so few votes for a complete ban on embryo-destructive research (including privately financed research on embryos taken from fertility clinics) that nobody in Washington has even proposed one.

Public opinion, or rather a misunderstanding of it, is one of the reasons politicians support embryo destruction. Polls routinely find that the public strongly favors embryonic stem-cell research. But most of the polls are systematically stacked to yield that result. Almost invariably, they have two or more of the following flaws: 1) They fail to tell respondents that the research destroys human embryos, even though that is the reason there is a dispute. 2) They fail to mention that taxpayer funding is at issue, thus counting as supporters of funding people who may wish only for the research to stay legal. 3) They wrongly suggest that the research is likely to have benefits for Alzheimer's patients.

Thus, for example, an August 2004 poll for the Annenberg Public Policy Center asked, "Do you favor or oppose Federal funding of research on diseases like Alzheimer's using stem cells taken from human embryos?" The pollsters got 64 percent of the public to say they favored the funding. The Catholic bishops did a poll the same month stacked the other way, and found a small plurality opposing funding. (Even its poll, however, found that supporters of the funding had gained ground during the previous three years.) Polls that mention "cloning," meanwhile, or the "creation of embryos for research purposes," or similar words, generally find strong opposition.[3]

The results of the polls are so heavily dependent on the wording of the questions as to suggest that many people don't have settled opinions and won't vote on the issue. A more important factor for politicians is that the biotech industry and patient lobbying groups, neither of which has been involved in the abortion debate, back taxpayer-funded stem cell research. The biotech companies are major campaign donors, and patient groups generate sympathetic news coverage and have members in every congressional district.

If people are convinced that only a federal subsidy stands between their son and certain death, politicians find it hard to tell them no. And patient lobbying groups play hardball. The Juvenile Diabetes Research Foundation arranged a meeting between a family pleading for funding and Indiana Republican Congressman Mark Souder. The family was pro-life, and when Souder explained to them that the research involved destroying embryos, they changed their minds.[4] After that, the JDRF required its members to pledge to support the organization's position or remain silent on the issue before it would set up any meetings with congressmen or their staff. Critics called it a "loyalty oath."[5]

Opposing embryo destruction, on the other hand, doesn't buy a politican any new friends. Almost all of the opponents are the same people who oppose abortion. Yet if the party of death holds the political high ground on embryo-destructive research, at least for now, it has been much worse at coming up with good arguments.

Not surprisingly, the worst arguments have come from those politicians who consider themselves pro-life but want to find a way to bless embryo-destructive research. Orrin Hatch solved the problem by deciding that embryos aren't human if they're not in a womb. Like real estate, the right to life turns out to be all a matter of location. Bill Frist, the Senate majority leader, picked a different

tactic: He just brazened through the contradiction. He said that he
believed that a human embryo is "nascent human life" that
"deserves to be treated with the utmost dignity and respect," indeed
"the same dignity and respect we bring to the table as we work with
children and adults to advance the frontiers of medicine and
health." In between those paeans to the embryo, he said, "I also
believe that embryonic stem cell research should be encouraged
and supported." It's as though he were giving two different speeches.
Perhaps he thinks being majority leader means never having to
explain yourself.[6]

But maybe Frist's non-explanation was a wise move, considering
the alternative explanations on offer.

Twin spin. One of the most sophistical arguments for embryo-
destroying research is that the early human embryo isn't a human
being because it could still split into twins.[7] Because there could be
two individuals there, there are really none. This is like saying that
a flatworm isn't a flatworm because it can be split into two flat-
worms. Besides, what is cloning but the creation of a twin? The
promise of cloning—or SCNT, or whatever the biotech companies
want to call it—is that an embryo with our genetic code can be
formed from the skin cells of any one of us. If an embryo has no
right to life because a twin can be formed from it, and a twin can be
formed from any of us, then it follows that nobody has a right to life.

Veggie tales. Molecular biologist Lee Silver, an evangelist for
using biotechnology to "remak[e] Eden," says,

> The confusion people have is with the meaning of the words *life*
> and *alive*. We use the words in two very different ways, one mean-
> ing vegetative life, the other conscious life. To biologists, *life* in a
> vegetative sense simply means the life of cells. In fact, in this
> beaker [gestures toward beaker containing a pinkish fluid], there
> are living human cells. Millions of human cells. They are per-

fectly alive and they are perfectly human, but they are not conscious. But when you talk about human beings and persons, we
are talking about consciousness. The best example of the difference that I know of is what happens when a person is shot with a
bullet in the heart—he dies almost instantly. And yet, most of his
body is still alive. So the person is dead, even though his body, for
the most part, is alive. That is the distinction between vegetative
life and conscious life. Human embryos are cells, and they are
alive in a vegetative sense, not a conscious sense.[8]

But the confusions here are Silver's own. He's confusing the distinction between "conscious" and "vegetative" organisms with the
distinction between organisms and parts of an organism.

The man who is killed by a bullet to the head does not go from
being "conscious" life to "vegetative" life. He becomes dead. He is
dead even if particular cells, tissues, and organs retain life for a
while, because those cells, etc., are no longer parts of a functioning,
integrated whole. The fact that an embryo isn't conscious doesn't
prove that it's not an organism—which is what it would have to do
for Silver's argument to work. Even if he abandons his point about
cellular life, he still has to justify making the right to life depend on
consciousness (a criterion that presumably does not distinguish
between humans and animals, and excludes unconscious humans).

Brainlessness. The libertarian journalist Ronald Bailey has
pointed out that we treat brain-death as the criterion for death, and
allow organs to be removed for the benefit of others after it has
occurred. Since embryos have not yet developed brains, he argues,
they are in the same position as the brain-dead. A version of this
argument has also been adopted by Michael Gazzaniga, a neurosci-
entist on the President's Council on Bioethics.[9]

The analogy doesn't work, simply because an embryo is not
dead. In a brain-dead person, the brain can no longer integrate the

body's functions. The corpse is no longer a living organism, and that's why we treat it as dead. The embryo, however, functions even before its brain emerges to take over most of that work.

Home wreckers. Gazzaniga is also fond of another analogy: "[I]t is a truism that the blastocyst has the potential to be a human being. Yet at that stage of development it is simply a clump of cells...An analogy might be what one sees when walking into a Home Depot. There are the parts and potential for at least thirty homes. But if there is a fire at Home Depot, the headline isn't thirty homes burn down. It's Home Depot burns down." *Science* magazine found this comparison so impressive it made it its "Metaphor of the Week."[10]

But the blastocyst (a young embryo) is a human at a very early "stage of development," as Gazzaniga himself puts it. The "parts" that go into it are the gametes (the sperm and egg cells).[11] It is the blastocyst itself that grows into the much larger clump of cells that becomes a person—like Michael Gazzaniga.

Enjoying the slippery slope. Senator Tom Harkin argues that anyone who supports in vitro fertilization (IVF) has no grounds for opposing embryo-destructive stem-cell research.[12] Mario Cuomo argues that since we tolerate abortion, we have no grounds for objecting to embryo-destructive research.[13]

In a series of columns, Michael Kinsley has vigorously argued that President Bush is "a hardened cynic, staging a moral anguish he does not feel, pandering to people he cannot possibly agree with." If he truly believed that embryos deserved legal protection, he would "oppose modern fertility treatments" that also involve the destruction of human embryos. Kinsley claims that people who picket fertility clinics are "entitled" to oppose stem-cell research. If you're not so "fanatical," he concludes, "please get out of the way."[14]

Some Americans—notably, orthodox Catholics—do consider IVF immoral because it reduces human life to the status of a product rather than a gift. A larger group is troubled by the IVF-clinic practice of creating "excess" embryos. But Harkin is clearly wrong to suggest that anyone who supports their creation must therefore bless their intentional destruction. Leaving an embryo frozen is not the same as killing it. Pro-life principles don't by themselves lead to a ban on IVF. They lead only to regulations that prevent fertility clinics from "discarding excess embryos," or implanting several and then aborting some fetuses.

It's true, as Cuomo and Kinsley note, that pro-lifers aren't proposing legislation to keep fertility clinics (or private-sector stem-cell researchers) from destroying embryos. Such legislation should be enacted, and pro-lifers ought to work toward that goal within the political process. It is not, however, presently achievable. Are pro-lifers therefore supposed to give up on what may be achievable?

Why can't pro-lifers concentrate on preventing the growth of a new evil (cloning) rather than on fighting a well-entrenched old one (the practices of IVF clinics)? If you've gone a long way down a slippery slope, are you obligated to keep sliding?

In Kinsley's world, pro-lifers are either hypocrites or fanatics. They can never be conscientious citizens. Their principles supposedly obligate them to act in self-defeating ways. They alone are not allowed (or "entitled") to take effective political action to promote their principles. But in truth, pro-lifers are morally obligated to attempt just that. They are under no special obligation to be politically obtuse. Not even when the pro-lifer in question is the president of the United States.

Keeping up with the Joneses. Congressman Mike Castle, a Delaware Republican, warns that because of Bush's funding restrictions, "We're falling behind other countries at this time." Senator Dianne Feinstein makes the same point.[15]

It's important, first, to remember that many countries go further than we do in protecting embryos from destructive experimentation. Fareed Zakaria said on ABC's *This Week* that "this debate is taking place in no other country." Not true. Canada has outlawed cloning. Germany, Austria, Ireland, Poland, and Lithuania have outlawed embryo-destructive research.[16]

Congressmen in favor of embryo-destructive research say that by keeping the research in America, we can ensure it follows ethical norms. But if you are not going to forswear killing human beings for research, what ethical norms remain to be imposed? And if restricting federal funding for research merely drives it overseas, why wouldn't imposing ethical norms do the same thing?

It may be that American restrictions on embryo-destructive research will impede it internationally. But if research proceeds in other countries, does that mean that American restrictions on cloning, or funding for embryo-destructive research, were for naught? No. Every day we ban the intentional destruction of human beings is a day that our laws come closer to justice. Every day that the federal government refrains from funding such destruction is a day that it has avoided complicity in injustice.

The crisis of everyday life. An advocate of embryo-destructive research, a man with Parkinson's disease, pleaded with a Senate subcommittee: "Please, please don't let time run out for me and the over 1.5 million Americans with Parkinson's, and the over 100 million Americans with diseases and conditions who are almost certain to benefit from regenerative medicine, including embryonic stem cell research. It is unconscionable to let time run out—especially now that the scientists tell us that the finish line might be within sight."[17]

It is a tone that advocates of the research often strike, and it is understandable that they strike it. For sufferers and their loved ones, diseases such as Parkinson's constitute a crisis. And during emergencies, people are often impatient with moral arguments. They're also unlikely to take a sober look at the real likelihood that a plan to end the crisis will actually work.

But what would be the consequences if society viewed the fight against disease as a crisis? Since "it is a struggle we can never expect fully to win," writes Yuval Levin,

> then we must always live in a state of emergency. We should be always in a crisis mode, always pulling out all stops, always suspending the rules for the sake of a critical goal. And that means, in effect, that there should be no stops and no rules; only crisis management and triage.
>
> Under crisis conditions, we allow ourselves to do things we would never otherwise contemplate...But if life is always at risk and we are always in crisis, then we must always do things that moral contemplation would suggest are wrong. If we are always in a mode of triage, then we must always choose the strong over the weak because they have a better chance at benefiting from our help."
>
> [T]he tragic fact is, of course, that people are always dying... If this means that there can never be a time for moralizing, then we are in trouble.[18]

As Paul Ramsey, a bioethicist before the field went sour, said, the moral history of mankind is more important than its medical history.

Which is not, of course, to say that we should do nothing for people suffering from Parkinson's, Alzheimer's, and other diseases. Research that does not cross important ethical lines should be encouraged: research using stem cells taken from adults and from umbilical-cord blood, for example.

Debate has raged about the relative potential of adult and embryonic stem-cell research. Many pro-lifers point out that only the former has resulted in clinical applications that have actually helped patients. Advocates of the embryo-destructive research see more potential in it, since the stem cells taken from embryos are "pluripotent"—capable of generating many types of cells (bone cells, liver cells, and others). Many scientists take this view. In many cases, there is no reason to question their sincerity.

In some cases, however, there may be a guild-protective instinct at work: an inclination to talk up research that is in danger of being restricted, or even of being unsubsidized. The *New England Journal of Medicine* exhibited this tendency when it ran an editorial supporting cloning (although it didn't use the word, of course, even misstating the science to avoid it). The journal announced that in order to fight a proposed ban on cloning, it would be "seeking out" papers that highlighted the potential of the research. It did not promise to seek out papers that highlighted the potential of research on adult stem cells.[19]

If there were no ethical objections to either type of research, the controversy over which should be pursued could be settled in the lab: Let the best course of research win. The question of potential, which really is strictly scientific, has gotten tangled up in the moral debate.

Recent scientific developments have, however, raised the possibility that pluripotent stem cells could be gotten without killing human embryos. One method involves the creation of biological entities that have the human genetic code but are not organisms. Instead, they are disordered growths, like teratomas (the tumors resulting from failures of fertilization).

Pro-lifers want to make sure this research really creates non-embryos, and doesn't end up creating severely disabled embryos. So they want it to proceed first among animals. Some proponents of embryo-destructive stem-cell research also favor this research, seeing it as a way to get moving now rather than continuing a political stalemate. But other proponents of embryo-destructive research have downplayed these nonlethal alternatives—and some have even opposed them.

Michael Sandel, a liberal member of the Bioethics Council and a professor at Harvard, has tried to put the sheen of principle on this position:

> As one who supports embryonic stem cell research, I do not regard the early embryo as inviolable. But neither do I regard it as disposable, open to any use we may desire or devise. For this reason, embryo research carries a special moral burden; it is justified only for the sake of saving human lives or curing devastating diseases. The proposal to genetically engineer a nonviable, embryo-like being would remove the moral burden by creating something that, lacking the capacity to develop into a human person, would be wholly disposable, presumably for any purpose, weighty or trivial. The very project of creating such a being is morally troubling...I therefore do not believe that this proposal should be encouraged or endorsed.[20]

So experimenting on "embryo-like beings" is *more* troubling than experimenting on human embryos...because it's *less* troubling. I guess you have to be a professor at Harvard to come up with an argument that profound.

Senator Harkin said that the proposal to create non-embryonic sources of stem cells was "monstrous" and "indefensible."[21] So, to review: Harkin is fine with creating and then killing human embryos for research purposes. But he's against creating biological artifacts that aren't embryos for research that would avoid any killing. It's as though he was eager to see killing for its own sake.[22] Monstrous is the right word.

CHAPTER 14

Weeding Out the Unfit

IN RECENT YEARS, many Americans have become concerned that our schools "overtest" children. In truth, however, the first test to which they are subject comes long before school, and it's the highest-stakes test of all. We test our children in the womb and, depending on the results, decide whether they live or die.

The number of children in this country with Down syndrome, for example, has fallen over the last fifteen years. That's not because a cure has yet been found. The rising number of older women having babies should, indeed, have increased the prevalence of the syndrome. The reason for the drop is the increased use of "second-trimester screening." When people find out that they are having a child likely to have the syndrome, more than 80 percent of them opt to abort the baby. Prenatal testing is routine, and its point is less to prepare parents for the challenges of raising a disabled child, or to determine whether the baby needs medical treatment in the womb, than to determine whether to kill the baby. We abort most children with Down syndrome, or Tay-Sachs disease, or spina bifida, or cystic fibrosis. And we abort some children who don't have those conditions because the tests aren't foolproof.[1]

Parents of children with Down syndrome often report that they were encouraged to have an abortion or, what might be worse, simply expected to have one. (Just as parents are simply expected to have prenatal testing, even when that testing poses risks to the baby. Physicians who don't offer the tests might later find themselves facing a "wrongful birth" lawsuit—a kind of legal action that itself reflects the influence of abortion on our mores.) Beth Allard reported that an obstetrician had told her that her child might have the syndrome, and then explained what that meant. "It could just be hanging off of you, drooling," the doctor said, and then "contort[ed] her face into a saggy, expressionless imitation of what a child [with the syndrome] might look like."[2]

A study released in 2005 found that a majority of mothers of children with Down syndrome reported that their doctors accentuated the negative, that many got out-of-date information about the trials of living with the condition, and that pressure to have an abortion was not uncommon.[3]

Parents also sometimes report that their decision *not* to abort elicits criticism, even from strangers. In the 2005 study, one woman related that after her baby was born, "the doctor flat out told my husband that this could have been prevented…at an earlier stage." Patricia Bauer wrote an op-ed about the phenomenon. "I see the way people look at [my daughter]: curious, surprised, sometimes wary, occasionally disapproving or alarmed."

> At a dinner party not long ago, I was seated next to the director of an Ivy League ethics program. In answer to another guest's question, he said he believes that prospective parents have a moral obligation to undergo prenatal testing and to terminate their pregnancy to avoid bringing forth a child with a disability, because it was immoral to subject a child to the kind of suffering he or she would have to endure. (When I started to pipe up about our fam-

ily's experience, he smiled politely and turned to the lady on his left.)

Margaret does not view her life as unremitting human suffering (although she is angry that I haven't bought her an iPod). She's consumed with more important things, like the performance of the Boston Red Sox in the playoffs and the dance she's going to this weekend. Oh sure, she wishes she could learn faster and had better math skills. So do I. But it doesn't ruin our day, much less our lives. It's the negative social attitudes that cause us to suffer.

Bauer's op-ed drew several letters decrying her as "sanctimonious."[4]

Senators Sam Brownback and Ted Kennedy, a pro-life Republican and a famously pro-choice Democrat, are co-sponsoring a bill to provide funding so that doctors can provide parents with better information, including contact information for support groups for parents of children with congenital diseases or syndromes. It's a worthy effort.

But the testimony of parents such as Bauer suggests that our country now has a reasonably strong social norm that disabled babies should be aborted. This type of diversity we do not wish to tolerate. In Chapter 17, I will go through poll data that suggest that Americans are much less supportive of abortion than is commonly thought. But no such claim can be made about abortion of the disabled. In every poll, Americans strongly support the right to abort *them*.

Leon Kass, who has thought deeply about medical ethics for years, concludes, "We are largely unaware that we have, as a society, already embraced the eugenic principle, 'Defectives shall not be born,' because our practices are decentralized and because they operate not by coercion but by private reproductive choice."[5] We are, however, occasionally given glimpses of the import of our choices.

When Joycelyn Elders was Governor Bill Clinton's surgeon general in Arkansas, she testified before Congress in favor of the Freedom of Choice Act. Abortion "has had an important and positive public-health impact," she said. It "has reduced the number of children afflicted with severe defects." She gave an example: "The number of Down's syndrome infants in Washington state in 1976 was 64 percent lower than it would have been without legal abortion."[6] The remark did not keep her from being nominated by Clinton, a few years later, to be the surgeon general of the United States, or from being confirmed.

We like to think that eugenics is a thing of the past, that it died in the ashes of Nazi Germany. Today's Supreme Court would not bless a forced sterilization with the words "Three generations of imbeciles are enough." (Also: "It is better for all the world, if instead of waiting to execute degenerate offspring for crime, or to let them starve for their imbecility, society can prevent those who are manifestly unfit from continuing their kind.")[7]

Yet the history of eugenics is worth reflecting on, not least because the history of abortion cannot be divorced from it. Consider the case of Margaret Sanger, the founder of Planned Parenthood, who is still revered by it. While she herself opposed abortion,[8] Planned Parenthood takes its support for it to be a straightforward extension of its support for birth control. And Sanger's crusade for birth control and "voluntary sterilization"[9] was openly eugenicist.

She worried about the "increasing race of morons" in the United States, and complained that "a moron's vote" was just as good as that of his betters. She told the New York legislature that "the Jewish people and Italian families" were "filling the insane asylums" and "hospitals" and "feeble-minded institutions." Taxpayers were thus subsidizing the "multiplication of the unfit" when they should have been spending money "on geniuses." She condemned eighty-five million Americans as "mediocre to imbecile."[10]

Lest we judge her too harshly, we should note that these sorts of sentiments were not unusual among the upper class and the intelligentsia in the first half of the last century. To take one example from hundreds: *The New Republic* editorialized in favor of contraception in a similar vein. "Few intelligent people would still maintain that it is better to have been born an imbecile than not to have been born at all." This "hideous doctrine," it continued, must be denounced "as a conspiracy by the superstitious against the race." The conspiracy resulted in "the multiplication of the unfit."[11]

This kind of thinking remained very much alive during the debate about abortion in the run-up to *Roe*. The respected scientist Ashley Montagu wrote:

> If life is sacred... then it is about time we began treating it as such, instead of continuing to commit the frightful tragedies we do in permitting individuals to be brought into the world who will suffer all the days of their lives from seriously disabling defects... The initial basic right of the individual should be to be born without handicap. Anyone who, in the light of the facts, assists in bringing a seriously handicapped child into the world in my view commits a crime against humanity.
>
> Abortion could prevent that "crime."[12]

A similar view was expressed by Bentley Glass in his 1971 presidential address to the American Association for the Advancement of Science. Defending "the right of every child to be born with a sound physical and mental constitution, based on a sound genotype," he looked forward to a "future time" when "[n]o parents will... have a right to burden society with a malformed or a mentally incompetent child."[13]

Traces, and more than traces, of the old eugenics live on in current attitudes and practices. The eugenic mindset has spread since

Roe. It can be seen in the popularity of *Freakonomics* and its specu-
lations about abortion and crime.[14] It can also be seen in the selective abortion of those whom we no longer label, but obviously still
consider, the unfit.

We frown on abortion for the purpose of sex selection (although
we don't prohibit it and it would be hard to do so while keeping
abortion generally legal), in part because we think it expresses a negative view of women. We don't seem to have that worry about people with disabilities.

Health is a basic human good. It is perfectly understandable that
disabilities should frighten (and sometimes even disgust) us. We
might look at a disabled person and, comparing his condition to our
own health, believe we wouldn't "want to live that way." This is
especially true if we have more fears than knowledge about what life
with a disability entails. Almost every parent of a disabled child
would wish that his child not have a disability or that a cure be
found. We are right to value health, but not by devaluing the
unhealthy. Notice the way our language sometimes slips into iden-
tifying a person with his affliction, as in Elders's reference to
"Down's syndrome infants." (We wouldn't call someone a "breast
cancer woman.") The medical project should be to make people
better, not to make better people.

The improved condition of people with Down syndrome over
the last few decades complicates both sides of the debate. Such people—at least those whom we allow to live—have better prospects
than ever before. Their life expectancies have risen, and most of
them can learn to read and hold a job (contrary to what some pregnant women are told).[15] Our society treats disabled children and
adults, in general, better than it used to, outside the contexts of abortion and euthanasia. So the worst pro-life fears about the dehuman-
ization of the disabled have not been realized. It may be, of course,

that our treatment of disabled children and adults would be even better if we did not routinely kill disabled fetuses in the womb.

But the same trends also make our treatment of disabled fetuses, in a way, more alarming. Down syndrome isn't a terminal illness, although it is a difficult (and expensive) condition. Yet we consider it something to be stamped out in the womb. We don't even protest at the starvation of infants who have it. In the "Baby Doe" case of 1982, a baby boy was born in Indiana with Down syndrome and a common symptom of that syndrome, an improperly formed esophagus. The baby's parents decided against surgery to fix the esophagus, opting instead to give him painkillers and let him die of starvation. The Reagan administration sought to intervene but was turned aside. It later promulgated regulations to ensure that babies receive medical care, but courts struck them down.[16] Perhaps some future society, no doubt with its own smugness and its own sins, will condemn our barbarity.

Or perhaps our eugenic tendencies will grow even stronger. One danger is that we will come to see children less as gifts than as products of manufacture. The commodification of human life is almost upon us: The biotech industry is looking at patenting early-stage human organisms pursuant to stem-cell research. Will we grow less and less tolerant of what we see as defective goods? Will we abort children who are deaf, or blind, or dumb, or short, or gay? How will the health and insurance industries treat us if we don't? How will our neighbors—or the strangers that we meet?

All over this country, there are people sitting in seminars at think tanks, colleges, and working groups, pondering these questions as though they concern the future. But these evils already exist, in embryonic form, today. Just ask Patricia Bauer. Or listen to Joycelyn Elders.

o   o   o

The party of death has corrupted the practice of medicine, turning healers into killers. Bernard Nathanson made that journey, and returned.

Nathanson was one of the founders of the National Association for Repeal of Abortion Laws. In the 1970s, he directed what was at the time the largest abortion clinic in the world, the Center for Reproductive and Sexual Health in Manhattan. He performed, he says, "many thousands" of abortions.

It was not a religious conversion, but technological and scientific advances, that changed his mind. His thinking about abortion, like that of many other people, was powerfully affected by the development of ultrasound technology. "When ultrasound in the early 1970s confronted me with the sight of the embryo in the womb, I simply lost my faith in abortion on demand," he later wrote. He was, at the time, an atheist.

It was not only the images that swayed him, but the new understanding of fetal development that ultrasound made possible. "As recently as [1969], we knew almost nothing of the fetus; when abortion on demand was unleashed in the United States, fetology essentially did not exist."

Nathanson went on to become a pro-life author, speaker, and documentary producer. His 1985 film *The Silent Scream* is misremembered today. It was not primarily an attempt to prove that abortion inflicts pain on a fetus (exactly when the fetus develops to the point of feeling pain is still a disputed question). It was a depiction of the violence of abortion.

> By 1984 ... I had begun to ask myself more questions about abortion: What actually goes on in an abortion? I had done many, but abortion is a blind procedure. The doctor does not see what he is doing. He puts an instrument into a uterus and he turns on a motor, and a suction machine goes on and something is vacu-

umed out; it ends up as a little pile of meat in a gauze bag. I wanted to know what happened, so in 1984 I said to a friend of mine, who was doing fifteen or maybe twenty abortions a day, "Look, do me a favor, Jay. Next Saturday, when you are doing all these abortions, put an ultrasound device on the mother and tape it for me."

He did, and when he looked at the tapes with me in an editing studio, he was so affected that he never did another abortion.[17]

CHAPTER 15

What's So Bad About Infanticide?: Child Murder and the Philosophers

"IN THINKING ABOUT [INFANTICIDE]," writes Peter Singer, "we should put aside feelings based on the small, helpless, and—sometimes—cute appearance of human infants...If we can put aside these emotionally moving but strictly irrelevant aspects of the killing of a baby we can see that the grounds for not killing persons do not apply to newborn infants."[1]

Singer believes that it can be morally permissible to kill infants. He believes that some animals have a greater claim to our protection than they do. He believes that sex between humans and animals is morally acceptable so long as it does not cause the animals pain or harm. He also holds a chair in bioethics at Princeton University—at the university's Center for Human Values, if you can believe it. And he has been treated with gross unfairness.

Singer has been arguing for infanticide for decades, at least since his 1979 book *Practical Ethics*, which in its various editions has been required reading in many college courses. Singer believes that "the traditional view of the sanctity of human life"—a view that treats all members of the human species as persons with rights and worth—is obsolete. It is an inescapably Christian doctrine, it cannot be rationally defended, and it is now collapsing. That view is, indeed, morally equivalent to racism. It is a biological bigotry: "speciesism."

According to Singer, there is nothing special about being a human organism, any more than there is something special about belonging to a particular race. It is consciousness of one's own existence over time that makes a person a person. Not every human being has that consciousness, and some non-human beings do. Hence the category of "persons" and "humans" are not identical, although they do overlap. There are animals who are persons and humans who are not. "[T]he concept of a person is distinct from that of a member of the species Homo sapiens, and that it is personhood, not species membership, that is most significant in determining when it is wrong to end a life."[2]

Hence Singer's support for abortion: Fetuses are not sentient. Hence his support for euthanasia when a human organism no longer has sentience. Hence his support for "animal liberation," the title of another influential book of his. Hence, also, his support for infanticide.

Rights require "characteristics like rationality, autonomy, and self-consciousness . . . Infants lack these characteristics. Killing them, therefore, cannot be equated with killing normal human beings, or any other self-conscious beings." Allowing the killing of fourteen-year-olds would inflict pain, especially in the form of fear, on much of the population. But allowing infanticide would not do so because the infants would not understand it.[3]

Singer notes that it may often be immoral to kill an infant. To kill someone else's infant is to do that person an injury. But it is not to do an injustice to the infant herself, since she is not a person. If the parents want the infant to be killed, it is not wrong.[4] It is not the unquestionable moral evil that, in Singer's view, eating meat is.

Singer is often misunderstood. He is taken (and sometimes presents himself) to be advocating the killing of severely disabled infants. He does indeed advocate that. But he advocates it merely to illustrate a larger point. He does not believe that severely disabled infants—he mentions those suffering from spina bifida—have *less* of a right to life than other infants. He does not believe that *any* infant has such a right. Parents have the right to kill any infant of theirs. If the infant has a severe disability, they also have a reason. "Parents may, with good reason, regret that a disabled child was ever born." Their lives "will be so miserable as not to be worth living." Killing them will not injure the parents, but help them. Singer also believes that nobody will want to adopt such infants, so no harm is done to possible adoptive parents, either.[5]

Singer goes on to discuss infants with Down syndrome or hemophilia: "disabilities that make the child's life prospects significantly less promising than those of a normal child, but not so bleak as to make the child's life not worth living." Killing them may be justified, too. Their continued existence may keep their parents from having other, healthier and therefore happier children.

> When the death of a disabled infant will lead to the birth of another infant with better prospects of a happy life, the total amount of happiness will be greater if the disabled infant is killed. The loss of happy life for the first infant is outweighed by the gain of a happier life for the second. Therefore, if killing the haemophiliac infant has no adverse impact on others, it would... be right to kill him.[6]

He allows that adoption may be easier in these cases than in cases of severe disability.

Severe and not-so-severe disability are not limiting cases for Singer. They may be the cases where people are most likely to be sympathetic to infanticide. But it would be easy to imagine other circumstances in which he would approve infanticide. Let's say a couple has just had a baby and then, days later, suffered a major financial reversal. If they kill the baby, they will be able to have another in a few years, when they are back on their feet. Singer could not possibly condemn them. The total amount of happiness will go up, and the newborn is not a person.

So it is not surprising that Singer has suggested that the killing of infants be allowed during their first month. At that time, perhaps, a ceremony would be held welcoming them—the survivors, any-way—to personhood. He has since decided that this approach is unworkable. Infants don't become aware of their existence over time at one month, after all. They do so during their first year, but exactly when depends on the infant. So a one-month rule would extend a right to life to too many infants who do not really deserve it. "So what do you do? I think you need to look at it on a case-by-case basis." That should work splendidly.[7]

Marvin Olasky found out how far Singer would be willing to go by interviewing him.

Question: What about parents conceiving and giving birth to a child specifically to kill him, take his organs, and transplant them into their ill older children? Mr. Singer: "It's difficult to warm to parents who can take such a detached view, [but] they're not doing something really wrong in itself." Is there anything wrong with a society in which children are bred for spare parts on a massive scale? "No."

When we had lunch a month after our initial interview and I read back his answers to him, he said he would be "concerned about a society where the role of some women was to breed chil-dren for that purpose," but he stood by his statements. He also reaffirmed that it would be ethically OK to kill 1-year-olds with physical or mental disabilities, although ideally the question of infanticide would be "raised as soon as possible after birth."[8]

Singer's lectures have occasioned many protests, especially in Germany and Austria, where his opponents say that his views are reminiscent of those of the Nazis. Singer bitterly protests this comparison. Unlike the Nazis, he is motivated by compassion for the disabled, whose suffering he wishes to end. Where the Nazis had the state make life-or-death decisions, Singer would keep the state from interfering in parents' decisions. Nor does he share the racial theories that underlay Nazi infanticide and euthanasia. The real Nazis, in his view, are those who have shouted him down, forced the withdrawal of lecture invitations, or contributed to a climate in which publishers decline to print his books.[9]

One need hold no brief for the disruption of lectures to reject Singer's comparison. The Nazis aren't reviled for having been energetic censors, but for having been energetic killers. Many of America's Founders supported censorship of opposing political views, but we do not therefore compare them to the Nazis. It is not true that Nazi infanticide was always imposed by the state on parents; it began in the "voluntary" fashion Singer favors.[10] Not that it matters from the perspective of the infant: "Choice," understood as a license to kill, is always tyrannical when judged from its perspective. Singer's remaining point about Nazi racism is question-begging. His critics believe it is immoral to deny the right to life to other human beings based on age and self-awareness, just as it is immoral to deny that right based on race.

Nevertheless, the opprobrium directed at Singer has been excessive for two reasons. The first is that Singer is hardly the only academic to defend infanticide. The second is that it is not at all clear that anyone who defends abortion can logically avoid legitimating infanticide, too.

The defense of infanticide is by now old hat in the academy. In the 1970s, philosopher Michael Tooley argued that the ban on infanticide is "a taboo rather than…a rational prohibition." His reasoning was very similar to Singer's (although Tooley wrote before Singer). To have a right to life requires having a desire to continue to exist. Not all members of the human species have this desire, and not all beings who do have it are members of the human species. Tooley makes the same leap from racism to speciesism, although he doesn't use that word.[11]

Mary Anne Warren, another philosopher, has, in the course of arguing for abortion, ended up arguing for a softer view of infanticide. She wrote a paper in 1973 arguing that personhood depends on the ability to reason, to communicate, and so forth. She writes, rather high-handedly, that she considers these criteria "to be so obvious that I think anyone who denied [them], and claimed that a being which satisfied none of [them] was a person all the same, would thereby demonstrate that he had no notion at all of what a person is—perhaps because he had confused the concept of a person with that of genetic humanity. If the opponents of abortion were to deny the appropriateness of these five criteria, I do not know what further arguments would convince them." She establishes that fetuses cannot meet these criteria.

In a postscript to the paper written in 1982, she noted that critics had raised the objection that newborns could not meet them, either. She conceded that these critics were, at least in part, correct: Infanticide does not "constitute the killing of a person" and is not "properly considered a form of murder." She allows that it is something very close to that, however, and that "to kill [infants] requires a very strong moral justification as does the killing of dolphins, whales, chimpanzees, and other highly personlike creatures." On the other hand, it may be acceptable in some societies. What is most important is that the "belief that moral strictures against killing should apply equally to *all* genetically human entities, and *only* to genetically human entities," which is an "error," must be "overcom[e]."[12]

The late Joseph Fletcher, a founder of the field of bioethics, best known to the public for his concept of "situational ethics," supported the killing of disabled infants as "postnatal abortion."[13] British bioethicist Jonathan Glover wrote in the 1970s, "The objection to infanticide is at most no stronger than the objection to frustrating a baby's current set of desires, say by leaving him to cry unattended for a longish period."[14] Another British bioethicist, John Harris, wrote in 1999 that the claim "that it is human beings that matter" is equivalent to valuing "whites over blacks, Nazis over Jews, and men over women." Having cast aside speciesism, he does not find it "plausible" to regard "the emerging human individual . . . during the neonatal period" as having a right to life.[15] Jeffrey Reiman, a philosophy professor at American University, has written, "I think (as do many philosophers, doctors, and parents) that ending the lives of severely handicapped newborns will be acceptable because it does not take from the newborns a life that they yet care about and because it is arguably compatible with . . . our natural love for infants."[16]

In the second edition of *Practical Ethics*, Singer was able to list several scholars who agreed with him, adding that "many more could be added."[17] Although they are not philosophers, two people whom he could have added are the co-discoverers of DNA. James Watson favors infanticide—or, to adopt the softening locution of the abortion debates, he is "pro-choice" on infanticide. Francis Crick, apparently, believes infanticide should be mandatory in some cases.[18]

The taboo against infanticide helps to protect us from falling into serious moral error. But the taboo is beginning to erode. Infanticide is starting to break through in the popular press. The first steps were timid. The celebrated evolutionary psychologist, Steven Pinker, wrote a curious essay on "neonaticide" for the *New York Times*

Magazine in 1997. Early on, he says that "[k]illing a baby is an immoral act." He spends the rest of the essay undermining that view. He explains how understandable it is that some people and societies have practiced infanticide, notes that birth is an "arbitrary...milestone," and dismisses the possibility of protecting all human beings with the familiar comparison to racism. He argues that neonates do not have any of the "morally significant traits" that "moral philosophers say" are necessary for a right to life. He concedes: "So how do you provide grounds for outlawing neonaticide? The facts don't make it easy...We will most likely muddle through, keeping birth as a conspicuous legal boundary but showing mercy to the anguished girls who feel they had no choice but to run afoul of it."[19] This is something less than a ringing affirmation of the ban on infanticide.

In 2005, Jim Holt went even further, again in the *New York Times Magazine,* arguing that infanticide might represent "moral progress." He mentioned the "Baby Doe" case discussed in the last chapter. Holt sees little sense in letting such malformed babies die but refusing to kill them. The Dutch, he suggested, are right to kill babies in cases of "unbearable and unrelievable suffering." Their policy is one of "unflinching honesty," and they are putting down guidelines to make sure that the diagnosis is certain, that the parents consent, "and so on." Only "sentiment" keeps us from adopting this policy of "reason."[20]

Holt is misinformed about "euthanasia for babies" in the Netherlands. The new guidelines apply to children under twelve, not just infants, as he implies. The preceding rules have been violated quite often with impunity. It is estimated that more than a fifth of Dutch infanticides take place without the parents' consent or request. Infanticide is common: At least eight percent of Dutch infant deaths result from it. Holt's own article slides down the slippery slope: If he wants euthanasia to end "unbearable and unrelievable suffering," why is he talking about Down syndrome?[21]

Singer himself made the case for infanticide on the Dutch model in the *Los Angeles Times*. He made two arguments. First, some sick infants are denied certain types of care even though it is known that denying it to them will kill them, and nobody protests. So why not just kill them directly? Second, a few cases of infanticide are a drop in the bucket given our infant mortality rate.[22]

The first argument ignores the fact that we can have reasons for withholding care other than a desire to see the patient die. We may forego painful, but life-extending, surgery or chemotherapy not to cause death but to avoid pain. Even if death is a likely outcome of the decision, it is not necessarily the goal. The second argument treats an act of killing as equivalent to a refusal to save someone's life. Singer's utilitarianism mandates such equivalence, but most people can see that the intent behind an act matters. A man who deliberately kills a child is more culpable than a man who isn't helping to reduce the infant mortality rate, assuming he even knows how to effect that goal.

The broader mistake of all of these defenders of infanticide is to assume that it is mere chauvinism to treat membership in the human species as conferring worth and rights. The obvious alternative to valuing all human beings because they are human beings is to value some human beings because of traits that they happen to possess and that other human beings do not: traits such as the ability to perform abstract mental functions. This view has unsavory implications: If basic human rights are built on that foundation, then it is hard to see why someone with more brainpower should not have those rights in greater degree than someone with less. This philosophy makes it hard, that is, to give any account of basic human equality.

In any case, it is not plausible that a human being's value is based on the *immediately exercisable* capacity to perform those functions. One need not be *actually* conscious, reasoning, deliberating, making choices, or doing whatever else it is that these philosophers value in order to be a human being who deserves full moral respect. Plainly people who are asleep, under anesthesia, or in reversible comas deserve such respect.

And once that alternative is rejected, it becomes more plausible to see that what is valuable about human beings is a different kind of capacity. Even human beings in the embryonic, fetal, and infant stages of development have the *radical* capacity (that is, the basic natural capacity in root form) to perform mental functions—and to laugh, sing, love, and mourn—because of the *kind* of beings they are; because they have a human, and therefore rational, nature. They have the capacity to develop themselves by a process of internal self-direction to the point at which the basic natural capacity is immediately exercisable.[23] And they have this radical capacity equally, because they are equally human beings.[24]

Yet what is perhaps most terrible about these apologias for child-murder is that they have a point. They are not correct about the justifiability of infanticide; but they are correct that if abortion is justified, so is infanticide. People who first hear of Singer's views are apt to respond that he is simply crazy. But if the philosophers of infanticide are insane, it is only in the Chestertonian sense: They are not people who lost their reason, but people who have lost everything but their reason. They are reasoning flawlessly from deeply flawed premises that they share with many people who avoid endorsing child-killing only by reasoning poorly from them.

Singer and the others have simply adopted the premises behind abortion and sought to apply them consistently. The ideas that there is a moral right to commit abortion and that there ought to be a legal right to do so are based on the notion that some human beings have no right not to be killed. Try to come up with criteria to rationalize withholding protection from human beings at the embryonic and fetal stages of development, and those criteria inevitably turn out to justify withholding protection from at least some human beings at later stages of development, too.

Note, for example, how Singer defends himself from the charge that he devalues the lives of handicapped people when he says that it would be a good idea to kill handicapped infants. He says that killing handicapped infants no more devalues the lives of handicapped adults than killing handicapped fetuses does. "That a fetus is known to be disabled is widely accepted as a ground for abortion." What's the morally important difference, he asks? Why should the only disabilities that justify killing be those that can be detected prenatally?[25] Good questions.

The truth is that it is extremely difficult to come up with a coherent explanation of why infanticide should be impermissible if abortion is permissible. And it is remarkable how few attempts have been made to devise one. Far fewer philosophers have sought to justify a distinction between abortion and infanticide than have tried to justify the latter. Singer's appointment at Princeton was widely said to be "controversial." Yet it was not controversial among the faculty. Almost none of the professors objected. Almost none of them condemned his views, or even voiced disagreement, even in the course of explaining why academic freedom protected his right to hold and proclaim them.

You would think that pro-choicers would denounce the likes of Singer if only because of the bad p.r. he gives them. Yet even outside the academy, how many pro-choicers have been moved to condemn Peter Singer or Jim Holt? It has been pro-lifers, such as former Princeton trustee Steve Forbes, who have spoken out against them. It will not do to say that Singer's views have no chance of prevailing, and that liberals are less inclined than conservatives to take offense at the harmless words of an intellectual. This is plainly untrue. People who would march against a professor who used the word "mankind" are silent about Singer.

Orthodoxies are marked not only by the views that most of their adherents believe but by the views that they consider reasonable, or tolerable, or unobjectionable. Supporting infanticide is not part of pro-choice orthodoxy. Neither is strongly opposing it.

None of this means that because our society allows abortion, it will inevitably come to allow infanticide too. But there is no reason to rule out the possibility that we will come to allow it—and legalized abortion doesn't make it *less* likely.[26]

Singer himself believes that "[d]uring the next 35 years, the traditional view of the sanctity of human life will collapse... By 2040, it may be that only a rump of hard-core, know-nothing religious fundamentalists will defend the view that every human life, from conception to death, is sacrosanct." The sanctity-of-life ethic will be replaced with a new one that recognizes the distinction between humans and persons.[27]

(This confidence in the historically inevitable triumph of his cause is, incidentally, another echo of the German doctors who paved the way for Nazi medicine. "A new age will arrive—operating with a higher morality and with great sacrifice—which will actually give up the requirements of an exaggerated humanism and overvaluation of mere existence," wrote Alfred Hoche in 1920. Hoche was not a Nazi, but pioneered concepts that the Nazis later employed.[28])

It is true that most people find the idea of infanticide revolting. It is also true that babies are ("sometimes," as Singer reminds us) cute, which makes it hard for us to imagine that we will ever be desensitized to their killing. But some societies, full of human beings with the same hard-wiring as us, have practiced infanticide— as do the Dutch today. Moreover, the fact that most people find the idea of allowing late-term abortions revolting has not moved them to take all legal measures to end the practice. If infanticide were imposed on the populace the way late-term abortion has been, are we sure that we would overturn it? What if infanticide started only with the severely disabled infants, the ones few of us could imagine having to raise, or to watch suffer?

It is easy, in advance, to imagine that our sensibilities will set limits on a moral innovation. We will liberalize the abortion laws, but only for the hard cases. We will allow euthanasia, but only when there is terminal illness and clear evidence of the patient's wishes. We will create human embryos for the purpose of experiments, but only up to the fourteenth day of life: We'll never create fetuses or infants for the same purposes. But crossing those limits is not so difficult once we have breached the principles that forbade all such actions. All it takes is a simple question: What's the difference? Why not? What changes at the fifteenth day? A Supreme Court justice may tell us one day that killing should be permitted until birth, and on another day forget why he once thought birth mattered. And there will always be Peter Singers to form the advance guard of a movement to erase the remaining limits. They are the symptoms; not the disease.

Part III

Life and the Parties

CHAPTER 16

Scribes of the Party of Death

IN THE SPRING OF 1989, as the Supreme Court considered the *Webster* case, and the historians offered their dubious help, supporters of abortion rights staged a big march in Washington, D.C. Many reporters were there, of course. But not all of them were there to cover it. Several journalists from prominent newspapers were there as marchers. Linda Greenhouse, who has long covered the Supreme Court for the *New York Times*, was one of them.

The journalists' participation in the rally became controversial. The editors of the *Times* said that Greenhouse should not have marched. Other reporters tut-tutted her for bringing her objectivity into question.[1] The dispute was somewhat otherworldly. No well-informed observer has ever thought that Greenhouse, or the *Times*, was unbiased, before or since the march. Conservatives even coined the phrase "the Greenhouse effect" to refer to the possibility that Supreme Court justices move left to get better coverage from her and like-minded scribes.

Greenhouse spent the second half of 1992 praising *Casey* in the *Times* as a "tightly reasoned" decision by "centrist" justices. She has described the dissenters—Scalia, Thomas, and Rehnquist—as "the Court's far right." She has written that *Roe* has "taken on a life of its own, evolving into something . . . in tune with the ideals of the American mainstream." And she has written an admiring biography of Harry Blackmun.[2]

If anything, the marching journalists had done everyone a favor by making their biases better known.

The major metropolitan daily newspapers and the big news networks are biased in favor of abortion, and euthanasia, and embryo-destructive research. And everybody knows it. In 1990, *Los Angeles Times* media critic David Shaw wrote a long series of articles documenting that bias.[3] He found that the media tended to identify with the advocates for abortion, describing political developments, for example, as "setback[s] for abortion rights" rather than "victories for pro-lifers." Reporters distorted polling, making public opinion seem more pro-choice than it actually was. They attributed pro-choice candidates' success to their position on abortion, while refusing to consider the possibility that winning pro-life candidates had gained any advantage from theirs. They had ignored news stories that cast abortion, and *Roe*, in a negative light. And they had described pro-life leaders less flatteringly than pro-choice ones.

The same year, Richard Harwood, then the ombudsman for the *Washington Post*, wrote that it was "probably" true that "our news coverage has favored the 'pro-choice' side" just as the newspaper's editorialists and columnists had.[4] The *Post*'s reporters were not only pro-choice themselves; they didn't even know anyone who was anti-abortion.[5] A few years later, *Post* writer Malcolm Gladwell commented on the question of marching reporters: "If you have a staff that is as totally unrepresentative of the national divide over abortion as ours is, you'd have to have a rule about not marching in a pro-abortion protest because the whole staff could conceivably be there."[6]

The story has not changed. In 2004, Daniel Okrent, the *New York Times*'s "public editor" (or ombudsman), discussing his newspaper's coverage of abortion and other social issues, wrote that "if you think The *Times* plays it down the middle on any of them, you've been reading the paper with your eyes closed."[7] Even liberals who deny that the media are biased in their favor across the board concede that they do exhibit a liberal bias on abortion and other social issues.[8] Robert Lichter and Stanley Rothman had found in the 1980s that journalists at the most prestigious media outlets were markedly more liberal on abortion than the public. In a 2001 update, Rothman and Amy Black found that 97 percent of media elites thought that women should have a right to abortion.[9] It's no wonder that most reporters and editors indignantly reject the charge to which Okrent cops. They can't be biased: All their colleagues agree.

In fairness to the media, it should be noted that it can be genuinely difficult to write neutrally about abortion, euthanasia, and embryo-destructive research. Should anti-abortion legislation be called "restrictive" or "protective"? Should it be called "anti-abortion," for that matter, with the emphasis on the negative, or "pro-life"? Reasonable people can disagree about journalistic choices on these matters. But the fact that the media consistently make the same choice—for "restrictive" over "protective," for example—is revealing. So is the fact that when reporters go outside the realm of reasonable disagreement, for example by describing anti-abortion legislation as "harsh," it is almost always to put a pro-abortion spin on a story.[10]

It is also worth noting that some reporters have produced excellent work. Ruth Padawer, David Brown, and Barbara Vobejda helped to uncover the truth about the incidence of partial-birth abortion and the typical reasons for it.[11] Cynthia Gorney has put the debate over partial-birth abortion in the context of the larger debate over abortion.[12] David Savage has explained what *Roe* really said to readers of the *Los Angeles Times*.[13] Karen Tumulty has written in

Time about how the politics of abortion have played out in Missouri.[14] Whatever these reporters' own views about abortion, they have managed to produce fair-minded and informative articles.

But they are the exception, not the rule. More reporters have contributed to the mythology of *Roe* than have debunked it. For example, the press perpetuated the myth that partial-birth abortion was rare—and only for medical (rather than elective) reasons—even when pro-lifers responded with facts that refuted the claim. The media didn't even acknowledge the existence of a dispute over the facts. Reporters debunked the myth only after Congress debated the partial-birth abortion bill and President Clinton vetoed it. Worse, many reporters continued to parrot the myth long after the debunking. In 2003, the *Wall Street Journal* reported that partial-birth abortion was "typically" performed "for medical reasons."[15] The *Boston Globe* and the *San Francisco Chronicle* made the same false claim.[16] The *Washington Post* and the Associated Press said that the procedure was "rarely" used—a characterization that pro-life lobbyist Douglas Johnson correctly terms "tendentious."[17]

Much of the press, led by the *New York Times*, avoided using the phrase "partial-birth abortion" (or placing it in distancing quotes) whenever possible. This impulse has led to some convoluted *Times* headlines: "House Acts to Ban Abortion Method, Making It a Crime"; "President Vetoes Measure Banning Type of Abortion"; "Bush Signs Ban on a Procedure for Abortion." The kids at Hogwarts speak the name of Voldemort more freely than the *Times* editors use the phrase partial-birth abortion.

Longtime *Newsweek* correspondent Kenneth Woodward points out that if the editors of the *Times* really believe the phrase should be avoided because it is not a medical term, they should remove references to "heart attacks" from their pages as well. If they want to avoid it because one side of the debate objects to it, "female genital mutilation" would have to go as well. The result is not only confusing stories; it is, as Woodward writes, that "every story is framed as a narrative of assault on *Roe* v. *Wade*." The *Times*'s choice of words helps to shield a political weak point for the abortion lobby.[18]

The *Chicago Tribune*'s official policy is to discourage references to "partial-birth abortion." The policy prompted public editor Don Wycliff to write: "If our purpose is to communicate clearly with our readers, should we not use the term they understand?"[19]

The press has not shown any general reluctance to adopt politically contested phrases. When Congress banned "assault weapons," the NRA bitterly protested that the phrase had been made up and referred to no distinct class of firearms. Yet the press adopted it without resorting to locutions such as "a class of guns called 'assault weapons' by advocates of gun control" or "Congress Bans Type of Gun."

When pro-life presidents cut off family-planning funding for groups that counsel women to have abortions, pro-choicers called the policy a "gag rule"—and the press did not handle the phrase with gloves and tongs. Headlines, including *New York Times* headlines, regularly used variants of the phrase.[20] Greenhouse casually referred to *Rust* v. *Sullivan*, which concerned the policy, as "the abortion gag-rule case."[21]

The conservative Media Research Center analyzed 217 stories about partial-birth abortion on ABC, CBS, and NBC that aired between 1995 and 2003. They found that only eighteen of those stories explained what took place in a partial-birth abortion (and only three of them explained it between 1998 and 2003). They reported on congressional votes and Supreme Court decisions about partial-birth abortion, but refused to provide the facts that would make it clear what the fuss was about.[22]

The bias was there from the start. Consider the *New York Times*'s role in its state's 1970 liberalization of its abortion law. The *Times* consistently referred to liberalization as "reform" and its advocates as "reformers." It referred—in the news pages—to the existing law against abortion as "rigid." Its articles stressed the Catholicism of abortion opponents without delving into the religious views of its supporters. They uncritically accepted Cyril Means's false claim that the state had banned abortion only to protect mothers' lives. (Greenhouse was one of the credulous reporters.)[23]

The paper ran puff pieces about the advocates of "reform." It even ran a long profile of Planned Parenthood president Alan Guttmacher in which the chief question was if voluntary birth control and abortion would suffice to fight the population explosion, or if coercive methods would also be needed. (Noting that a birth took place somewhere in the world every half second, the reporter called it "a frightening statistic.") It was during this period, incidentally, that the *Times* editorial page established the tone of contempt with which it treats pro-lifers. When its favored bill passed, it credited its leading proponent, who had previously been the subject of one of the puff pieces, with "calm, persuasive argument in the face of intense emotional opposition."[24] In all the years since, the newspaper's op-ed page has never featured a regular columnist who is pro-life.

The press has not gotten notably more even-handed in the years since. The *Times* still runs puff pieces about abortion advocates. Its readers discovered in 2005 that Kelli Conlin, the executive director of NARAL Pro-Choice America's New York branch, is a "dedicated mother hen." "If Ms. Conlin, with her blue eyes, green chinoiserie blouse, and pearly white earrings looks as if she grew up healthy, shy and straitlaced on a 400-acre farm in Michigan, attending only Catholic schools all the way until Northwestern University for a master's in journalism, it's because she did." A similarly sympathetic portrait of a pro-life activist will have to await the apocalypse.[25]

The major change has been that the bias has been imported to new areas, such as the debate over stem-cell research. When Ronald

Reagan died in 2004, *Newsweek* ran the obligatory commemoration issue. The next week's edition carried *three* articles making the case for federal funding of embryo-destructive research. First, Reagan's daughter Patti Davis wrote that the research could cure Alzheimer's. She even wrote that promoting the research could be God's redemptive purpose for her family's suffering. Second, the magazine ran a news article playing up the potential benefits of the research for the treatment of Alzheimer's. Third, the magazine's columnist Jonathan Alter speculated that Reagan would have favored it.[26]

In reality, as we have seen, the research is highly unlikely to yield any benefits for Alzheimer's patients. As for Reagan's views, nobody can say with certainty what they would have been, and trying to hold a séance is not an especially fruitful way to think about the ethics of the research. But any serious inquiry would have to take note of the fact that Reagan's administration blocked federal funding of research on human embryos and that Reagan proclaimed his belief in the personhood of human beings from their earliest stages of life.

Newsweek was only slightly less biased the first time embryonic stem-cell research made the news, in the summer of 2001. At that time it ran an issue with cover text that read, from top to bottom: "The Stem Cell Wars: Embryo Research vs. Pro-Life Politics: There's Hope for Alzheimer's, Heart Disease, Parkinson's and Diabetes. But Will Bush Cut Off the Money?" This counts as restraint only if the alternative text were: "Science vs. Pro-Life Fanatics: Will Bush Condemn Millions of People to Lingering, Painful Deaths?"

The lead story, by Sharon Begley, let proponents of the research make their case at length. Opponents got exactly two words (eleven letters) in. And that quote was immediately rebutted, unlike any of the pro-research quotes. The piece concluded thus: Not funding stem-cell research would amount to "squelching what is, more than anything, a quest for knowledge. We simply don't know how embryonic cells might help people who are suffering and dying today. By banning the research, we uphold the most extreme view of the sanctity of life, but at a price: foreclosing the possibility of doing all we can to improve the lot of the living."

Set aside that bit about extremism. Any research, including research on humans that most people would find objectionable, can legitimately be described as "a quest for knowledge." And the reference to "the living" stacked the deck: It assumes, falsely, that the embryos are not also alive.

Next came three pages on the politics of the research from Evan Thomas and well-known liberal Eleanor Clift. The subhead suggested that "[t]he president is trapped between religion and science over stem cells." The president was "expected to ban federal funding" because of "pure politics." Yet "[b]y a 3–1 margin, the public wants to go forward with research that has the potential to provide magical [!] cures for a host of neurological and other diseases." The article concluded with some helpful suggestions on how President Bush could betray pro-lifers without suffering too much political damage.

Only after those articles did the magazine run a short essay on the ethics of the research that refused to pound the readers' heads with a conclusion.[27]

The Terri Schiavo case showed the same bias at work. Sometimes it was blatant, as when Peter Jennings referred to congressional "interference" in the case or a CBS correspondent referred to the involvement of "the far right."[28] At other times, the media made it hard for consumers of the news to figure out the facts of the matter. Schiavo was described as "brain dead" and terminally ill, although she was neither until her starvation.[29] Then there were the media's omissions. The facts that Michael Schiavo had a fiance and had had children with her was rarely mentioned, even though they could reasonably be taken to be relevant to his ability to represent his wife's wishes. Nor were his earlier courtroom promises to care for her for the remainder of her life.

The media's coverage of euthanasia has also exhibited the tendentious gullibility that has characterized its abortion coverage. Mike Wallace of *60 Minutes*, a supporter of euthanasia and of Jack Kevorkian, ran footage of Kevorkian's "mercy killing" of Thomas Youk. Wallace accepted Kevorkian's claim that he was acting to keep Youk, a man with Lou Gehrig's disease, from choking to death on his own saliva. Proper medical care can prevent this from happening, but viewers of *60 Minutes* didn't find that out. At least the publicity ended up serving a useful purpose: The videotape contained enough evidence for prosecutors to put Kevorkian away— something Wallace bitterly protests.[30]

Jack Lessenberry reported on Kevorkian for the *New York Times*. In other media outlets, he expressed strong support for the man and his mission. He even wrote a column about why a jury should acquit him—and then covered the trial for the *Times*. Not surprisingly, his coverage was favorable to Kevorkian.[31]

Whether or not its members realize it, America's journalistic elite is a functional ally of the party of death.

CHAPTER 17

The Tide Turns

THE TWENTIETH ANNIVERSARY OF *Roe* was the high tide of the pro-abortion movement. The day before witnessed the inauguration of Bill Clinton; there had never been a president more favorably disposed to abortion rights. On that first day in office, Clinton issued a series of executive orders liberalizing abortion law. The Supreme Court had re-affirmed *Roe* the year before. Since most of the leaders of the House and Senate favored abortion rights, pro-choice activists had high hopes of enacting the Freedom of Choice Act. By the end of the year, Clinton would propose a health-care plan featuring subsidized abortion. "The great abortion debate is over," wrote columnist Charles Krauthammer: The pro-lifers had lost.[1]

For the twenty years after *Roe*, both the abortion rate and public support for abortion had crept steadily up. In February 1979, 22 percent of Americans told Gallup that abortion should be "legal under any circumstances." That number had risen to 29 by July 1989, and to 34 by July 1992. Clinton's support for legal abortion was widely described as a factor in his victory, and Republicans were warned that they would have to soften their opposition to return to power.

But pro-choice dreams quickly turned to ashes. Congress never even voted on the Freedom of Choice Act or the Clinton health plan. Within two years, both the House and Senate had Republicans opposed to abortion as their leaders—and the abortion lobby found itself having to fight legal restrictions rather than fighting for government subsidies. The abortion rate peaked in 1990 (at 1.6 million), and public support for abortion peaked soon thereafter.

In retrospect, it is easy to see that even at its height the pro-choice movement had major weaknesses—some of them hidden, most of them growing. Evidence of these weaknesses could be found in the polls, in the culture, and in the behavior of politicians and voters.

The polls on abortion can be confusing. NARAL and its allies have long claimed that there is a "pro-choice majority," and their spin has largely prevailed. The *Washington Post* reports, for example, that "polls have consistently found support for fundamental abortion rights, even while the public backs some efforts to restrict access to the procedure."[2] But that conventional wisdom is based on a highly selective reading of the polls.

Several polls have shown that when presented with the options of keeping abortion legal, prohibiting it, or prohibiting it with exceptions when pregnancies result from rape or incest or endanger the mother's life, majorities of the public choose the two prohibitionist alternatives. In what follows, when I use a specific number, it will be both the most recent number available and in the same neighborhood as other poll findings on the same subject. Although the data is recent, the overall picture will be the same as the one that prevailed in the early 1990s.[3]

A CBS News poll from late July 2005 found that 53 percent of the public thought that abortion should be illegal, period, or illegal with those exceptions. That finding has been repeated fairly consistently. The exact same number turns up in a *Los Angeles Times* poll from March 2001. There appears to be no gender gap: In 1998, the Center for Gender Equality, a feminist group, found that 53 percent of women believed that abortion should either be illegal altogether or with the rape/incest/life-of-the-mother exceptions.[4]

Gallup has long asked people whether they think abortion should be "legal under any circumstances," legal "only under certain circumstances," or "illegal in all circumstances." A majority always picks the middle option. For the last ten years, it has subdivided that middle option, asking the moderates whether they think abortion should be legal in "most" or "only in a few" circumstances. The May 2005 results were typical: 23, 12, 40, and 22, respectively, for always, mostly, rarely, and never legal. So a combined 62 percent of the public thought abortion should be either illegal or legal only in a few circumstances. A *Los Angeles Times* poll also found (in January 2005) that 53 percent of the public thinks abortion should be either "illegal without exceptions" or "illegal with a few exceptions."

Large majorities of the public favor mandatory waiting periods, parental-consent laws, spousal-notification requirements, and prohibitions on abortion after the first three months of pregnancy. A small majority of the public says that it believes that life begins at conception, and roughly half the public thinks abortion is murder. Small majorities also think abortion should not be available simply because the mother is single, is poor and cannot afford more children, or simply does not want more children.

There is no "pro-choice majority."

But there isn't a pro-life majority, either, exactly. A majority sides with pro-choicers on some questions. If you ask people whether they support *Roe*, for example, almost two-thirds of them will say that they do and that it should not be overturned. A very similar number say, if asked, that abortion should be legal in the first three months, and that they oppose a constitutional amendment to prohibit abortion. If you ask them whether the abortion decision should be between "the woman and her doctor," about 55 percent of the public says yes. Something like 75 percent of the public favors a right to abortion when "there is a strong chance of a serious defect in [the] baby." A slightly higher percentage favors it when the pregnancy results from rape.

And if you ask Americans whether they consider themselves "pro-life" or "pro-choice," the results fluctuate. At all times, fewer people consider themselves "pro-choice" than think that abortion should often be legal in the first trimester. Also at all times, fewer people consider themselves "pro-life" than think that abortion should be illegal with at most a few restrictions.

The differences among these results cannot be completely resolved. Wanting to ban abortion under most circumstances isn't really compatible with thinking of it as a matter between a woman and her doctor. The public has some ambivalence about the subject of abortion, along with, perhaps, a reluctance to think it through in detail.

But some of the mystery can be cleared up. The numbers on the *Roe* and first-trimester questions match up so closely as to suggest that when people say they support *Roe*, they mean that they oppose a ban on all first-trimester abortions. There is no reason to think that most people know that *Roe* effectively creates a constitutional right to late-term abortions, or that overturning it would not by itself prohibit anything.

Other results may reflect a widespread overestimation of the percentage of abortions that result from rape and incest. Finally, some people who think that abortion should generally be illegal may not consider themselves "pro-life" because they associate the pro-life movement with militancy and even violence. A tiny number of anti-abortionists, by taking up the gun and the bomb, have done enormous damage to their cause.

There is a clear majority for legal abortion only in particular cases that account for a small proportion of abortions (rape, incest, life of the mother, and severe fetal abnormality). Even the polls that seem to show that the public supports first-trimester abortion are open to question. There is not much polling that asks people whether they support first-trimester abortions for reasons other than rape, life, and incest. In November 2004, however, pollster Richard Wirthlin found that 55 percent of the public thought abortion should either be illegal altogether or illegal with the rape, incest, and life exceptions. Forty percent thought that it should be legal for any reason in the first trimester. (That 40 percent includes nine percent who would keep it legal afterward, too.)[5]

It is undeniable that the public supports a legal regime that is far more protective of unborn life than we have now, and it is possible that it narrowly supports a ban on most abortions. The abortion lobby has had good reason to keep the issue in the courts: It never could count on the public's being in its corner.

Nor did the culture reflect the party of death's views, even at its high point. Perhaps most important, abortion has never been normalized, never become just another medical procedure for most Americans. Many doctors have not wanted to perform it. The standard pro-choice explanation for their reluctance has been fear of harassment and violence by pro-lifers. These fears have surely inhibited some doctors, but moral objections, distaste, and social pressures must have done so as well.[6]

Qualms about abortion also help to explain why characters in prime-time television shows almost never have abortions—and even then, most are shown on medical dramas where the act is incidental to the plot. The last high-profile prime-time abortion took place in 1972, on *All in the Family*—and even that was the result of a population-control group's offering a $10,000 prize for scripts dealing with its concerns. On soap operas, characters are much more likely to return from the dead than to have an abortion.[7] "[W]e might as well be living in an era before *Roe* v. *Wade* as far as TV is concerned," writes one frustrated feminist. "Characters these days rarely even say the word *abortion* when confronted with an unplanned pregnancy—let alone have one."[8]

o   o   o.

In early 1992, the Arthur S. DeMoss Foundation began running a television ad campaign called "Life: What a Beautiful Choice." One ad showed children laughing and smiling while an announcer said, "All these children have one thing in common. All of them were unplanned pregnancies. Pregnancies that could have ended in abortion. But their parents toughed it out, listened to their hearts and discovered...that sometimes the best things in life aren't planned. Life: What a beautiful choice." Another ad showed more children playing while, in voice-overs, their mothers said that they couldn't believe they had considered not having them.

Still another ad showed a picture of a baby in a crib and an image of a fetus in the womb. The announcer checked off the similarities: beating hearts, arms, toes, and so on. "The difference is, the baby on the left is just born—and the baby on the right would very much like to be. Life. What a beautiful choice."

The ads didn't include gruesome images of aborted fetuses. They said nothing about what the government should do about abortion. They were attempts to persuade people to choose life. But pro-choice groups were furious nonetheless. The headquarters of Planned Parenthood got phone calls from several affiliates asking "whether or not there's a way of blocking" the ads. Critics denounced the ad campaign as "slick." (Ad campaigns often are.) They said that the ads presented an idealized picture of adoption and parenthood.

Two years later, the foundation started running the occasional ad that suggested that the availability of abortion was a "problem." But the focus remained on persuading people not to have abortions.

Pro-choice groups eventually responded with their own ad campaign, which showed, in the words of a pro-choice writer, "a phalanx of grim, graying, suited white men trail[ing] a young, biracial urban woman throughout her day, monitoring and correcting her every move....When she drops her change into a street-corner soda machine and reaches for a can, they grab her finger and guide it to their favorite cola."

The ads worried pro-choicers. Kate Michelman recalls:

In the mid-1990s, prominent national polls began to show growing support for restrictions on abortion, a trend that Harrison Hickman's polls for NARAL confirmed...Harrison scrutinized the numbers, analyzing the views of various demographic groups, searching for a coherent explanation for the slippage, but he found none. He then serendipitously stumbled onto a list of media markets in which the anti-abortion Arthur DeMoss Foundation was running [its ad campaign]...Harrison found that the most significant declines in support for the right to choose [abortion] coincided precisely with the markets in which the DeMoss campaign was running.

There's no question that the ads got people thinking. Perhaps, in some small way, the abortion lobby's reaction to them also had an impact—by suggesting, as Maria McFadden put it, that keeping the baby is the choice pro-choicers aren't pro.[9]

o   o   o

By the 1990s, medical developments were starting to weaken further the hold of abortion on society. In the early years of the debate it was common for advocates of legal abortion to dismiss the human fetus as a mere "blob of tissue" or as "protoplasm." But as more and more people looked at ultrasound images of their children, nephews and nieces, or grandkids in the womb, they could see even early in pregnancy that those descriptions were grossly inadequate.

The date of viability kept (and keeps) moving back, too. Many people have thought that this date mattered morally: that it is somehow permissible to kill a young human being before, but not after, it can survive "on its own." That standard has never made much sense, since infants (and, in some respects, much older people) are not self-sufficient either. It also makes the permissibility of killing turn in principle on the technological or economic circumstances of a particular time and place—which is not how we usually think about killing. But even people who believe in the viability standard could see, as doctors saved the lives of increasingly premature infants, that more and more fetuses met the test. Some of them could not help but take note of the incongruity: A doctor would take heroic measures, and even perform surgery, on a fetus who, depending on the mother's wishes, could just as legally be killed by him.

Even when it came to elections, pro-choicers were not riding as high as they thought. What political professionals sometimes call the "intensity factor" worked against them. Pro-life voters are more likely than pro-choice ones to vote on the issue of abortion. The number of people who vote on abortion varies from election to election, as does the margin by which pro-lifers dominate that group. But in most elections, they are a majority of the voters who consider abortion a top issue.

In 1988, CBS found that voters to whom abortion was "one of the issues that mattered most" went 65 percent for pro-lifer George H. W. Bush and 33 percent for pro-choicer Michael Dukakis. The *Los Angeles Times* reached a similar conclusion. In 1992, media exit polls found Bush beating Clinton 55 to 36 percent among these voters. In 1996, Dole beat Clinton among them 60 to 34. In 2000, 14 percent of voters told the *Times*'s pollsters that abortion was one of the issues they considered most important—and they voted for George W. Bush over Al Gore, 58 to 41 percent. That translates to an advantage for Bush worth 2.3 percent of the national electorate. In a close race, the pro-life advantage can make a difference.

That advantage exists even in relatively pro-choice states. In 1998, abortion voters went 55 percent for the pro-life Republican Senate candidate in Illinois and 58 percent for his counterpart in New York.[10]

The electoral dynamics of abortion are, to be sure, more complicated than those numbers suggest. Most voters don't consider abortion one of their top issues, but a candidate's position on abortion may still have a great influence on their view of him. They may, for example, associate the pro-life position with intolerance. On the other hand, they may associate it with family values. Given the one-dimensional shape of American politics—politicians who are pro-life are more likely to be anti-tax and pro-defense spending—they may associate it with all kinds of things they like or dislike. To the extent that a candidate's position on abortion affects the tone of media coverage of him and therefore voters' views, the pro-life position probably hurts. But the data does suggest that voters who are pro-choice are more ambivalent about it than voters who are pro-life. For one thing, other types of polls—asking voters whether they would think better or worse of a candidate if they heard he is pro-life—also generally suggest a marginal pro-life advantage.

Politicians have understood the dangers of appearing to be pro-abortion. Bill Clinton's campaign slogan in 1992—repeated many times thereafter—was that abortion should be "safe, legal, and rare." The message wasn't that abortion was a liberating choice. "Once the pro-choice movement sent the message that abortion was undesirable, we were on a slippery slope headed downhill," says David Garrow, a pro-abortion historian.[11] By 1996, pro-choice politicians were running away from the word abortion. At the party conventions, both Al Gore and Colin Powell said only that they supported "a woman's right to choose," pretending that this verb requires no object. (Clinton did use the word, but returned to the safe, legal, and rare mantra.)

Even the abortion lobby distanced itself from the word. NARAL, the leading group, began its life in 1969 as the "National Association for the Repeal of Abortion Laws." After *Roe* it became the "National Abortion Rights Action League." The sidelining of abortion began in 1993, when the group became the "National Abortion and Reproductive Rights Action League." In 2003, it adopted its current official name: "NARAL Pro-Choice America." The letters "NARAL" literally no longer stand for anything. Champions of free speech, of freedom of religion, or of the right to own guns unfurl their banners proudly. Abortion is the right that dare not speak its name.

Pro-life candidates can certainly approach the issue in ways that backfire politically. The public doesn't want officials to be crusaders on abortion. Its discomfort at seeing the issue raised works in favor of the status quo and against attempts either to ban or to subsidize abortion.[12] But taking a pro-life position has helped many candidates, and the Republican party generally. Republicans would probably not have become the nation's majority party without the abortion issue. Abortion wasn't the only issue that swept them to control of Congress in 1994. But it's notable that amidst the upheaval not a single pro-life incumbent lost to a pro-choice challenger that year.

In the mid-1990s, the politics turned worse for the abortion lobby with the emergence of the issue of partial-birth abortion. That issue highlighted the pro-choice movement's extremism. It also represented a change of strategies for pro-lifers. Previously their legislative agenda had centered on a Human Life Amendment. The public's fear of sweeping change and support for abortion in some instances made it a non-starter. Every year it made a constitutional amendment the center of discussion, the pro-life movement was highlighting an issue where the public sided with pro-choicers. An amendment-centered pro-life movement also faced a seemingly insoluble chicken-or-egg problem. The culture would have to become much more pro-life before an amendment could be enacted. But law affects culture: The legality of abortion, and its status as a supposed constitutional right, made that kind of massive cultural change less likely.

The campaign against partial-birth abortion represented a decisive turn to an incrementalist strategy. Pro-lifers would work to protect lives where they could, starting with the issues that generated the largest consensus and moving forward. This strategy was controversial among pro-lifers. Some felt that it amounted to an abandonment of the goal that all lives should be protected. Most pro-lifers, however, concluded that it was not an abandonment of that goal but rather the only way to get closer to it. The law would little by little change the culture, and as the culture changed it would become possible to change the law more.

The strategy has been successful so far. Pro-lifers made significant victories in state legislatures during the 1990s, and those victories appear to have reduced the number of abortions. Economist Michael New has found that restrictions on government funding and informed-consent laws—which typically require that women seeking abortions be told about the facts of fetal development and the support available to mothers—have significantly reduced the abortion rate. States did not have much time to implement bans on partial-birth abortion before the Supreme Court struck them down, but New found some evidence that those bans also drove the numbers down.[13] (Those state-level victories have continued. NARAL reported that states passed fifty pro-life bills in 2005 alone, albeit modest ones.[14])

The polling began to change, too—most strikingly, on the question of whether voters considered themselves "pro-life" or "pro-choice."

In September 1995, Gallup found that 56 percent of the public thought of itself as pro-choice and 33 percent identified as pro-life. By August 1997, however, the pro-choice advantage on that measure had shrunk from 23 points to only three (47–44). With one exception, which looks like a blip, it stayed in the single digits from then through May 2005 (48–44).

UCLA conducts a nationwide poll of incoming college freshmen every fall. It has shown declining support for legal abortion among young people. In 1992, 67 percent believed that abortion should be legal. In 2004, only 54 percent did—the lowest number since the question started to be asked in 1977.[15]

In 2005, the women's magazine *Glamour* ran a story on the "mysterious disappearance of young pro-choice women." It noted that a 2003 CBS/*New York Times* poll had found that 35 percent of young women (aged 18-29) thought that "abortion should be available to anyone who wants it." Fifty percent of the young women of 1993 had thought that. It quoted Alexander Sanger of Planned Parenthood: "I've seen the numbers and I find them unbelievably shocking. Isn't it obvious that young women have to be at the forefront of fighting for their reproductive rights because they're the ones who need them?" It isn't obvious to many young women.[16]

o   o   o

The pro-choicers suffered another blow during the 1990s, as well. Norma McCorvey, the Jane Roe of *Roe* v. *Wade*, announced that she was pro-life—joining Sandra Cano, the Jane Doe of *Doe* v. *Bolton*.

McCorvey was twenty-two at the time of the case. Her pregnancy was not a result of rape, as she claimed at the time in trying to get an abortion. But her actual history of abuse and rape, including a marriage at sixteen to a violent twenty-four-year-old man, was grim enough.

In the years after *Roe*, McCorvey moved from job to job and place to place. She drank heavily. By 1995, McCorvey had gone public with her identity as the lead plaintiff in *Roe* and written a book defending *Roe*. She was working at an abortion clinic in Dallas when Operation Rescue, an anti-abortion protest group, moved to the office next door.

"I will never forget the call I received on March 31, 1995, informing me about the move," she later wrote. "I immediately lit up a second cigarette, even though I already had one burning. They don't make nicotine strong enough for situations such as these."

She talked to Flip Benham, the head of Operation Rescue, when the protests coincided with her smoke breaks. It was the most banal of conversations that started her on a new path.

> I goaded Flip, "What you need is to go to a good Beach Boys concert." Flip answered, "Miss Norma, I haven't been to a Beach Boys concert since 1976." The seemingly innocuous response shook me to the core. All at once, Flip became human to me.
>
> Before, I had thought of Flip as a man who did nothing but yell at abortion clinics and read his Bible. In fact, I even pictured him sleeping with his hands across his chest, Dracula-like, with a big Bible tucked under his arms. The thought that he was a real person—a guy who had once even gone to a Beach Boys concert—never occurred to me. Now that it had, I saw him in a new light.

They became friends. McCorvey also befriended Emily, the seven-year-old daughter of one of Benham's colleagues. McCorvey had never been comfortable with children: That fact that her own three children had been placed for adoption, and her history of abortion activism, made her "fearful of bonding with anyone so young."

McCorvey had already had some doubts about her involvement in *Roe*. She recalls being haunted, some time in the 1980s, by the sight of an empty playground. Her doubts grew when she found out that Emily's mother, Ronda, had faced pressure to abort Emily and almost did. "Abortion was no longer an 'abstract right.' It had a face now, in a little girl named Emily."

Emily and Ronda took McCorvey to church, and she converted to Christianity. A few weeks later, while looking at a poster on fetal development in the Operation Rescue office, she acknowledged to herself something she had spent years pretending not to know: "Abortion wasn't about 'products of conception.' It wasn't about 'missed periods.' It was about children being killed in their [mothers'] wombs. All those years I was wrong. Signing that affidavit, I was wrong. Working in an abortion clinic, I was wrong."

Pro-choice leaders dismissed McCorvey's change of heart when they heard about it. Kate Michelman said that *Roe* "isn't about any single individual." (That is surely correct: It is about at least forty-five million individuals—former individuals. That's why McCorvey defected.) Sarah Weddington, McCorvey's lawyer in *Roe*, told CNN that if she could do it over again, "she would have picked a different plaintiff, who might have better represented the case."[17]

o   o   o

At the start of the 1990s, the Republican party was extremely nervous about its pro-life stand. When the Supreme Court narrowed the scope of *Roe* in 1989, Republicans feared that the supposed "pro-choice majority" would awaken and turn on them. But the campaign against partial-birth abortion helped to solidify their opposition to abortion. In addition to making pro-lifers seem in tune with public opinion, it marginalized Republican pro-choicers. The most vocal ones, such as Governor Christine Todd Whitman of New Jersey, opposed bans on partial-birth abortion—but most pro-choice Republicans weren't willing to go that far. Already a minority faction among Republican officeholders, they now found themselves divided, too. And the pro-choicers against partial-birth abortion could unite with their pro-life colleagues on that issue. The Whitmans of the party became marginalized.

When she was elected in 1993, Whitman was supposed to herald the future of the Republican party. She was a pro-choice tax-cutter: just the mix the party supposedly needed to make it in the suburbs. But nothing came of all her glowing press. It didn't help that while her pro-abortion convictions were deep and genuine, her tax-cutting was a campaign tactic abandoned in the middle of her term. It also didn't help that she failed to win a majority of women's votes in her state in any of her campaigns.

In 1996, three Republican governors—Whitman, Bill Weld of Massachusetts, and Pete Wilson of California—tried to change the party's platform so that it would no longer declare opposition to legal abortion. By 2004, pro-choice Republican governors such as Arnold Schwarzenegger of California and George Pataki of New York were not willing to put up a fight. Support for partial-birth abortion effectively ended the careers of Whitman and Weld. Today's Republican party includes pro-choicers, but they are not investing their careers in a challenge to the pro-life definition of the party. The party's big donors (like the Democrats' big donors) are more pro-choice than the party rank-and-file, but they too have largely thrown in the towel.

At the turn of the millennium, pro-choicers found themselves doing something they had never expected to do: playing defense.

CHAPTER 18

Pro-Life Democrats

KRISTEN DAY EXPLAINS THE decline of the Democratic party with just a few numbers.

In 1978, she points out, there were 292 Democratic members of the House of Representatives: a large majority. One hundred twenty-five of them were pro-lifers.

By 2004, there were only about thirty pro-life Democrats in the House—and only 203 House Democrats, period.[1]

The Democrats have lost eighty-nine seats, and there are ninety fewer pro-life Democrats. Day thinks it's no coincidence. The executive director of Democrats for Life of America, she means to reverse both trends.

The thirty or so pro-life Democrats who remain in the House play an important legislative role. There are around twenty-five pro-choice Republicans. So without the pro-life Democrats, very few pro-life bills (and many pro-choice bills) would pass. But there is no denying that they have been a marginal influence on their party.

In 2002, they even lost the support of the flaky left-wing congressman Dennis Kucinich. He had compiled a very consistent pro-life voting record. But he decided he wanted to run for president as a kind of protest candidate within the Democratic primaries. A left-wing magazine ran a column complaining about his pro-life stand. So like Joe Biden, Jesse Jackson, Dick Gephardt, and all the rest before him, Kucinich flipped on the issue. (He even promised that he would appoint Supreme Court justices who would strike down the pro-life laws he had spent his career voting for.) This time, history was repeated both as tragedy and farce. Kucinich abandoned the unborn and, in return, received the support of alt-rocker Ani DiFranco. It's a sad day when a man can be corrupted by power he is never going to have.[2]

The nadir of the pro-life Democrats' influence probably came in 2003, when Terry McAuliffe, then the chairman of the Democratic National Committee, refused to include a link to Day's organization on the DNC website. Mark Shields, a pro-life liberal columnist, pointed out that the DNC's site posted 261 links, "including ones to such longtime party stalwarts as Easter Seals, the Veterans of Foreign Wars, the U.S. Forest Service and the Oneida Indian Organization."[3]

McAuliffe explained, "I do not think it would be appropriate to use official party resources such as the DNC website on behalf of organizations whose purpose is to reverse the current platform and/or to enact legislation that contradicts that platform." Shields responded: "'Official party resources?' Democrats for Life is not asking for a desk and a phone at party headquarters or even access to the postage meter. All it asks from the Democratic Party (which views 'diversity as a source of strength') is to be the 262nd link on its Web site."

Eventually the DNC just removed all the links.[4] It was an elegant solution to the problem, one that neatly illustrated the instincts that have brought the party to minority status: better to cut off all ties to the outside world than to include pro-lifers.

Few as they are, pro-life Democratic congressmen come in several varieties. Some are relatively conservative on a broad range of issues, compared to their parties. By the end of his political career, Senator Zell Miller of Georgia was practically a Republican as well as a pro-lifer. John Murtha of Pennsylvania is another pro-life conservative Democrat.

Other pro-life Democrats are liberal. In 2003 and 2004, Representative Dale Kildee of Michigan voted the way the National Right to Life Committee wanted 91 percent of the time. In 2004, he also voted with the liberal Americans for Democratic Action 90 percent of the time—more than most House Democrats. Representatives Michael McNulty of New York and Mike Doyle of Pennsylvania are among the other pro-life liberals in Congress. Like Kildee, they tend to keep a low profile.[5]

A similar grab-bag of pro-lifers who don't fall into the conventional political categories can be found outside Congress. Feminists for Life is home to both Republicans and Democrats who believe that abortion is a symptom of a social failure to meet the needs of women. ("Women Deserve Better than Abortion" is one of their slogans.) The anti-euthanasia activists at Not Dead Yet don't even accept the pro-life label, regarding themselves as fighting for the rights of the disabled alongside liberal Democrats such as Tom Harkin. The Pro-Life Alliance of Gays and Lesbians ("Human rights start when human life begins!") keeps the culture warriors confused just by existing.

Such groups, however multifarious and small, serve the valuable purpose of bringing the pro-life point of view to people who might otherwise be predisposed against it. If that point of view is ever to prevail, it will have to come to include within its tent people who disagree about other political matters. Only in that way could a consensus ever be forged.

While there are certainly exceptions to the trend, pro-life Democrats are more likely than pro-life Republicans to oppose capital punishment and to regard that position as integral to being pro-life. Day's organization, for example, includes opposition to the death penalty as part of its mission.

Pro-life Democrats tend to think that pro-life Republicans are also inconsistent because they don't value life after birth. Pro-choice Democrats make that charge, too, of course. But when they make it, it is usually a debater's point: *You people on the other side are a bunch of hypocrites.* (The rejoinder is obvious: You don't have to adopt a child to campaign for laws against child abuse.) Pro-life Democrats want the charge to be a challenge. They want laws against abortion *and* they want assistance to make it easier for women in difficult situations to choose life.

They're right on both counts. Both ambitions should be part of a consistent ethic of life. The pro-life movement has, in fact, invested many of its resources in crisis pregnancy centers that seek to provide material and emotional support for pregnant women in trouble. (America now has more crisis pregnancy centers than abortion clinics.[6]) A Democratic think tank estimates that 22 percent of women who choose abortion do so because of "inadequate finances." While that number suggests obvious limits to a strategy of material support in bringing down the abortion rate, it also suggests that it could do some good.[7]

Feminists for Life points out that many colleges offer an array of services to help students get abortions, but do nothing to help them take care of children (let alone to help integrate mothers into the life of the campus). They have succeeded in getting a few colleges to alter those policies.

What role the government should play in supporting women who choose life is open to legitimate debate. Reasonable people can disagree, for example, about whether it makes more sense to have the federal government offer health insurance to pregnant women, to change regulatory and tax policies so the private sector or the states can do the job, or to try some mix of both approaches. Similar questions arise with regard to health care at the end of life.

In the mid-1990s, for example, as welfare reform was being debated, pro-lifers found themselves divided. Many social conservatives favored a "family cap": Welfare payments to single mothers would not rise as they had more children. The National Right to Life Committee, Feminists for Life, and the Catholic bishops objected that the cap would increase abortions. (Pro-choice groups sided with them, reasoning that a restriction on funding violated welfare recipients' "reproductive rights.") Nobody had much data to go on.

I myself favored the family cap. Its introduction by many states does not seem to have caused the abortion rate to increase. More to the point, the experience of the last thirty years does not suggest that there is a social trade-off between abortion and illegitimacy rates: They rose together, and then they fell together.

Noting the complexity of the issues can sometimes be a cop-out for conservatives. If there is good reason to think that providing federal funds to colleges that can't afford to offer child care will help drive down the abortion rate, that is a good reason to support such funding, and it may be a decisive one. Some colleges, on the other hand, have plenty of wallet but no will. Some regulation may be called for. When conservatives fail to address, or even consider, these questions, they deserve to be called to account.

But pro-life liberals do not always acknowledge that there are reasons besides miserliness and hard-heartedness to prefer private-sector solutions. They treat every budget cut as "anti-life," just as though it were a vote to make killing legal. That can't be right. (If it were that simple, we would be obligated to increase public health and welfare budgets *ad infinitum*.) Pro-life liberals sometimes argue that creating jobs is a pro-life policy. But even if it is true that abortion rates rise with unemployment—something that is by no means clear—that hardly tells us what economic policy would do the most good.

Sadly, some pro-life liberals let their liberalism, and their difficult political circumstances, compromise their pro-life stand. Mark Roche, a dean at the University of Notre Dame, illustrated this phenomenon during the 2004 election. He wrote an op-ed for the *New York Times* that declared, "History will judge our society's support of abortion in much the same way we view earlier generations' support of torture and slavery." Yet the purpose of the essay was to argue for the pro-choice candidate in the presidential race.[8]

It would be one thing to argue against single-issue voting. Roche attempted, however, to argue that voting for the candidate who favored legal and tax-funded abortion, who pledged to appoint only justices who would keep states from offering any protection to the unborn, and encouraged the development of an industry in the production and destruction of embryos in biomedical research—that voting for this man was *the pro-life thing to do.*

The argument unfolded this way: Abortion rates had stayed stable under Republican presidents between 1980 and 1992, and then fallen under a Democratic president between 1992 and 2000. This evidence suggested that Democratic support for a "social safety net" reduced the abortion rate better than "criminal prosecution."

Unfortunately for this argument, Bill Clinton didn't invent the sonogram—and the drop in the abortion rate predated his presidency. Roche is wrong to deny the importance of anti-abortion legislation. Abortion rates have responded to legal changes in the past. And if abortion is the unjust killing of a human being, then the unborn deserve the "safety net" of legal protection as a matter of justice.

A few months later, Glen Harold Stassen, a professor of Christian Ethics, took Roche's argument a step further. In a left-wing Christian publication, he claimed that the abortion rate had risen during George W. Bush's presidency. He found twelve states that had reported increased abortion rates from 2001 to 2002, and four that had reported declines. Based on those numbers, he estimated that Bush's economic policies had driven an additional 52,000 women a year to abortion.[9]

Stassen's statistical analysis was laughable. He had surveyed only sixteen states. He did not name most of these states, and his numbers changed as he told the story. Nor did he explain how he derived the 52,000 figure. He used dubious data.[10]

Still, Hillary Clinton adopted Stassen's analysis as her own. In a major speech on abortion in January 2005, examined in more detail in the next chapter, she repeated the claim that abortion rates had gone up in twelve states under Bush—and implied that they had gone up nationally. In a later CNN interview, she said that "during the Clinton administration, abortions went down" and have "gone back up under the Bush administration."[11]

John Kerry, too, claimed that "in fact" abortion had "gone up in these last few years." The press repeated the line, too. Columnist Nicholas Kristof wrote that abortion rates had "increased significantly."[12]

Howard Dean, as is his wont, went even further. The chairman of the Democratic National Committee claimed that "abortions have gone up 25 percent since George W. Bush [became] president."[13] It's not clear where Dean got that number, which is five times larger than anything Stassen claimed.

Dean spoke, and Clinton gave her CNN interview, a few days after the Alan Guttmacher Institute had released a report thoroughly debunking Stassen's numbers. The institute is the research arm of Planned Parenthood and has the best numbers on the incidence of abortion. Its report pointed out that Colorado, where Stassen had claimed that the abortion rate had "skyrocketed 111 percent," had recently changed its counting method because it had undercounted previously. The state had specifically cautioned analysts that its statistics would show an apparent increase in the abortion rate which could not be taken at face value. AGI's overall conclusion: Contrary to Stassen's claims, abortion rates had continued to fall in 2001 and 2002.[14] The Centers for Disease Control confirmed that conclusion.

Stassen conceded that the AGI study was better than his. He was reduced to arguing that the rate of decline had fallen under Bush, thus demonstrating that the president's economic policies were causing abortions.[15] It's a strange argument, which seems to assume, for no good reason, that the abortion rate has a natural tendency to fall at a constant rate.

The original charge was strange enough coming from the mouths of Hillary Clinton and Howard Dean. They were saying that the pro-life strategy of restricting abortion had failed to reduce the abortion rate. But Clinton, Dean, and their allies have fought every step of the way to prevent any such strategy from being implemented. And they have largely fought successfully. Thanks in large part to their efforts, and with their approval, the courts have vetoed important restrictions on abortion. If the abortion rate *had* gone up "under Bush," it would hardly prove anything against pro-life policies.

Unlike Dean or Clinton, Congressman Tim Ryan usually votes with pro-lifers. The Ohio Democrat is also the leading congressional advocate of the Democrats for Life initiative called "95–10." (The goal is to reduce the abortion rate by 95 percent over the next ten years, although neither DFLA nor Ryan claims that the intiative would actually accomplish this goal.) The initiative is a list of mostly worthy ideas: making the adoption tax credit permanent, requiring pregnancy counselors who receive federal funds to offer adoption referral information, and providing funds for nonprofit groups that need ultrasound equipment.

Conservatives will find little with which to disagree in the initiative. Supporters of legal abortion will not find much with which to disagree, either. The initiative contains no legal acknowledgment of the right to life of the unborn, and no legal restrictions on abortion. That doesn't mean it's not worth passing as a consensus measure. But it is a little remarkable that an explicitly pro-life organization should choose, as its defining initiative, such a weak set of proposals.

The political goal of the initiative is clearly to create common ground. But among whom? It seems well designed for creating common ground between pro-life and pro-choice Democrats. The pro-choice majority of the party won't mind the bill and may even see it as a way to moderate the party's image and to help pro-life Democratic congressmen burnish their image without doing any real damage to the abortion license. But the goal is clearly not to create common ground among pro-lifers and pro-choicers generally. If it were, the bill would include the legal restrictions that have overwhelming support from Americans. There is nothing in it about partial-birth abortion, or parental consent.

If the initiative merely papers over differences within the Democratic coalition, then it will be another chapter in the decline of pro-life Democrats. This time, it will be they themselves who have written the chapter. Day crows about how the party let Representative Jim Langevin, a foe of abortion, tell the Democratic convention in 2004 that life should be protected. But Langevin wasn't on the podium to make the case against abortion. He was there to make the case for embryo-destructive research, and to introduce Ron Reagan's speech doing the same thing. That pro-life Democrats present his inclusion on the convention roster as a triumph suggests that they will take any scraps from the table.[16]

The trajectory of Jim Wallis is another sobering lesson in the limits of pro-life liberalism. Wallis is an evangelical left-winger (although he would reject that description) and the editor of *Sojourners*, where Stassen's article appeared. In 1996, Wallis signed a pro-life manifesto that called for *Roe* to be overturned or a pro-life constitutional amendment to be enacted.[17]

After the 2004 election, Wallis was much sought-after as a sage who could explain how the Democratic party could re-connect to "values voters." He wrote a book, which turned out to be a bestseller, outlining his own "prophetic" approach to politics. Did he use the moment to urge the Democrats to protect the unborn?

No. His discussion of abortion in *God's Politics* was "strikingly evasive," as one reviewer commented. He suggested that the Democrats should be "much more respectful and welcoming" of pro-lifers, and that they "becom[e] anti-abortion without criminalizing an agonizing and desperate choice." This is equivocal. Either Wallis wants Democrats to oppose abortion without seeking jail time for women who get abortions, in which case he ought to simply say that he wants Democrats to adopt the position of the pro-life movement. Or he is saying that Democrats should not legally restrict the procedure, in which case he is merely taking the "personally opposed" line that the Democrats have long followed. His refusal to clarify seems studied. And he's not even running for anything![18]

Pro-life Democrats claim that the party is newly open to their ideas. Let's hope so. But so far, the party has made mostly cosmetic concessions. The real change may be that now pro-life Democrats are complicit in their own marginalization.

CHAPTER 19

Dancing with Death

JOHN KERRY'S FIRST SPEECH on the floor of the Senate, in 1985, was a defense of the right to abortion. He has a perfect record, from NARAL's perspective. He was against bans on partial-birth abortion, against recognizing assaults on pregnant women as crimes with two victims. He has said that if he were president, he would appoint only judges who would re-affirm *Roe*. During he presidential campaign in 2004, he didn't retreat an inch from those commitments.

He did, however, work furiously to downplay them.

His own Catholicism was one of the reasons for his nervousness about the issue. He was the first Catholic presidential nominee since John F. Kennedy, and his disagreement with his church on the issue was the cause of some awkwardness. Some bishops had suggested that Kerry's support for legal abortion was so sinful that it made him ineligible for communion. Others said that it might be sinful for Catholics to vote for him. Catholics had been a Democratic constituency since forever, but Republicans were taking an increasing share of their votes, not least because of abortion. Kerry didn't want to give fence-sitting Catholics an additional reason to defect.

And it wasn't just Catholic voters he had to worry about. For years the press had made it sound as though the voters in the middle of the electorate were social liberals and fiscal conservatives. But in 2004 it was obvious that the real swing voters were the blue-collar social conservatives of Pennsylvania, West Virginia, Ohio, Iowa, Wisconsin, and Minnesota. These voters caused President Bush to softpedal his positions on free trade and the minimum wage—and Kerry to do the same on same-sex marriage and abortion.

The 2002 elections had gone unexpectedly poorly for the Democrats. Abortion wasn't the only reason for their losses. But polling by John Zogby and Fox News indicated that abortion had hurt their defeated Senate candidates in Georgia, Minnesota, Missouri, and North Carolina. (It could have been worse. Just after the September 11 attacks, three of the Democrats' top strategists wrote a memo suggesting that the party should get voters to see the terrorists as enemies of the "freedom of choice," just like Republicans. That outrageous tactic would surely have compounded the party's losses.)[1]

While campaigning in the Midwest, Kerry explained that he was "very serious about [his] faith," believed that life began at conception, and personally opposed abortion. "But I can't take my Catholic view and legislate it on a Protestant or Hindu." His comments distressed some of his pro-abortion supporters, and led others to question his consistency. He tried to clarify his views in an interview with Peter Jennings. It was his "personal belief" that fertilization formed a "human being": "[T]hat's when life begins." But "that's not a person yet."[2] In order to defend his position, Kerry had taken up residence in Peter Singer-land, where the concept of a "human non-person" makes sense.

Neither Kerry nor his running mate John Edwards pledged to defend abortion rights in his convention speech. The presidential nominee, the vice-presidential nominee, or both had made that pledge at the three previous Democratic conventions. Kerry not only refused to utter the word "abortion"; he did not even use the euphemism "the right to choose."

Other convention speakers were slightly less reticent. Kerry's daughter Alexandra said that "we want our children...to control their own bodies." New York congresswoman Louise Slaughter, who has devoted much of her career in the House to abortion rights, had a line about it. But for the most part, the speakers, and especially the prime-time speakers, followed the ticket's lead in not mentioning the subject. Even Nancy Pelosi, the liberal House Democratic leader. The convention also shied away from the topic of judges. Blocking Bush's judges was a top priority of the Democratic delegates, but Al Gore was the only major speaker to discuss the issue. Embryonic stem-cell research was the only social issue about which Democrats were aggressive—and it's an issue that engages fewer voters than abortion does.

During the second presidential debate, Bush effectively called Kerry on his attempts to paint himself as a moderate. Bush pointed out Kerry's support for taxpayer funding for abortion, his effective support for partial-birth abortion, his opposition to Laci and Conner's Law, and his opposition to parental-notification laws. Kerry responded, "I'm not going to require a 16- or 17-year-old kid who's been raped by her father and who's pregnant to have to notify her father." Kerry said he had voted against parental-notification laws because they included no exception for these cases. In fact, Kerry had repeatedly voted against such laws even though they contained that exception (and other exceptions).[3]

By the third debate, Kerry was back to explaining that he could not impose his "articles of faith" on others. In the next breath, he said that his faith guided him to fight poverty and pollution, and that "faith" without "deeds" is "dead." So, in short, he would happily "impose his faith" on taxpayers and businesses. But when it came to protecting the unborn, he would settle for a faith without deeds. He regarded the view that a human fetus is a living human being as true, but an "article of faith," like belief in the Trinity. Requiring people not to kill fetuses would therefore be like compelling religious belief.

Kerry was better off ducking the issue. Democrats disinvited Kate Michelman, the longtime head of NARAL, from a rally. Kerry's advisers, she later complained, thought that "his support of a woman's right to choose was a liability to him."[4]

The tactical pirouettes didn't work. Kerry lost. Republicans gained four more seats in the Senate. Since one of the Democrats replaced was pro-lifer Zell Miller of Georgia, pro-lifers gained three seats. Barbara Boxer acknowledged the setback: "There is no question that pro-choice forces have lost ground in the U.S. Senate. There was a time when the Senate was the protector of a woman's right to choose. I believe those days are gone, and I say that with a heavy, heavy heart."[5]

Bush won the Catholic vote—the first time a Republican presidential candidate had done so since 1988. Indeed, he did better among Catholics than non-Catholics (it had been the other way around in 1988). Post-election analysis by Democratic pollster Stanley Greenberg fingered abortion as one reason white Catholics had left the Democrats.[6] Another postmortem, by William Galston and Elaine Kamarck, concluded that Democrats should "continue to support the core of Roe v. Wade while dropping their intransigence on questions such as parental notification and partial-birth abortion."[7]

Emily's List, a pro-abortion activist group, put out its own analysis, arguing that the "pro-choice majority" still existed. But many Democrats acknowledged that their abortion stance was a problem. One of them was John Kerry. A few weeks after the election, he addressed a gathering of liberals. The president of Emily's List asked him about the party's future. Kerry, *Newsweek* reported, "told the group they needed new ways to make people understand they didn't *like* abortion. Democrats also needed to welcome more pro-life candidates into the party, he said. 'There was a gasp in the room,' says Nancy Keenan, the new president of NARAL Pro-Choice America."[8]

Chris Matthews, a former House Democratic aide turned pundit, complained about "fanatically pro-choice women's groups, who insist that the Democrats say 'pro-choice' every five words."[9]

Senator Dianne Feinstein lamented that Republicans had "been successful at painting the view of the pro-choice movement as abortion on demand—and nothing can be farther from the truth." Donna Brazile, who had managed the Gore campaign in 2000, added, "All these issues that put us into the extreme and not the mainstream really hurt us with the heartland of the country. Even I have trouble explaining to my family that we are not about killing babies."[10]

Michael Lind, another pundit, wrote an insightful column for a liberal website.

> As a social liberal party with economic liberal and economic conservative wings, the Democrats are doomed to perpetual minority status. As an economic liberal party with social conservative and social liberal wings, the Democrats might have a chance... Between 1968 and 2004 the Democrats went from dominating U.S. government at all levels to being the minority party at all levels. Their 36 year downfall was a direct result of the fact that they define themselves by social liberalism... Social liberals can be the minority in a majority party. Or social liberals can be the majority in a minority party. But social liberals can't be the majority in a majority party—not in the United States, not in the foreseeable

future. There just aren't enough social liberals in the American electorate.[11]

By embracing the party of death, the Democrats were committing assisted suicide. After years in which Republicans had been warned that they needed to have a "big tent" on abortion, suddenly it was the Democrats' turn to hear that advice.

Simon Rosenberg, head of the New Democratic Network, said, "All Democrats are united around the idea that we should make abortion safe, legal, and rare," but added, "we also have to be open to people who are pro-life."[12] The comment reflected both the Democrats' intention to reposition themselves and the habits of mind that would make that repositioning difficult: How open could the party be if all of its members had to support legal abortion?

Still, Senate Democrats did elect Harry Reid, a moderate pro-lifer, as their leader. Reid, a senator from Nevada, has voted for many pro-life bills and has twice in recent years voted against resolutions expressing the Senate's support for *Roe*. On the other hand, he rarely speaks in favor of legal protection for the unborn, and has often tried to water down pro-life bills before voting for them. He voted for the Daschle bill on partial-birth abortion, with its broad health exception, and for an alternative to Laci and Conner's law that refused to recognize that assaults on pregnant women have two victims.[13]

Senator Charles Schumer of New York also recruited a pro-life candidate, Bob Casey Jr., to run against Senator Rick Santorum in Pennsylvania. Pro-abortion groups howled, but tolerated it since a Casey win would be an improvement for them. Santorum has not only voted for pro-life bills but led the fight for them. Casey, the son of the pro-life governor the Democrats refused to let speak in 1992, may not play the same role. Howard Dean, the head of the Democratic National Committee, thinks he won't: "It's unlikely, for example, that Bob Casey in the Senate would support these extreme nominees [President Bush] has for the courts. It's a qualitative improvement for the community that believes in a woman's right to choose."[14]

Reid has not made it a priority to seek a Court that might overturn *Roe*, either. When the first Supreme Court vacancy of the new century came up, Reid sent the president a list of nominees he would consider unacceptable. John Roberts was not on it. But after meeting with representatives of forty liberal groups, including the National Organization of Women, Reid announced that he would vote against Roberts. Kim Gandy, the head of NOW, told the press, "He got the message loud and clear, didn't he?"[15]

The leash could be yanked only so far. In order to advertise the party's new openness, Reid and Nancy Pelosi, the House Democratic leader, tried to help former congressman Tim Roemer, a prolifer, become head of the DNC. But the party's activists rejected him in favor of Dean, who had vocally opposed even parental-notification laws. (Dean argued against them by saying that as a doctor he had seen a pregnant twelve-year-old patient whose father had impregnated her. Later, it came out that the father was not the guilty party and that Dean had known it when he told the story.[16]) In both parties, the biggest donors tend to be more pro-choice than the rank-and-file membership—and in the Democratic party, the biggest donors are extremely pro-choice.

Greater openness to pro-lifers, however slight, however qualified, is an improvement. The rest of what the Democrats are offering, unfortunately, is just spin. They have been working hard at coming up with new buzzwords and legislative initiatives to fix their abortion problem. They seem to be willing to do anything—anything, that is, except adjust their position.

Dean is the most transparent of the party's new marketers. "We're not the party of abortion," he told Tim Russert a month after the

2004 elections. A few months later, he was back on Russert's show. "I'm not advocating we change our position," he explained.

> We have been forced into the idea of "We're going to defend abortion." I don't know anybody who thinks abortion is a good thing. I don't know anybody in either party who is pro-abortion. The issue is not whether we think abortion is a good thing. The issue is whether a woman has a right to make up her own mind about her health care, or a family has a right to make up their own mind about how their loved ones leave this world. I think the Republicans are intrusive and they invade people's personal privacy, and they don't have a right to do that.

Here Dean was simply taking the "personally opposed" line on abortion, which has been the dominant note in Democratic rhetoric on the topic for a generation. He seemed to think he had invented the wheel.[17]

Dean went on to claim, falsely, that late-term abortions are generally done for health reasons. Interestingly, however, he was willing to go very far in his attempted rhetorical makeover. He was prepared not only to banish the word "abortion," but even "choice." In a later appearance on *Hardball*, host Chris Matthews asked Dean six times whether he or his party were "pro-choice" or supported "abortion rights." Dean refused to associate himself or his party with either phrase, instead saying variants of "the government should stay out of the personal lives of families and women."[18]

Hillary Clinton has not been quite as ham-handed. To the contrary, she has gotten rave reviews for her alleged attempt to find "common ground" with pro-lifers on abortion.[19] In a January 2005 speech, just after *Roe*'s anniversary, she claimed to "respect" pro-lifers. She said that both pro-lifers and pro-choicers favor reducing the number of abortions. ("[A]bortion in many ways represents a sad, even tragic choice to many, many women.") She said that they should therefore join forces to reduce the number of unwanted pregnancies by promoting contraception.[20]

Amid the paeans to Clinton's alleged centrism, political brilliance, and willingness to seek compromise, it seems to have escaped almost everyone's attention that her speech began by implicitly comparing pro-lifers to the brutal communist dictators of Romania and China. Nicolae Ceausescu wanted to raise Romania's birth rate. So, Clinton explained,

> Once a month, Romanian women were rounded up at their workplaces. They were taken to a government-controlled health clinic, told to disrobe while they were standing in line. They were then examined by a government doctor with a government secret police officer watching. And if they were pregnant, they were closely monitored to make sure you didn't do anything to that pregnancy. If a woman failed to conceive, her family was fined a celibacy tax of up to 10 percent of their monthly salary.

China's communists, meanwhile, used forced sterilization and forced abortion to further its population-control policy. The moral of these examples? "Now with all of this talk about freedom as the defining goal of America, let's not forget the importance of the freedom of women to make the choices that are consistent with their faith and their sense of responsibility to their family and themselves."

The idea that the alternative to abortion-on-demand is Ceausescu's Romania is the kind of thing one would expect in a paranoid feminist novel, and hardly qualifies as nuance.[21]

The notion that Clinton is a moderate on abortion will come as a surprise to the man she defeated to win her Senate seat. Former Republican congressman Rick Lazio is pro-choice. But he opposed partial-birth abortion and federal funding of abortion, favored parental notification, and refused to rule out voting for anti-*Roe* judges. Clinton hit him from the left on each of those issues.

For many politicians and journalists, of course, the key question about Clinton's approach to abortion is not whether it represents a good-faith effort to find common ground but whether it will work politically. Was Clinton's speech really "a political masterstroke"?[22] Will the strategy it reflects drive a wedge between pro-lifers who oppose contraception and those who don't? Will it transform the politics of abortion in favor of pro-choice Democrats such as herself?

If it could, shouldn't it have done so already? It is certainly politically shrewder for Clinton to call abortion a tragedy than it would be for her to celebrate it as liberation. But pro-choice politicians have been saying that type of thing for years. Bill Clinton said that abortion should be "safe, legal, and rare" back in 1992, and stuck to it over the next decade—which did not stop pro-choicers from losing ground over the period. Al Gore tried to use contraception as a wedge issue. In 1997, he told a NARAL conference that he had reached out to pro-life leaders four years earlier and asked them to work with him to reduce abortion through increased contraception. Supposedly they refused. Yet no pro-life leader remembers Gore ever making such an offer.[23]

Hillary Clinton's speech didn't represent new ground even for her. In a 1999 speech to a pro-abortion group, she had already said that abortion was a tragedy, pro-lifers were to be respected, and contraception was the answer. (She cited Romania and China back then, too. But she also cited Nazi Germany. Maybe she *has* mellowed.)[24] Clinton's fans bring up the continuity of her views themselves, to defend her against the charge that she is a political chameleon. But that defense nullifies the claim that she is bringing anything new to the table. Why should pro-lifers treat it as a concession when pro-choicers reiterate their long-held positions?

Clinton's position is that abortion is such a terrible, terrible tragedy that it has to be defended against any legal restrictions and, indeed, subsidized. Her strategy will backfire to the extent that it raises the question: What's so tragic about abortion anyway? It can't be just that many women feel bad after having abortions, which is the closest she has come to an explanation. If that were the only problem, the solution would be to counsel the women and to do what could be done to change the culture so that people regarded abortion the way they do appendectomies.

Abortion is regrettable, and needs to be minimized, for the same reason that abortion is wrong and unjust: because it kills an innocent human being. That is also the reason it should be prohibited. Clinton casts pro-lifers as rigid ideologues who pursue legal restrictions but don't take practical steps to reduce the incidence of abortion (as if legal restrictions weren't practical steps). But it's not as though Clinton is simply trying to figure out the most effective way to reduce the abortion rate. Her record is full of opposition to even incremental restrictions—such as ending taxpayer funding of abortion—that have already reduced the abortion rate.

In the days after Terri Schiavo died, as pro-choice Democrats savored the pro-lifers' defeat, one Democratic operative warned, "We can't just be the party of death."[25] That's right. But it is not a fate from which Hillary Clinton or Howard Dean seems prepared to deliver them.

CHAPTER 20

Life after *Roe*

THE CONVENTIONAL WISDOM IS that overturning *Roe v. Wade* would be a political disaster for pro-life Republicans.

Democratic pollster Peter Hart says, "I can think of nothing that would galvanize and anger a wide segment of the American public more than overturning *Roe v. Wade*. I can't think of another issue that would generate as much intensity not only from the active left and feminists, but also from a lot of people in the middle."[1]

Cass Sunstein, the liberal law professor, agrees: "[I]f *Roe* were overruled, Democrats would also certainly be helped and Republicans would almost certainly be hurt. Everyone knows that if abortion really becomes an active issue again—if abortion might actually be a crime—then countless Americans will vote for pro-choice candidates. A judicial decision to overrule *Roe* would immediately create a major crisis for the Republican Party. Some red states would undoubtedly turn blue or at least purple."[2]

Gloria Feldt, the former head of Planned Parenthood, says, "If *Roe* is overturned, I think women will take to the streets." They "will be so angry" that they might succeed in passing a constitutional amendment "securing abortion as a permanent right."[3]

The respected legal journalist Stuart Taylor, who is not a reflexive liberal, writes, "[I]t seems pretty clear that headlines such as

'Bush Court Overrules *Roe v. Wade*' would be a disaster for the Republican Party... [I]ts candidates would then have to choose between alienating most voters by mounting a futile push to outlaw abortion... and alienating the most loyal Republican voting bloc by not doing so."[4]

Many Republican politicians fear that these predictions are right. Congressman Tom Davis says, "If *Roe v. Wade* is overturned, you're going to have a lot of very nervous suburban [Republican] candidates out there." When *National Journal* surveyed "political insiders," it found that most Republicans thought a reversal of *Roe* would hurt them and most Democrats thought it would help them.[5]

Nobody will know for sure, of course, unless *Roe* actually falls, but this conventional wisdom is highly suspect.

There is, however, a kernel of truth in it. The public would likely find the overturning of *Roe* unsettling. The mere discussion of the possibility was enough to move the polls in a pro-choice direction in the summer of 2005.

Pro-lifers had made gains over the previous decade. When Gallup asked people if they were "pro-life" or "pro-choice," pro-choicers usually won. But the margin had shrunk from 23 points in September 1995 to 4 points in May 2005.

Then Justice Sandra Day O'Connor announced that she was retiring, and Chief Justice William Rehnquist died. President Bush had to nominate replacements for each vacancy and the Senate had to consider whether to confirm the nominees. The process ensured several months of speculation about the possibility that Bush's appointments would bring about the end of *Roe*.

Much of that speculation was ill-informed. Many people seemed to think that these nominees might overturn *Roe* by themselves. In fact, even if they wanted to overturn *Roe*, they would not have the votes unless a third new anti-*Roe* justice joined them. In addition, the mythology of *Roe* was alive and well. Reporters and pollsters continued to suggest that *Roe* protected only first-trimester abortions, and that overturning it would prohibit them. Republicans, cowed by the popularity of the mythical *Roe*, failed to challenge these notions.

Soon after O'Connor's announcement, Gallup found that 54 percent of the public considered itself "pro-choice" and 38 percent "pro-life." Pro-choicers had, at least temporarily, won back much of the ground they lost over the preceding decade. Apparently some people thought of themselves as pro-life when the top abortion issue was partial-birth abortion, but thought of themselves as pro-choice when a prohibition on all first-trimester abortions seemed to be on the table. As sharp a swing as this was, its practical effect was limited: It did not stop most people from favoring the confirmation of Bush's nominees.

As it becomes clear that Chief Justice John Roberts and Justice Samuel Alito do not put *Roe* in immediate jeopardy, the pro-choice advantage is dissipating. The only abortion issues on the Court's current agenda are partial-birth abortion and parental notification, and both issues play to pro-life strengths. If there is another vacancy at the Court, the pro-choice advantage in the polls would return—but, again, would not by itself prevent confirmation of a conservative nominee.

But what would happen if some future Court, with an additional conservative justice, took a case in which *Roe* itself were at issue?

Many people would be afraid that in overturning *Roe*, the Supreme Court would be prohibiting all abortions. The press would do its usual bang-up job of deepening that confusion. The public's aversion to sudden change would increase the anxiety. And some pro-life politicians would therefore be inclined to panic.

These are Republicans who are nominally pro-life because they want to get ahead in the party, but have no deep convictions about the sanctity of life. The Court has insulated them from ever having to take any real responsibility for abortion policy. And many have absorbed the conventional wisdom about the "pro-choice majority" and fear overturning *Roe*. In 1989, the Supreme Court signaled that it was retreating from *Roe*. The leading pro-life official of the day—the first President Bush—offered no guidance to lower-ranking pro-life politicians. Many of the weak pro-lifers flipped their positions. The same thing could happen if the Court abandoned *Roe*.

But if *Roe* were overturned, it would quickly become clear that the Supreme Court had not outlawed abortion. Nor would state legislatures across the country have immediately taken the opportunity to outlaw it. Still less would the country have split in two over the issue. The sky would not have fallen.

Supporters of *Roe* would start campaigning for Supreme Court nominees who would reinstate the decision. But much of the debate over abortion would move away from the Court, and from Washington. There would be too many legislative battles going on in state capitols for either pro-lifers or pro-choicers to concentrate as heavily on D.C. as they do now.

Each side would probably retain enough strength in Congress to block the other from imposing its policy nationally (especially if Republicans didn't panic). Some congressmen would attempt to impose a national compromise, such as requiring all states to allow first-trimester abortions but prohibit later abortions. But some pro-choicers and some pro-lifers would oppose that bill to preserve their ability to win bigger in some states. Some congressmen would think a federal policy unwise, or want to kick the issue back to the states so as to continue avoiding any responsibility for it. The safe bet is for stalemate.

The conventional wisdom assumes that once the debate moves away from the federal level, pro-lifers would exhibit less political sophistication than pro-choicers, and go further than the public will tolerate. That is certainly a possibility—in Louisiana in the early

1990s, the state government was on the verge of enacting a ban on abortion when pro-life purists, who opposed any ban that made an exception for rape and incest, blew up the bill. (The Supreme Court would have struck it down anyway, of course, had it passed.)

But pro-lifers have grown more tactically flexible and incrementalist since 1990. And pro-choicers are capable of making political mistakes of their own. Insisting on public funding for abortion cost pro-choicers their chance to enact a federal Freedom of Choice Act in the first two years of the Clinton administration. If *Roe* falls, maybe it's *pro-choice* politicians who will be caught between a public that wants second- and third-trimester abortions banned and a liberal activist base that doesn't.

But suppose pro-lifers do overreach and pro-life politicians get defeated in droves at the next election. The pro-life movement would not simply cease to exist at this point. In a very short time, it would be back, fighting for whatever it could get. Compared to the legal regime of *Roe*, remember, any protection for unborn human life would be progress. It is inconceivable that Americans will support unrestricted abortion-on-demand for all nine months of pregnancy from sea to shining sea. There is a reason that pro-choicers have invested so heavily in keeping this issue in the courtroom. Outside it, they can only lose ground.

What if *Roe* were reversed not in one dramatic decision but rather in a series of cases? The Supreme Court might start by narrowing its definition of "health" and giving legislatures authority to restrict most abortions in the second half of pregnancy. Such decisions would, perhaps, lead to exaggerated worries about what the Court would do next. But it would make legislative overreach impossible. If legislatures regain their authority bit by bit, a spectacular collapse of pro-life political fortunes is highly unlikely.

In any of these scenarios, the situation will be complicated in some states by state courts that, mimicking the activism of the

Supreme Court, have divined a right to abortion in state constitutions. If *Roe* were to fall, other states' courts would no doubt create their own versions. Pro-lifers in those states will have to work either to amend those constitutions, to limit the power of the state courts to rewrite the law, or to change the composition of the state judiciary.[6]

The end of *Roe* would not hand pro-lifers victory in all the political debates over abortion policy. It would give them the right to have those debates in the first place.

The result might be a surprising return to political moderation. It would be surprising for two reasons. First, many of the people who decry the absence of moderation in our politics—editorialists, affluent voters, "centrist" thumbsuckers—treat support for legal abortion as part of the definition of moderation. So for increased moderation to accompany the achievement of many pro-life goals would contradict much of the official discourse about political temperance. Second, abortion is obviously an emotionally polarizing issue. I suspect that one reason many people are happy to let judges set abortion policy is fear that the issue is too hot for the political process to handle.

Debates would be passionate, certainly, but would they really be explosive? Neither side would have any reason to feel that the deck had been stacked against them: that they and their goals were unfairly being shut out of the political process. No state or region would have reason to feel that outside forces had imposed on it an abortion policy alien to its mores. Neither side would have the incentive that exists today to impose rigorous tests of commitment on presidential candidates. If it became clear that the federal courts were going to stay out of abortion policy, pro-lifers would cease to care as much if the Republican nominee disagreed with them. Eventually—though perhaps after losing some elections—Democrats would be freed to embrace some restrictions on abortion.

In state legislatures, Republicans in relatively pro-choice states and Democrats in relatively pro-life ones would be more likely to vote with their constituents than with their parties. Compromise and tolerance of dissent are easier in an atmosphere of legislative give-and-take than in courtroom battles over constitutional principle.

Abortion is a clear partisan dividing line today. That line could be blurred in a post-*Roe* world. Abortion, more than any other issue, has driven religious traditionalists into the Republican camp and religious (and irreligious) progressives into the Democratic one. If *Roe* goes, it might become more acceptable for a Southern Baptist to vote for a Democrat, or for a Reform Jew to vote for a Republican. Americans would remain divided over social issues such as same-sex marriage, the role of religion in public life, and abortion. But party divisions might not fall so cleanly along those lines.

If the end of *Roe* goes a long way to defusing America's "culture wars," Republicans might suffer some losses after all. Opposition to abortion has netted them votes over the years, as has the related religious realignment. Less partisanship on abortion might reduce this advantage. In this one respect, the conventional wisdom could prove correct: not because opposition to abortion proved wildly unpopular, but because it became less controversial; not because the issue hurt Republicans, but because it stopped helping them as much.

A less partisan divide over abortion might yield one further benefit for the pro-life side. Blacks, and to a lesser extent Hispanics, have been the great exception to the realignment of American politics wrought by abortion. Blacks have tended to oppose abortion more than whites. But white and black pro-lifers have been largely unable to make a political alliance because white pro-lifers have largely joined a Republican party that the vast majority of blacks reject. The efforts of social conservative groups to bridge the divide have largely failed; other conservative groups haven't even made much of an effort, preferring instead to cultivate the same old list of reliable donors in the white suburbs and exurbs.[7] The end of *Roe* might make an effective alliance possible—in which case pro-lifers would be hard to beat.

At every stage of the post-*Roe* debate, pro-lifers' legislative goals should be first to provide the maximum feasible legal protection that can be sustained over time, and second to expand the limits of what is feasible.

A few states would be willing, as soon as the Supreme Court made it possible, to ban almost all abortions, making exceptions when the pregnancy results from rape, endangers the mother's life, or is likely to yield a severely disabled baby. Even states that agreed with one another on the broad outlines of policy might differ in the details. One state might conclude that it can protect unborn human beings by removing the medical licenses of anyone who commits an illegal abortion, and imposing steep fines on anyone who commits one without a medical license. If that legal regime sufficed to provide effective protection—if it deterred abortion and communicated the state's and the public's hostility to abortion—there would, in my view, be no need to go further.[8] No state, it seems pretty clear, will "throw pregnant women in jail."

Another state might be willing to protect unborn human beings after the fifteenth week of pregnancy. If so, pro-lifers should get it enacted. The year after, they should introduce a bill protecting fetuses in the fourteenth week. And so forth.

The incrementalist strategy will, at least in the beginning, do more to protect the children of the poor than the children of the rich. If Alabama restricts abortion and New York doesn't, some women in Alabama will be able to fly to New York to get abortions and some won't. Pro-choicers often lodge the obverse of this objection ("anti-abortion laws discriminate against the poor who, unlike the rich, cannot afford to travel to states with permissive laws to obtain abortions") to a federalist replacement of *Roe*. But how much force does this objection really have? Do any of those who make it take it so seriously that they would urge New York to ban abortions for out-of-state residents, or to tighten up its own laws, in a post-*Roe* world? To ask is to answer.

The more resources a person has, the easier it is for him to get away with crimes. That is a sad reality to fight against, but it is not a reason to refrain from treating crimes as crimes.

Would the back alley return? There would certainly be some black-market abortions. But the number of women who were dying as a result of abortions dropped dramatically before *Roe*, and even before states liberalized their laws. The repeal of *Roe* would not mean the repeal of antibiotics.

Abortion-on-demand has created a sizable constituency for itself. People support legal abortion for all sorts of reasons. For some people, it is almost part of middle-class respectability. Orderliness is the quintessential bourgeois virtue, after all, and everyone knows that children tend to upset order. Abortion allows young women to continue with their plans, which usually include having children later—when the women have planned for it. Thus abortion turns social morality inside out, protecting "family values" by killing members of the family. As Frederica Mathewes-Green has observed, "In the land where women kill their unborn children, every lesser love grows frail."[9]

By some estimates, one in three American women will have had an abortion by the age of forty-five.[10] An awful lot of women, and men, have been complicit in the evil of abortion. Others have quietly approved of abortions involving their friends and loved ones. While some of these people later change their minds, many do not. The more marginal a practice abortion becomes, the fewer supporters it will have. That is one of the reasons to have hope for an incrementalist strategy.

Perhaps in this new climate, it will even be possible to restore a sense of the sanctity of life to America. Over the last decade, pro-lifers have gained ground on abortion, while losing it on embryo research. People have turned against abortion based on the gut-level appeal of babies and revulsion toward ripping them apart. That's why ultrasounds and the campaign against partial-birth abortion have moved the debate. So far, pro-lifers have not been able to reach people in that way in the debate over stem-cell research. The case for not killing embryonic human beings has had to stand on its own—and against our own interest in cures that might be had by killing them, and our sadness at the suffering of people we know. (The balance could change if the debate moves to harvesting stem cells from cloned fetuses.)

Yet it is possible to progress, or regress, on all fronts. If abortion had not become the law of the land, we might not now be debating euthanasia or the killing of human embryos for research purposes. The same process might work in reverse. The more we reject abortion, the more we might come to reject other choices for death, too. That is surely what pro-lifers should work for.

Most Americans already know that abortion is wrong. If *Roe* falls—when it falls—pro-lifers will be able to demonstrate another truth about abortion: We can live without it.

Acknowledgments

THIS BOOK WOULD NOT have been possible if I had not had the kind assistance of many people.

Robert P. George has done more to shape my thinking on the subject of this book than any other person. Jonah Goldberg, Ross Douthat, and he each suggested many improvements to the manuscript, for which I am grateful. The chapters on partial-birth abortion benefited from Shannen Coffin's careful eye.

John Virtes, Liz Fisher, Doug Johnson, Dorothy McCartney, Yuval Levin, Tim Graham, and Anthony Paletta each helped with research. For the trickiest questions, I sought assistance from Bradford Short, who could not have been more enthusiastic about the work.

Matt Continetti and Reihan Salam offered early encouragement.

Harry Crocker and Ben Domenech at Regnery Publishing were ideal editors. Together with Marji Ross, they made the process of writing a first book easier than I had any right to expect.

My colleagues at *National Review* have also been unfailingly supportive, allowing me to take time off to work on *Party of Death*. I owe special thanks to William F. Buckley Jr., Ed Capano, Rich Lowry, Jay Nordlinger, Kate O'Beirne, and Kathryn Lopez.

My wife, April Ponnuru, has been my editor, muse, therapist, and cheering section. Her patience and love have sustained me in this project. I'm afraid that Mary Lakshmi Ponnuru has often seemed indifferent or even hostile to the progress of this book, but I have enjoyed her sweet small presence throughout the writing nonetheless.

Finally, I would like to thank the millions of pro-lifers who have kept this great cause alive, from political leaders such as Henry Hyde to writers such as Francis Schaeffer to the unsung volunteers helping women at crisis pregnancy centers. The National Right to Life Committee, the pro-life office of the Catholic bishops' conference, Focus on the Family, the American Life League, the Family Research Council, and a hundred allied organizations may not agree with every word in this book, nor I with all of their views, but I honor their commitment and labor in what is, as I have hoped to show, a great work of social justice.

Notes

Introduction

1. Lou Cannon, *Gov. Reagan: His Rise to Power* (Public Affairs, 2003), p. 213; interview with Judge William Clark, Feb. 27, 2006.

2. Gloria Steinem, *Outrageous Acts and Everyday Rebellions* (Henry Holt, 1995), p. 165.

3. Warren Weaver Jr., "National Guidelines Set by 7-to-2 Vote," *New York Times*, Jan. 23, 1973.

Chapter 1

1. *Doe* at 192.

2. In what might be regarded as an attempt to limit the damage of *Roe* and *Doe*, Supreme Court justice Clarence Thomas has argued that *Doe*'s language about the many dimensions of "health" was an interpretation of the Georgia law at issue, not a constitutional ruling. (See *Voinovich v. Women's Professional Medical Corp.*, 520 U.S. 1036, 1039 [1998], dissent from denial of cert.) But for several reasons, Thomas's claim does not affect my argument about the real scope of the Court's abortion jurisprudence. 1) His interpretation of *Doe* does not appear to command a majority of the Court. 2) Blackmun may well have been suggesting that Georgia's law should be read to contain a broad health exception because a narrower one would be unconstitutional. So the effect on abortion law would be the same as I indicated in the text. 3) As I note in the text, the performance of late-term abortions have almost never drawn successful prosecutions since *Roe* and *Doe* came down. Their practical effect has been to make it impossible for legislators to prohibit abortion at any stage of pregnancy. Descriptions of *Roe*—and especially descriptions of *Roe* that purport to summarize the Court's abortion jurisprudence generally—are misleading to the extent that they gloss over this effect.

3. Gallup/CNN/USA *Today* poll, www.aei.org/publicopinion15, p. 15.

4. I am aware of only one case of a successful prosecution—the case of Abu Hayat, "the butcher of Avenue A" in New York. In 1992 he was prosecuted for performing an abortion at 32 weeks along with several other crimes. Perhaps because he was an unsympathetic defendant—he had botched several abortions, run an unclean clinic, and was accused of sexually abusing patients—abortion-rights groups did not protest the prosecution. Had Hayat performed the abortion in a hospital and claimed that he thought the abortion was necessary to protect the woman's health, he would probably have been able to dodge conviction on this charge.

5. "*Roe* v. *Wade* and the Right to Privacy," third edition, Center for Reproductive Rights, 2003, pp. 54-8.

6. Russell Hittinger, "Abortion Before Roe," *First Things*, Oct. 1994, pp. 14-15. Hittinger's account is drawn from David Garrow, *Liberty and Sexuality* (University of California Press, 1998), esp. pp. 316-19, 325, 329, 347-48, 370-71, 412, 483, 496, 544-47, 566-67, 577. I have used ellipses and brackets to correct minor mistakes by Hittinger.

7. A Harris poll asking whether abortion should be legal in the first four months of pregnancy came back 46 percent no, 42 percent yes in August 1972. Eric Uslaner and Ronald Weber, "Public Support for Pro-Choice Abortion Policies in the Nation and States," 77 *Michigan Law Review* (Aug. 1979), pp. 1773-5. Women were markedly less supportive of legal abortion than men.

8. John Hart Ely, "The Wages of Crying Wolf: A Comment on *Roe* v. *Wade*," 82 *Yale Law Journal* 920, 935-937 (1973).

9. Edward Lazarus, "The Lingering Problems with *Roe* v. *Wade*. . ." *FindLaw*, Oct. 3, 2002.

10. See Reva B. Siegel, "Reasoning from the Body: A Historical Perspective on Abortion Regulation and Questions of Equal Protection," 44 *Stanford Law Review* 261 (1992); Andrew Koppelman, "Forced Labor: A Thirteenth Amendment Defense of Abortion," 84 *Northwestern University Law Review* 480 (1990).

11. James S. Witherspoon, "Reexamining *Roe*: Nineteenth-Century Abortion Statutes and the Fourteenth Amendment," *St. Mary's Law Journal*, Vol. 17 No. 1 (1985), p. 59 n90.

12. See Chapter 9 for more on how Blackmun misread the historical evidence.

13.   Warren Weaver Jr., "National Guidelines Set by 7-to-2 Vote," *New York Times*, Jan. 23, 1973; "Respect for Privacy," editorial, *New York Times*, Jan. 24, 1973.

14.   www.nrlc.org/abortion/Roe_scope_New_York_Times.pdf

15.   David Brown, "Viability and the Law," *Washington Post*, Sept. 17, 1996.

16.   Mike Allen, "Abortion, Cloning Are on Bush Agenda," *Washington Post*, Jan. 23, 2003, p. A4.

17.   Manny Fernandez, "Abortion Protest Draws Thousands," *Washington Post*, Jan. 23, 2004, p. B1; Jo Becker and Chris Jenkins, "Va. House Acts to Restrict Clinics Offering Abortions," *Washington Post*, Jan. 23, 2004, p. B4.

18.   "Romney's Choice," editorial, *Boston Globe*, July 27, 2005, p. A14.

19.   Scott Stossel, "Separation Anxiety," *Boston Globe*, May 23, 2004, p. L1.

20.   "Bush working to keep truth hidden," editorial, *Atlanta Journal-Constitution*, Nov. 3, 2000, p. 18A.

21.   http://www.tnr.com/easterbrook.mhtml?pid=865

22.   Peter Berkowitz, "The Court, the Constitution, and the Culture of Freedom," *Policy Review*, August-September 2005.

23.   Leslie Goldman, "Key Supreme Court Rulings on Abortion," *Chicago Tribune*, Jan. 22, 2003, p. C1.

24.   Bill Clinton, *My Life* (Knopf, 2004), p. 229.

25.   See, e.g., Charles Babington and Amy Goldstein, "Nominee Dismisses Speculation on Roe," *Washington Post*, Oct. 18, 2005, p. A17 (subheadline refers to possibility that Harriet Miers, if confirmed to the Supreme Court, "Would Vote to Outlaw Abortions"); and *Hardball*, Oct. 17, 2005 (host Chris Matthews suggests that Miers might "actually operate on the court as someone who tries to outlaw [abortion] by getting rid of *Roe* v. *Wade*").

26.   "Judging Samuel Alito," editorial, *New York Times*, Jan. 8, 2006.

Chapter 2

1.   Jesse Jackson, "How we respect life is the over-riding moral issue," *Right to Life News*, Jan. 1977.

2.   Colman McCarthy, "Jackson's Reversal on Abortion," *Washington Post*, May 21, 1988.

3.   Letter from Sen. Joseph Biden to Juanita Sonnier, Aug. 2, 1982; Rep. Simon's bill, H.J. Res 356, can be seen at thomas.loc.gov; Simon's 1987 questionnaire is on file with Douglas Johnson, legislative director for the National Right to Life Committee.

4. Mary Meehan, "Democrats for Life," *Human Life Review*, Summer 2003, quotes Gephardt's 1977 statement. Gephardt 2003 speech: www.dickgephardt2004.com/plugin/template/gephardt/8/215.

5. Michael Kramer, "The new (low) levels of the game," *U.S. News & World Report*, March 7, 1988, p. 29.

6. Gov. Bill Clinton letter to Earlene Windsor, Sept. 26, 1986. If Clinton meant to suggest that his opposition to abortion were merely "personal," and not meant to have any effect on policy, he did not say so in the letter.

7. Bob Kerrey letter to Bernice Labedz, June 9, 1982.

8. Sen. Kennedy letter to Thomas Dennelly, Aug. 3, 1971.

9. "Durbin for Congress" letter, March 14, 1982; Rep. Richard Durbin letter to Frank Tureskis, Aug. 14, 1989; House Roll Call Vote 756, Nov. 1, 1995.

10. Muskie: Joseph Kraft, "The Muskie Problem," *The Atlantic Monthly*, June 1971, p. 12. Humphrey: Steven Hayward, *The Age of Reagan, 1974-1980* (Prima Lifestyles, 2001), p. 341.

11. Louis Bolce and Gerald De Maio, "Our Secularist Democratic Party," *The Public Interest*, Fall 2002.

12. Hayward, pp. 341-2.

13. Maris Vinovskis, "Abortion and the Presidential Election of 1976," *Michigan Law Review*, Vol. 77, No. 7, p. 1762.

14. Greg Adams, "Abortion: Evidence of an Issue Evolution," *American Journal of Political Science*, Vol. 41, No. 3 (July 1997), pp. 730-31.

15. Alan Abramowitz, "It's Abortion, Stupid," *Journal of Politics*, Vol. 57, No. 1 (Feb. 1995), pp. 177-8, 182-3, 185 (salience of abortion for voters, ignorance of pro-life Democrats); Bolce and DeMaio (delegates' attitudes).

16. William Galston and Elaine Kamarck, "The Politics of Polarization," report for ThirdWay, October 2005, pp. 42-51. The trend described in this paragraph and the next one is most pronounced among white voters, who are still the great bulk of the electorate.

17. David Nyhan, "Cuomo's Call to Community," *Boston Globe*, Feb. 24, 1999, p. A21.

18. See Cuomo's remarks in E. J. Dionne, Jr., *et al*, ed., *One Electorate Under God?* (Brookings Institution Press: Washington, D.C., 2004), pp. 13-18, 24-35, and his exchange with Kenneth Woodward in *Commonweal*, Sept. 24, 2004.

19. See Chapters 7 and 8.

20. See Chapter 17 for evidence that restrictions reduce the abortion rate.

21. Robert P. George, "Cuomological Fallacies," in Dionne *et al*, pp. 104-5 (emphasis in original).

22. Robert Casey, *Fighting for Life* (Word Publishing: Dallas, 1996), Ch. 16, p. 186.

23. Michael Crowley, "Casey Closed," *The New Republic*, Sept. 16, 1996, p. 12.

24. *Crossfire*, June 28, 2004, quoted by mediamatters.org/items/200406290002. Media Matters has aggressively pushed the Democratic spin, not pausing to note the contradiction between two confident accounts it reported within four days of each other (see mediamatters.org/items/200406250007).

25. Casey, Ch. 16, p. 191. Crowley argues unpersuasively that Brown was a special case as "one of the party's highest-profile women."

26. Cuomo, speech to the Democratic convention, July 15, 1992.

Chapter 3

1. Gil Bliss, "Clark camp backs off abortion statement," (Manchester) *Union Leader*, Jan. 11, 2004, p. A1.

2. Paul Schwartzman, "Clark Moves to Clarify His Abortion Views," *Washington Post*, Jan. 23, 2004, p. A10.

3. "Strong at Home, Respected in the World: The 2004 Democratic National Platform for America," p. 42 (emphasis added).

4. See, e.g., "ISSUES '92," *Orange County Register*, June 29, 1992, p. A14.

5. "Boxer Introduces Legislation to Codify Roe v. Wade On The 31st Anniversary Of The Decision," press release of Sen. Boxer, Jan. 22, 2004.

6. Statement of NOW president Kim Gandy, Jan. 22, 2004.

7. boxer.senate.gov/about/index.cfm

8. Justin Norton, "Boxer: Filibuster to block anti-abortion Supreme Court candidate," Associated Press, July 5, 2005.

9. "Press Conference of Democratic Women Senators," July 28, 2005.

10. See www.factcheck.org/article336.html and Clarke Forsythe, "The Effective Enforcement of Abortion Law Before *Roe v. Wade*," in Brad Stetson, ed., *The Silent Subject* (Praeger, 1996), pp. 198-99.

11. Cecil Adams, May 28, 2004, column at straightdope.com. Ellen Goodman's original column appeared in the April 25, 2004, *Boston Globe*. She issued a correction on May 13, although she still didn't realize that the 1936 estimate was retracted six years later. See also afterabortion.blogspot.com/2004/05/ellen-goodman-has-recanted.html.

12. Forsythe, pp. 199-200. See Chapter 6 for more about pro-choice exaggerations about illegal abortions.

13. *Ibid.*, p. 200. Naturally, the *New York Times* treats the 1.2-million figure as a fact. ("Abortion: Where Are the Doctors?" [editorial], Oct. 13, 1994, p. A26.)

14. Paul Chavez, "Rejection Urged For Bush Appellate Court Nominee," *The Associated Press*, May 8, 2003.

15. Juvenile Law Center *et al*, brief to the Supreme Court in *Roper* v. *Simmons* (2005), Appendix B, pp. 17-18, 27-28.

16. Fox News/Opinion Dynamics poll, April 2005 (72 percent); CNN/USA *Today*/Gallup poll, Jan. 2003 (73 percent).

17. *Congressional Record*, May 1, 2003, p. S5620.

18. *All Things Considered*, NPR, Oct. 21, 2003, quoting Boxer on the Senate floor.

19. Judy Pasternak, "Abortion Restrictions Were Efforts Long on the Rise," *Los Angeles Times*, Nov. 21, 2004, p. A31.

20. NOW press releases, Feb. 26, 2004, and April 26, 2001.

21. Douglas Johnson, "Seeing 1 When There Are 2," *National Review Online*, Feb. 5, 2004.

22. Jack Torry, "Killing Fetus Is Murder in Bill Sent to Bush," *Columbus Dispatch*, March 26, 2004, p. 3A.

23. Sharon Rocha statement, Feb. 26, 2004.

24. "Four Accused of Murder in Fetus' Death," *Chicago Tribune*, Sept. 3, 1999, p. N8.

25. "Senate Passes Unborn Victims Bill," Foxnews.com, March 26, 2004; Debra Rosenberg, "The War Over Fetal Rights," *Newsweek*, June 9, 2003.

26. Alan Cooperman and Amy Goldstein, "HHS Proposes Insurance for Fetuses," *Washington Post*, Feb. 1, 2002, p. A1.

27. Kimball Perry, "Teen's Abortion Prompts Lawsuit," *Cincinnati Post*, March 30, 2005; Richard Walton, "Judge: Give kids' medical records to state," *Indianapolis Star*, May 31, 2005.

Chapter 4

1. Deborah Orin, "Moynihan will vote to override prez's abortion-ban veto," *New York Post*, May 3, 1996, p. 2. Moynihan would later say that the procedure "is not just too close to infanticide; it is infanticide, and one would be too many" (*Meet the Press*, March 2, 1997).

2. Martin Haskell, "Dilation and Extraction for Late Second Trimester Abortion," paper presented at the National Abortion Federation Risk Management Seminar, September 13, 1992.

3.   Cynthia Gorney, "Gambling With Abortion," *Harper's*, Nov. 2004.
For a slightly different account, see Kate Michelman, *With Liberty and Justice for All* (Penguin, 2005), p. 142.

4.   William Saletan, "The 'Partial-Birth' Myth," *Slate*, Oct. 22, 2003.

5.   Diane Gianelli, "Shock-tactic ads target late-term abortion procedure," *American Medical News*, July 5, 1993, p. 21.

6.   Planned Parenthood Federation of America, news release, Nov. 1, 1995.

7.   Gianelli, "Medicine adds to debate on late-term abortion," *American Medical News*, March 3, 1997, p. 54.

8.   Marilyn Rauber, "Leading doc tells Congress pro-choicers 'misinformed,'" *New York Post*, March 22, 1996.

9.   Edwin Chen, "Abortion Foes See Major Gains in House," *Los Angeles Times*, June 16, 1995, p. A32; Chen, "House Votes To Ban Rare Form of Abortions," *LAT*, Nov. 2, 1995, p. A1.

10. Jerry Gray, "Issue of Abortion Is Pushing Its Way to Center Stage," *New York Times*, June 19, 1995, p. A1.

11. "Attack on rare abortion procedure invites misery" (editorial), *USA Today*, Nov. 3, 1995, p. 10A; "The right to choose" (editorial), *New York Daily News*, Dec. 15, 1995, p. 68; Ellen Goodman, "The abortion art gallery," *Boston Globe*, November 12, 1995, p. 87.

12. *Congressional Record*, Nov. 1, 1995, p. 31160; Nov. 8, 1995, p. 31661.

13. *Nightline*, Nov. 7, 1995. Boxer also claimed that "every single state has rules and regulations that apply to the second and third trimester," going on to suggest strongly, and falsely, that some are not allowed.

14. Transcript of *American Medical News* interview, nrlc.org/abortion/pba/AmericanMedicalNews1993.pdf.

15. Dr. Norig Ellison, testimony to House subcommittee on the Constitution, March 21, 1996.

16. President Clinton, press conference, Dec. 13, 1996. A leading practitioner of partial-birth abortion, Dr. James McMahon, testified in June 1995 that hydrocephaly, the condition to which Clinton alluded, accounted for a small proportion of the procedures he had performed. Dr. Watson Bowes, a respected authority on fetal medicine, wrote to the chairman of the House subcommittee on constitutional matters that the size of an enlarged fetal head could be reduced without the intentional killing of the fetus. Dr. Bowes, letter to Rep. Charles Canady, July 11, 1995.

17. Ruth Padawer, "The Facts on Partial-Birth Abortion, *The Sunday Record* (Bergen County, N.J.), Sept. 15, 1996.

18. David Brown and Barbara Vobejda, "Discomfitting Details of Late-Term Abortions Intensify Dispute" and "Late Term Abortions: Who Gets Them and Why," *Washington Post*, Sept. 17, 1996.

19. Transcript of *American Medical News* interview, nrlc.org/abortion/pba/AmericanMedicalNews1993.pdf.

20. David Stout, "An Abortion Rights Advocate Says He Lied About Procedure," *New York Times*, Feb. 26, 1997, p. A11; Gianelli, "Medicine adds to debate on late-term abortion," *American Medical News*, March 3, 1997, p. 54.

21. *Nightline*, Feb. 27, 1997.

22. Tamar Lewin, "Study on a Late Term Abortion Finds Procedure Is Little Used," *New York Times*, Dec. 11, 1998, p. A12.

23. Douglas Johnson, "Letters to the editor," *Washington Times*, Nov. 4, 2003.

24. *Ibid.*

25. Steven Waldman, "John Kerry's Abortion Ban," www.beliefnet.com/story/155/story_15523_1.html.

26. *McNeil-Lehrer Newshour*, May 15, 1997.

27. Frank Murray, "Daschle bill may not ban anything," *Washington Times*, May 15, 1997.

28. Glen Johnson, "Kerry Vows Court Picks To Be Abortion-Rights Supporters," *Boston Globe*, April 9, 2003.

29. President Clinton, veto message, Oct. 10, 1997.

30. Letter from P. John Seward, AMA executive vice president, to Sen. Rick Santorum, May 19, 1997.

31. Sen. Boxer appears to be referring to an exchange between Sen. Santorum and Sen. Russ Feingold (D., Wisc.) on Sept. 26, 1996. Santorum conjured a hypothetical situation in which a doctor tried to perform a partial-birth abortion but accidentally delivered the baby's whole body, including the head. Santorum asked whether the doctor could "kill the baby." Feingold answered, "I am not the person to be answering that question. That is a question that should be answered by a doctor, and by the woman who receives advice from the doctor. And neither I, nor is the Senator from Pennsylvania, truly competent to answer those questions. That is why we should not be making those decisions here on the floor of the Senate." Feingold took advantage of his prerogative to alter his words in the *Congressional Record*. See *National Right to Life News*, Nov. 14, 1996, p. 24.

32. *Congressional Record*, Oct. 20, 1999.

33. Jesse Holland, "House approves bill to give legal protection to some fetuses after abortion," Associated Press, March 13, 2002.

34. Rep. Charles Canady (R., Fla.) entered the press release into the *Congressional Record*, Sept. 26, 2000.

35. Hadley Arkes, *Natural Rights and the Right to Choose* (Cambridge University Press, 2002), pp. 260-62.

Chapter 5

1. *Planned Parenthood Federation of America*, et al., v. *Ashcroft* (N.D.Cal. 2004).

2. CNN/USA *Today*/Gallup poll taken Oct. 24-26, 2003.

3. O'Connor dissent from *Thornburgh* v. *American College of Obstetricians & Gynecologists* (1986).

4. Section II-A of Justice Thomas's dissent from *Stenberg* v. *Carhart* (2000) makes a good case for a straightforward reading of the statutes.

5. ACOG Statement of Policy, Sept. 2000.

6. Posner dissent from *Hope Clinic* v. *Ryan* (1999).

7. *Planned Parenthood of Central New Jersey* v. *Farmer* (2000).

8. Stevens concurrence in *Thornburgh* v. *American College of Obstetricians & Gynecologists*. I am indebted for this point to Richard Stith, "Location and Life: How *Stenberg* v. *Carhart* Undermined *Roe* v. *Wade*," 9 *William & Mary Journal of Women and the Law* 255 (2003), although he makes a slightly different one.

9. Shannen Coffin, "The Abortion Distortion," *National Review*, July 12, 2004.

10. *Ibid.*

11. *National Abortion Federation* v. *Ashcroft* (2004).

Chapter 6

1. Nicholas von Hoffman, "Understand That Pro-Abortion Is Pro-Life and Vice-Versa," *Philadelphia Inquirer*, July 10, 1992.

2. Von Hoffman in *Slate*: http://slate.msn.com/id/2000038/entry/1001488/.

3. Steven Levitt and Stephen Dubner, *Freakonomics: A Rogue Economist Explores the Hidden Side of Everything* (HarperCollins, 2005).

4. He is also "devilishly clever," according to his book jacket.

5. Gregg Easterbrook, *Washington Post*, May 1, 2005, p. T7; Michael Shermer, *Los Angeles Times*, May 15, 2005, p. R3; Steven Landsburg, *WSJ*, April 13, 2005, p. D14.

6. Michael Maiello, *Forbes*, May 13, 2005 (www.forbes.com/economy/2005/05/13/cz_mm_0513freakonomicsreview.html); *The Economist*, "Curious and Curiouser," May 12, 2005.

7. John Tierney, *NYT*, April 16, 2005, p. A13; Jim Holt, *NYT*, May 15, 2005, Book Review, p. 12; Roger Lowenstein, *NYT*, June 19, 2005, Business Section, p. 6.

8. Steve Sailer, "Pre-Emptive Executions?" *The American Conservative*, May 9, 2005. See also his follow-up comments at www.isteve.com/abortion.htm.

9. See also John Lott and John Whitley, "Abortion and Crime: Unwanted Children and Out-of-Wedlock Births," Yale Law School Program for Law, Economics and Public Policy Working Paper # 254, 2001.

10. Ted Joyce, "Further Tests of Abortion and Crime," National Bureau of Economic Research Working Paper 10564, 2004.

11. Christopher Foote and Christopher Goetz, "Testing Economic Hypotheses with State-Level Data," Federal Reserve Bank of Boston, Working Paper 05-15. This research led *The Economist*, to its credit, to take a more skeptical look at the *Freakonomics* theory. "Oops-onomics," Dec. 1, 2005.

12. Laurie Elam-Evans et al, "Abortion Surveillance—United States, 2002," Centers for Disease Control, Table 13. (I'm assuming, conservatively, that where the number of abortions a woman has had is unknown, she has had only one.)

13. Jonathan Klick and Thomas Stratmann, "The Effect of Abortion Legalization on Sexual Behavior: Evidence from Sexually Transmitted Diseases," *Journal of Legal Studies*, vol. 32 (June 2003).

14. *Freakonomics*, p. 139.

15. George Akerlof and Janet Yellen, "An Analysis of Out-of-Wedlock Births in the United States," Brookings Policy Brief #5, 1996 (www.brook.edu/comm/policybriefs/pb05.htm). It is based on a paper by Akerlof, Yellen, and Michael Katz with the same title, published in the *Quarterly Journal of Economics* that year.

16. For a review of the literature, see Jonathan Klick, "Econometric Analyses of U.S. Abortion Policy: A Critical Review," *Fordham Urban Law Journal*, vol. 31 (2004).

17. Information in this paragraph comes from Sailer's website.

18. Sharon Cohen, "Freakonomics in Chicago," *Northwest Indiana Times*, May 6, 2005.

19. See www.isteve.com/abortion.htm

20. Joyce, *op. cit.*

21. *Freakonomics*, pp. 142-44.

22. Bernard Nathanson with Richard Ostling, *Aborting America* (Doubleday, 1979), p. 193.

23. Lilo Strauss, et al., "Abortion Surveillance—United States, 2001," Centers for Disease Control.
24. Candace Crandall, "The Fetus Beat Us," *The Women's Quarterly*, Winter 1996, p. 20.
25. Mary Calderone, "Illegal Abortion as a Public Health Problem," *American Journal of Health*, Vol. 50 (July 1960), p. 949.
26. Crandall, *op. cit.*, p. 20.
27. Rachel Benson Gold, "Lessons from Before *Roe*," *The Guttmacher Report on Public Policy*, March 2003, pp. 8, 10, 11, available at www.guttmacher.org/pubs/tgr/06/1/gr060108.pdf.
28. The National Cancer Institute held a workshop in February 2003 that concluded that there was no link, but Dr. Joel Brind wrote a dissenting report on this finding.

Chapter 7

1. Ronald Dworkin, *Life's Dominion* (Vintage, 1993), Ch. 1, p. 3. The full sentence reads: "Abortion, which means deliberately killing a developing human embryo, and euthanasia, which means deliberately killing a person out of kindness, are both choices for death."
2. *Ibid.*
3. Some examples: 1) "In this text, we begin our description of the developing human with the formation and differentiation of the male and female sex cells or gametes, which will unite at fertilization *to initiate the embryonic development of a new individual*" (emphasis added). William J. Larsen, *Human Embryology*, 3rd edition (Philadelphia: Churchill Livingstone, 2001), p. 1. (2) *"Human development begins at fertilization*, the process during which a male gamete or sperm (spermatozoon) unites with a female gamete or oocyte (ovum) to form a single cell called a zygote. This highly specialized, totipotent cell marked the beginning of each of us as a unique individual." Keith Moore and T. V. N. Persaud, *The Developing Human* (6th edition, 1998), p. 18, emphases in original. (3) "It needs to be emphasized that life is continuous, as is also human life, so that the question, 'When does (human) life begin?' is meaningless in terms of ontogeny. Although life is a continuous process, fertilization (which, incidentally, is not a 'moment') is a critical landmark because, under ordinary circumstances, *a new, genetically distinct human organism is formed* when the chromosomes of the male and female pronuclei blend in the oocyte" (emphasis added). Ronan O'Rahilly and Fabiola Mueller, *Human Embryology and Teratology*, 3rd edition (New York: Wiley-Liss, 2000), p. 8. (4) In Scott F. Gilbert, *Developmental Biology* 6th edition (Sunderland, MA: Sin-

auer Associates, 2000), Chapter 7 is entitled: "Fertilization: Beginning a New Organism." The first sentence of that chapter reads: "Fertilization is the process whereby two sex cells (gametes) fuse together *to create a new individual* with genetic potentials derived from both parents" (emphasis added) (p. 185).

4.   Nobody, that is, except for Jack Kevorkian. See Chapter 11.

5.   Morton Kondracke, "Can GOP Moderates Exert Power in Party Dominated by Right?" *Roll Call*, Aug. 9, 2005.

6.   E.g., the members of the Religious Coalition for Reproductive Choice, or the churches and religious bodies (such as Presbyterian Church USA) that co-sponsored the pro-abortion "March for Women's Lives" in 2004.

7.   To be more precise: Anyone who reads a Biblical passage as condemning embryo-destructive research is doing so because he holds premises, not explicitly stated in the Bible, that inform his reading.

8.   George McKenna, "Bearing Witness," *Human Life Review*, Winter 2004, pp. 31-32.

9.   Jonathan Alter, "The 'Pro-Cure' Movement," *Newsweek*, June 6, 2005.

10. Anna Quindlen, "A New Look, An Old Battle," *Newsweek*, April 9, 2001, p. 72.

11. Michael Kinsley, "If You Believe Embryos Are Humans. . ." *Time*, June 25, 2001, p. 80; Kinsley, "One Reason Not to Like Bush," *Washington Post*, Oct. 24, 2003, p. A25. Feminist writer Barbara Ehrenreich also makes the argument from miscarriage: See http://slate.msn.com/id/2000038/entry/1001488/.

12. Michael Sandel, "Embryo Ethics," *New England Journal of Medicine*, July 15, 2004. The argument is echoed by Richard Cohen, "Life vs. Life," *Washington Post*, May 26, 2005, p. A27.

13. Ellen Goodman, "Weathering the Embryo Debate," *Boston Globe*, June 12, 2005, p. D11.

14. Jeffrey Hart, "The Magazine is Wrong," *National Review*, April 19, 2004.

15. Nor need we conclude that every type of killing is equally blame-worthy. Take the case of a man who performs an abortion out of compassion for a pregnant woman in distress. Anyone who recognizes that the baby has an equal right not to be killed as an adult would judge that compassion misplaced and seek to prohibit the abortion. But the act might also be judged less culpable than, say, the murder of a business rival out of greed, and it might be thought just to impose less severe punishments.

16. Judith Jarvis Thomson, "A Defense of Abortion," *Journal of Philosophy and Public Affairs*, vol. 1 no. 1 (1971).

Chapter 8

1. Chapter One treats the constitutional claim. The Court's point about people's reliance on abortion in the event of contraceptive failure hardly closes the case against allowing state legislatures around the country to restrict abortion gradually.

2. I owe this view of *Casey* to Gerard Bradley, "Shall We Ratify the New Constitution?" in Terry Eastland, ed., *Benchmarks* (Washington, D.C.: Ethics and Public Policy Center, 1995), Ch. 6, pp. 117-40.

3. Mario Cuomo, giving the official Democratic response to one of President Bush's weekly radio addresses, claimed that Republicans want "ownership of the Supreme Court and other federal courts, hoping to achieve political results on subjects like abortion, stem cells, the environment and civil rights that they can not get from the proper political bodies." This is a lie. Judicial imposition of pro-life policy on abortion or stem cells is not on the table, and Cuomo knows it. It is the party of death that has used the courts to impose its views when it could not win in the "proper political bodies." Cuomo, April 30, 2005.

4. See Robert Nagel, *The Implosion of American Federalism* (Oxford University Press, 2001), Ch. 7, pp. 99-111.

5. "Respect for Privacy," editorial, *New York Times*, Jan. 24, 1973.

6. Conclusion to Scalia's dissent from *Hill* v. *Colorado* (2000).

7. Conclusion to Kennedy's dissent. See also *Madsen* v. *Women's Health Center* (1994), *Schenck* v. *Pro-Choice Network of Western New York* (1997).

8. Public Agenda's July 2002 poll asked if abortion should be "generally available to those who want it," "available but under stricter limits," or "not. . . permitted." The results were nearly identical by sex. Two percent more men than women picked the first option, and one percent more women than men picked each of the relatively pro-life options.

9. See, for example, the Annenberg Election survey released on July 2, 2004. There was almost no difference between the sexes on whether all abortions should be banned: 32 percent of men and 31 percent of women favored a ban, while 62 percent of men and 64 percent of women opposed one. Married people opposed abortion more than single people by 15 percentage points. (The gap between married and single men was 18 points; the gap between married and single women was 14 points.)

10. Sen. Dianne Feinstein, speech to the Los Angeles County Bar Association and Public Counsel, August 24, 2005 (feinstein.senate.gov/05speeches/s-supreme-ct.htm). See also Nicole Brodeur, "Nail-biting times for women," *Seattle Times*, Jan. 26, 2006.

11. Press release from CAW: "Is Your Mother's Feminism Dead?" June 24, 2003 (www.advancewomen.org/for_reporters/press_releases.php).

12. Michael Finnegan, "Dean Says Democrats Will Make Schiavo Case an Election Issue," *Los Angeles Times*, April 16, 2005, p. A17.

13. Ron Reagan, speech to the Democratic convention, July 27, 2004.

14. *Meet the Press*, Aug. 7, 2005.

15. John Rawls, *Political Liberalism* (Columbia University Press, 1996), Lecture VI, pp. 212-254.

16. Peter Beinart, "Morally Correct," *The New Republic*, Nov. 29, 2004, p. 6.

17. Stevens concurrence in *Thornburgh* v. *American College of Obstetricians & Gynecologists* (1986).

18. Joseph Bottum, "John Kerry, in the Catholic Tradition," *Weekly Standard*, April 26, 2004.

19. Robert P. George and Christopher Wolfe, "Natural Law and Public Reason," in George and Wolfe, ed., *Natural Law and Public Reason* (Georgetown University Press, 2000), p. 57. I used the word "knowledge," not opinion, advisedly. This book presupposes, though it does not defend, both the existence of moral truths and the inclusion within that category of the wrongness of murder. Almost everyone acknowledges both of these things in practice.

20. Rawls, p. 243.

21. Rawls (paperback edition), p. lv.

Chapter 9

1. Sylvia A. Law, Jane E. Larson, and Clyde Spillenger, "Brief of 281 American Historians as *Amici Curiae* Supporting Appellees," filed in *Webster v. Reproductive Health Services, Inc.*, 1989 (hereinafter referred to as "the historians' brief"), p. 1.

2. Sylvia A. Law, Jane E. Larson, and Clyde Spillenger, "Brief of 250 American Historians as *Amici Curiae* in Support of Petitioners and Cross-Respondents Planned Parenthood of Southeastern Pennsylvania, *et al.*," filed in *Planned Parenthood of Southeastern Pennsylvania v. Casey*, 1992, hereinafter referred to as "the *Casey* brief".

3. Cyril C. Means, Jr., "The Phoenix of Abortional Freedom: Is a Penumbral or Ninth Amendment Right About to Arise From the Nineteenth-Century Legislative Ashes of a Fourteenth-Century Com-

mon Law Liberty?" *New York Law Forum*, Vol. 17 (1971) No. 2, pp. 335-410.

4.   Joseph Dellapenna, "Brief of the American Academy of Medical Ethics as *Amicus Curiae* in Support of Respondents and Cross-Petitioners Robert P. Casey *et al.*," filed in *Planned Parenthood of Southeastern Pennsylvania v. Casey*, 1992; Robert M. Byrn, "An American Tragedy: The Supreme Court on Abortion," *Fordham Law Review*, Vol. XLI No. 4 (May 1973).

5.   See Dellapenna; Byrn; Lyle Koehler, *A Search for Power: The "Weaker Sex" in Seventeenth-Century New England* (Chicago, IL: University of Illinois Press, 1980), pp. 329, 336 n132; John Keown, *Abortion, doctors, and the law: Some aspects of the legal regulation of abortion in England from 1803 to 1982* (Cambridge: Cambridge University Press, 1988), Ch. 1, pp. 7-8.

6.   James C. Mohr, *Abortion in America: The Origins and Evolution of National Policy, 1800-1900* (New York: Oxford University Press, 1978), Ch. 1, p. 3. The *Casey* brief (p. 5) revised this footnote: Instead of citing pages irrelevant to the point, it refers to the whole book without specifying any page numbers.

7.   Angus McLaren, *Reproductive Rituals: The perception of fertility in England from the sixteenth century to the nineteenth century* (London: Methuen & Co., 1984), p. 5 n9. The same passage appears, without the allusion to witchcraft, in the *Casey* brief (p. 6 n6).

8.   Mohr, *Abortion in America*, Ch. 1, pp. 3-4.

9.   Courts treating pre-quickening abortion as illegal: William Hand Browne, ed., *Archives of Maryland* (Baltimore, MD: Maryland Historical Society, 1891), Vol. 10, p. 464; Marvin Olasky, *Abortion Rites: A Social History of Abortion in America* (Wheaton, IL: Crossway Books, 1992), Ch. 1, p. 22; George W. Harris, reporter, *"Mills v. The Commonwealth," Pennsylvania State Reports* (Lancaster, PA: Hamersly & Co., 1850), Vol. XIII, pp. 631-36 at p. 633. Courts treating it as legal: See Dudley A. Tyng, reporter, *"Commonwealth v. Isaiah Bangs," Reports of Cases Argued and Determined in the Supreme Judicial Court of the Commonwealth of Massachusetts* (Boston, MA: Charles C. Little and James Brown, 1850), Vol. IX, pp. 386-7; Theron Metcalf, reporter, *"Commonwealth v. Luceba Parker," Reports of Cases Argued and Determined in the Supreme Judicial Court of Massachusetts* (Boston, MA: Little, Brown and Company, 1853), Vol. IX, pp. 263-68; Dellapenna, p. 24 n59.

10. Francis Wharton, *A Treatise on the Criminal Law of the United States* (Philadelphia, PA: Kay and Brother, 6th rev. ed. 1870), Vol. II, Ch. VI, §1220, pp. 210-11; Dellapenna, p. 24 n59.

11. Byrn, "An American Tragedy," at p. 824, quoting 170 Eng. Rep. 1310 (N.P. 1811).

12. Wharton, A *Treatise on the Criminal Law of the United States*, Vol. II, Ch. VI, §1223, p. 214.

13. Mohr, *Abortion in America*, Ch. 1, p. 4. Mohr believes that the common law reflected medieval treatments of quickening as a morally as well as practically important moment. He cites two sources for this view: Means, "The Law of New York Concerning Abortion and the Status of the Fœtus, 1664-1968," at pp. 411-19; and John T. Noonan, Jr., "An Almost Absolute Value in History," in Noonan, ed., *The Morality of Abortion: Legal and Historical Perspectives* (Cambridge, MA: Harvard University Press, 1970), pp. 1-59. Means, however, confuses the phrases "quick with child," "with quick child," "formation," and "animation," and thus cannot be relied upon. Noonan writes throughout of formation and "ensoulment," rather than quickening, and concludes, contrary to Mohr, that the medieval theologians "on one basis or another condemned abortion at any point in the existence of the fetus" (at p. 26).

14. Byrn, "An American Tragedy," at pp. 815-16.

15. McLaren, Ch. 5, p. 136.

16. John D'Emilio and Estelle B. Freedman, *Intimate Matters: A History of Sexuality in America* (New York: Harper & Row, 1988), Ch. 2, p. 26. Freedman has acknowledged the inaccuracy of the brief on this point: See Freedman, "Historical Interpretation and Legal Advocacy: Rethinking the *Webster Amicus* Brief," *The Public Historian*, Vol. 12 No. 3 (Summer 1990), pp. 27-32. The *Casey* brief weakens the claim, describing abortion as "far from unknown" at the time of the Founding. By then the earlier version had, however, already made its way into Laurence Tribe's influential book *Abortion: The Clash of Absolutes* (New York: W.W. Norton & Company, 1992) (Ch. 3, pp. 28-29).

17. Mohr, Ch. 2, p. 44.

18. Rosalind Pollack Petchesky, *Abortion and Woman's Choice: The State, Sexuality, and Reproductive Freedom* (Boston, MA: Northeastern University Press, rev. ed. 1990), Ch. 2, p. 53.

19. *Ibid.*, p. 10 n27. This footnote does not appear in the *Casey* brief, though the corresponding text remains.

20. John B. Beck, "Infanticide," in Theodric Romeyn Beck and John B. Beck, *Elements of Medical Jurisprudence* (Albany, NY: Little & Co., 10th rev. ed. 1850), Vol. I, pp. 425-26. See also pp. 521-33.

21. Means, "The Law of New York Concerning Abortion and the Status of the Fœtus, 1664-1968," pp. 443-53.

22. Mohr, Ch. 2, pp. 28-30.

23. *Ibid.*, Ch. 6, pp. 160-64.

24. Olasky, Ch. 6, pp. 126-28.

25. Mohr, Ch. 2, pp. 34-6.

26. Kristen Luker, *Abortion and the Politics of Motherhood* (Berkeley, CA: University of California Press, 1984), Ch. 2, pp. 29-32, argues that the anti-abortion laws' life-of-the-mother exceptions showed that the physicians did not really believe in fetal life but were trying to create an oligopoly over abortions. The argument is plainly erroneous. People can sincerely oppose abortion in general while supporting an exception for the life of the mother.

27. Paul Starr, *The Social Transformation of American Medicine* (New York: Basic Books, Inc., 1982), p. 451 n25.

28. Barbara Ehrenreich and Deirdre English, *For Her Own Good: 150 Years of the Experts' Advice to Women* (Garden City, NY: Anchor Press/Doubleday, 1978), Chs. 2-3, pp. 29-88.

29. *1750 to 1950* (New York: Oxford University Press, 1986).

30. Linda Gordon, *Woman's Body, Woman's Right: A Social History of Birth Control in America* (New York: Grossman Publishers, 1976), Ch. 5, p. 97.

31. *Ibid.*, Ch. 5, p. 108. *Cf.* Tribe's curious formulation: "Intriguingly, abortion rights. . . were not really on the agenda of the early feminists" (Tribe, *Abortion*, Ch. 3, p. 33).

32. Carl Degler, *At Odds: Women and the Family in America from the Revolution to the Present* (New York: Oxford University Press, 1980), Ch. 10, p. 243.

33. Mohr, Ch. 4, pp. 111-13.

34. "Marriage and Maternity," *The Revolution*, Vol. IV No. 1 (July 8, 1869), p. 4.

35. "The Slaughter of the Innocents," *Woodhull & Claflin's Weekly*, Vol. VIII No. 3 (June 20, 1874), pp. 8-9.

36. See, *e.g.*, J. J. Mulheron, "Fœticide," *The Peninsular Journal of Medicine*, Vol. 10 (Sept. 1874), p. 391; J. C. Stone, "Report on the Subject of Criminal Abortion," *Transactions of the Iowa State Medical Society*, Vol. 1 (1867), p. 29; Joseph Taber Johnson, "Abortion and Its Effects," *American Journal of Obstetrics and Diseases of Women and Children*, Vol. 33 (1896), pp. 87-88.

37. The characterization is Mohr's (*Abortion in America*, Ch. 7, p. 186 — one of the pages the brief cites in reference to Storer). Storer also lauded the Catholic position on abortion: "[T]here can be no doubt, that the Romish ordinance, flanked on the one hand by the confessional, and by denouncement and excommunication on the other,

has saved to the world thousands of infant lives" (Horatio R. Storer and Franklin Fiske Heard, *Criminal Abortion: Its Nature, Its Evidence, and Its Law* [Boston, MA: Little, Brown, and Company, 1868], Book I, Ch. III, p. 74 n2).

38.   See brief signatory Michael Grossberg, *Governing the Hearth: Law and the Family in Nineteenth-Century America* (Chapel Hill, NC: University of North Carolina Press, 1985), Ch. 5, pp. 169-70, 193.

39.   "The Evil of the Age," *New York Times*, August 23, 1871, p. 6.

40.   "Hellish Earll," *National Police Gazette*, Vol. 36 No. 155 (Sept. 11, 1880), p. 10.

41.   B. G. Jefferis and J. L. Nichols, *Light on Dark Corners* (New York: Grove Press Inc., 1894), Part V, p. 139.

42.   James Witherspoon, "Reexamining *Roe*: Nineteenth-Century Abortion Statutes and the Fourteenth Amendment," *St. Mary's Law Journal*, Vol. 17 No. 1 (1985), pp. 36, 40, 42, 48-50.

43.   Dellapenna, "Brief of the American Academy of Medical Ethics," p. 25. For a list of early twentieth-century cases holding that the law sought to protect fetal life, see Byrn, "An American Tragedy," pp. 828-29.

44.   This chapter is based on my senior thesis in college, which I will make available upon serious request.

45.   Law, "Conversations Between Historians and the Constitution," p. 14.

46.   See James Davison Hunter, *Before the Shooting Begins: Searching for Democracy in America's Culture War* (New York: The Free Press, 1994), Ch. 6, pp. 178-79, for interviews with (unnamed) signatories who confess their ignorance.

47.   E.g., Dennis Hevesi, "How Debate Over Abortion Evolved With Changes in Science and Society," *The New York Times*, July 4, 1989, p. 11.

48.   Walter Dellinger, "Day in Court," *The New Republic*, May 8, 1989, pp. 11-12.

49.   George Will, "Abortion Is A State Question," *Washington Post*, June 18, 1989, p. C7.

50.   Ronald Dworkin, "The Great Abortion Case," *The New York Review of Books*, June 29, 1989, p. 50.

51.   Ronald Dworkin, *Life's Dominion: An Argument about Abortion, Euthanasia, and Individual Freedom* (New York: Alfred A. Knopf, 1993), Ch. 4, p. 112; p. 248 n8.

52.   Tribe, *Abortion*, Ch. 3, p. 27; p. 258 n1.

53.   Laura Flanders, "Abortion: the Usable Past," *The Nation*, Vol. 249 No. 5 (Aug. 7/14, 1989), p. 176.

Chapter 10

1. For a critique of the Florida courts' role, see Andrew McCarthy, "Death by Court Order," *National Review*, April 25, 2005.
2. Two notable exceptions were the Rev. Jesse Jackson, perhaps returning to his pro-life roots, and Ralph Nader.
3. "Praise God but defend secularism," editorial, *Financial Times*, March 26, 2005; Hendrik Hertzberg, "Matters of Life," *The New Yorker*, April 4, 2005.
4. Eric Cohen, "How Liberalism Failed Terri Schiavo," *Weekly Standard*, April 4, 2005.
5. Christopher Hitchens, "Easter Charade," *Slate*, March 28, 2005. (Note the echo of Monty Python's dead-parrot routine.) Al Franken, who freely accuses others of being "liars," repeatedly claimed that Schiavo was "brain dead": *Scarborough Country*, May 23, 2005.
6. Anna Quindlen, "The Culture of Each Life," *Newsweek*, April 4, 2005; Glenn Reynolds on *Kudlow & Company*, CNBC, March 24, 2005.
7. Immanuel Kant, *Lectures on Ethics* (Peter Heath and J. B. Schneewind, eds., Heath trans., Cambridge University Press, 1997), p. 124. See Bradford Short, "History 'Lite' in Modern American Bioethics," *Issues in Law & Medicine*, vol. 19 no. 1 (Summer 2003), pp. 45-76, for examples of how some bioethicists have distorted the anti-suicide teachings of Kant and John Locke.
8. See, for example, Andrew Sullivan, "An age-old moral lifeline out of the Terri Schiavo torment," *Sunday Times* (London), April 3, 2005; also Neal Boortz, "Because she's earned it," Townhall.com, March 24, 2005, a column Sullivan commended.
9. Sen. Hubert Humphrey, *Congressional Record*, Nov. 4, 1977, vol. 123, p. 37287; Cohen, op. cit.
10. Michael Finnegan, "Dean Says Democrats Will Make Schiavo Case An Election Issue," *Los Angeles Times*, April 16, 2005, p. A17.

Chapter 11

1. Dean Koontz, "Author's Note," *One Door Away from Heaven* (Bantam, oversize edition, 2001), pp. 897-8.
2. Wesley Smith, *Culture of Death* (Encounter Books, 2002), pp. 161-2.
3. R. Hoffenberg et al, "Should Organs from Patients in Permanent Vegetative State Be Used for Transplantation?" *The Lancet*, Vol. 350, No. 9087 (Nov. 1, 1997), p. 1321.
4. Smith, *op. cit.*, pp. 178-9 (emphasis in original); D. Alan Shewmon et al, "The Use of Anencephalic Infants as Organ Sources: A Cri-

tique," *Journal of the American Medical Association*, Vol. 261 (1989), p. 1775; Robert Steinbrook, "Frank Admissions End Infant Organ Harvesting," *Los Angeles Times*, Aug. 19, 1988, p. 3.

5.   CourtTV.com online debate, March 24, 2005.

6.   Michael Beltzold, "The Selling of Doctor Death," *The New Republic*, May 26, 1997; Stephen Drake, "The All-Too-Familiar Story," *Ragged Edge Online*, Vol. 2, 2001.

7.   Betzold, *op. cit.*; Adam Wolfson, "Killing Off the Dying?" *Public Interest*, Spring 1998.

8.   Randi Goldberg, "Coroner calls kidney removal from Kevorkian client mutilation," Associated Press, June 8, 1998; Smith, *op. cit.*, pp. 181-82.

9.   Linda Johnson, "Study: Newborn euthanasia often goes unreported in Netherlands—and probably other countries," Associated Press, March 9, 2005; Tara Burghart, "Study Examines Euthanasia in the Netherlands," Associated Press, Aug. 8, 2005.

10. Smith, *op. cit.*, p. 110.

11. Brief of Not Dead Yet et al in *Gonzales* v. *Oregon* (2005).

12. Carol Gill and Larry Voss, "Views of Disabled People Regarding Legalized Assisted Suicide Before and After a Balanced Informational Presentation," *Journal of Disability Policy Studies*, vol. 16, no. 1 (2005), pp. 6-15.

13. Smith, *op. cit.*, p. 108.

14. Stephen Drake, "Euthanasia Is Out of Control in The Netherlands," *Hastings Center Report*, Vol. 35, No. 3 (2005); Chief Justice William Rehnquist's majority opinion in *Washington* v. *Glucksberg* (1997); Smith, *op. cit.*, p. 111.

15. Smith, *op. cit.*, pp. 70-71.

16. *Ibid.*, pp. 123-24.

17. Marcia Angell, "After Quinlan," *New England Journal of Medicine*, Vol. 330 (May 26, 1994), p. 1525.

18. "Withholding and Withdrawing Life-Sustaining Therapy," official statement of the American Thoracic Society, published in *Annals of Internal Medicine*, Sept. 15, 1991.

19. Richard John Neuhaus, "The Return of Eugenics," *Commentary*, April 1988, p. 19.

20. Robert Arnold and Stuart Youngner, "The Dead Donor Rule," *Kennedy Institute of Ethics Journal*, vol. 3, no. 4 (1993), pp. 271-72.

Chapter 12

1.   Ronald Reagan, *Abortion and the Conscience of a Nation* (Thomas Nelson, 1984).

2. William Clark, "For Reagan, All Life Was Sacred," *New York Times*, June 11, 2004.

3. Andrea Stone and Dan Vergano, "Congress looks again at stem-cell research," *USA Today*, June 9, 2004, p. 5A (quoting Orrin Hatch); William Safire, "Reagan's Next Victory," *New York Times*, June 7, 2004, p. A27; Jonathan Alter, "Reagan's Last Political Gift," *Newsweek*, June 21, 2004, p. 45.

4. Ron Reagan Jr., speech to the Democratic convention, July 27, 2004.

5. Charles Krauthammer, "An Edwards Outrage," *Washington Post*, Oct. 15, 2004, p. A13.

6. Rick Weiss, "Stem Cells An Unlikely Therapy for Alzheimer's," *Washington Post*, June 10, 2004, p. A3; John Kerry, radio address, July 12, 2004. The Democratic platform was also finalized after Weiss's article appeared.

7. Polls making misleading claims about cures and effects of "information" on public opinion: Results for America poll, June 16, 2004; Civil Society Institute poll, March 2004; Juvenile Diabetes Research Foundation poll, Nov. 17, 2004. News coverage: Rick Weiss, "Looser Rules for Stem Cells Sought," *Washington Post*, April 29, 2004; Michael Crowley, "Stem Sell," *The New Republic Online*, June 2, 2004; Charles Babington and Ceci Connolly, "Minor Mutiny in GOP Ranks Fails to Derail Tom DeLay," *Washington Post*, Nov. 21, 2004, p. A5.

8. Compare Antonio Regalado and Bob Davis, "Kerry Treads Cloning Tightrope," *Wall Street Journal*, Aug. 10, 2004, p. A4, to Diedtra Henderson, "Scientists, engineers seek virtual audience with candidates," *USA Today* (online), Aug. 20, 2004.

9. Specter statement on *The Edge with Paula Zahn*, June 21, 2001; Daschle statements, July 31, 2001, and Aug. 1, 2001 ("I'm very uncomfortable with even cloning for research purposes"); Dodd statement, Sept. 5, 2001 ("I vehemently oppose" research cloning); Harkin statement, Sept. 14, 2000; Hatch answer to pro-life group questionnaire signed April 14, 2000; Hatch statement in Senate subcommittee on criminal justice, July 17, 2001.

10. See William Saletan, "The Organ Factory," *Slate*, July 25-29, 2005.

11. *Meet the Press*, February 24, 2002.

12. Barton speech on House floor, May 24, 2005.

13. See, e.g., Rick Weiss and Mary Fitzgerald, "Kerry, First Lady at Odds on Stem Cells," *Washington Post*, Aug. 10, 2004, p. A11.

14. Specter comment at press conference, April 30, 2002; Neil Munro, "Cloning Begets Diverse Factions," *National Journal*, April 27, 2002.

15. All the related arguments—nobody grieves when an embryo dies, nat-
     ural miscarriages kill embryos all the time—have also been made. In
     this chapter and following one, I give little or no attention to a num-
     ber of common arguments for embryo-destructive research that I
     have already discussed in Chapters 7 and 8.

16. See William Saletan, "Killing Eve," *Slate*, Dec. 31, 2002; Mary Cur-
     tius and Peter Wallsten, "Bush Objects to Stem-Cell Bill," *Los Ange-
     les Times*, May 20, 2005, p. A1; statement by Sen. Feinstein, Senate
     Judiciary Committee hearing, March 19, 2003; statement by Rep.
     Anna Eshoo, Feb. 27, 2003.

17. Rick Weiss, "Firm Aims to Clone Embryos for Stem Cells," *Washing-
     ton Post*, July 12, 2001, p. A1. Rep. Peter Deutch (D., Fla.) made this
     claim at a press conference on Feb. 26, 2003, about his pro-cloning
     legislation—only to be contradicted by one of the scientists on hand
     to talk about his support for the legislation. See letter by Rep.
     Christopher Smith (R., N.J.), dated the same day. See also *Nature*,
     July 7, 2005, p. 2 (editorializing against the redefinition of the word
     "embryo").

Chapter 13

1.   See, for instance, Peter Slevin's use of the phrase "stem cell propo-
     nents" in this little masterpiece of propaganda: "Mo. May Vote on
     Stem Cell Research," *Washington Post*, Dec. 25, 2005, p. A4.

2.   Robert P. George and Patrick Lee, "Acorns and Embryos," *The New
     Atlantis*, no. 7 (Fall/Winter 2005), p. 91.

3.   National Annenberg Election Survey, released Aug. 9, 2004; U.S.
     Conference of Catholic Bishops, release, Aug. 23, 2004; Matthew
     Nisbet, "Public Opinion About Stem Cell Research and Human
     Cloning," *Public Opinion Quarterly*, Spring 2004, pp. 131-154.

4.   See my article, "A Stem-Cell Defection," *National Review Online*,
     Aug. 16, 2004.

5.   Amy Fagan, "Republicans irked by group's 'loyalty oath,'" *Washington
     Times*, July 15, 2005.

6.   Sen. Bill Frist, speech, July 28, 2005 (*Congressional Record*, p.
     S9325). Frist later told the *Huntsville Times* that his experience as a
     heart surgeon informed his policy: "[H]e's dealt with trading life for
     life because when a heart is removed from one body and put in
     another, that first body will certainly die" (Patricia McCarter, "Frist
     discusses stem cells, taxes, but not Lott book, Aug. 19, 2005). But did
     Frist take hearts out of healthy patients?

7.   See Kyla Dunn, "Cloning Trevor," *The Atlantic*, June 2002, for an example of a biotech executive making this argument (and a journalist uncritically repeating it).

8.   Ron Bailey, "Liberation Biology" (interview with Silver), *Reason*, May 1999, p. 46 (emphasis in original). Silver is the author of *Remaking Eden: Cloning and Beyond in a Brave New World* (William Morrow, 1997). See Peter Singer, "Germ of a new debate on the ethics of life," The Australian, Dec. 23, 2005, for a related argument. He points out that cloners could create a new human being out of any of our skin cells, and attempts to use that fact to erase the distinction between an embryo and a skin cell. He fails. A skin cell isn't an organism, even if a scientist can combine its nucleus with an enucleated egg to create an embryonic organism.

9.   Ronald Bailey, *Liberation Biology* (Prometheus Books, 2005), p. 125; William Saletan, "Wiggle Room," *Slate*, July 25, 2005; Clive Thompson, "How to Farm Stem Cells Without Losing Your Soul," *Wired*, June 2005. Bailey (pp. 123-27) offers examples of almost every fallacious argument discussed in this chapter, and several discussed in Chapter 7.

10. *Science*, vol. 295, no. 5560 (March 1, 2002), p. 1637. Gazzaniga repeats the Home Depot analogy in Michael Gazzaniga, "The Thoughtful Distinction Between Embryo and Human," *Chronicle of Higher Education*, April 8, 2005; William Saletan, "Drugstore Cowboys," *Slate*, April 4, 2005.

11. In sexual reproduction, at least. In cloning, the "parts" would be the nucleus of a somatic cell and an enucleated egg.

12. Sen. Harkin statement at labor/health appropriations subcommittee hearing, July 12, 2005.

13. Mario Cuomo, "Not on Faith Alone," *New York Times*, June 20, 2005.

14. Michael Kinsley, "The False Controversy of Stem Cells," *Time*, May 31, 2004, p. 88; Kinsley, "Taking Bush Personally," *Slate*, Oct. 23, 2003. See also Michael Sandel, "Embryo Ethics," *New England Journal of Medicine*, July 15, 2004.

15. Rep. Castle, press conference, May 23, 2005. See also his letter to the president, Aug. 9, 2005. Sen. Feinstein, press conference, April 21, 2005.

16. *This Week*, May 22, 2005; Michael Woods, "U.S. relatively hospitable to stem-cell research," *Pittsburgh Post-Gazette*, June 5, 2005.

17. James Cordy, testimony to the labor/health appropriations subcommittee, May 22, 2003.

18. Yuval Levin, "The Crisis of Everyday Life," *The New Atlantis*, No. 7, Fall 2004/Winter 2005. Recall that Ellen Goodman asks us to imagine ourselves in a burning building when thinking about embryo ethics.

19. Dr. Jeffrey Drazen, "Legislative Myopia on Stem Cells," *New England Journal of Medicine*, Vol. 349, No. 3 (July 17, 2003), p. 300.

20. Michael Sandel, personal statement accompanying report of the president's council on bioethics on "alternative sources of pluripotent stem cells." My ellipses replace "for reasons that are well-stated in the ethical analysis (pp. 38-45 above)." The reference to those pages does not rescue Sandel's position. It drags it deeper into the muck. For example, the report notes that the creation of these biological entities could involve the exploitation of women for their egg cells—an objection that applies equally to the cloning research that Sandel favors.

21. Rick Weiss, "Contentious Hearing Focuses on Stem Cells," *Washington Post*, July 13, 2005, p. A19.

22. Anna Quindlen welcomes the stem-cell controversy because she thinks it will increase support for abortion. "A New Look, An Old Battle," *Newsweek*, April 9, 2001, p. 72.

Chapter 14

1. "The Year in Medicine," *Time*, Dec. 5, 2005; Amy Dockser Marcus, "A Brother's Survey Touches a Nerve in Abortion Fight," *Wall Street Journal*, Oct. 3, 2005, p. A1; Tucker Carlson, "Eugenics, American Style," *Weekly Standard*, Dec. 2, 1996, p. 20.

2. Jonathan Finer, "Study: Negativity Often Tied to Down Syndrome Diagnoses," *Washington Post*, April 29, 2005, p. A3.

3. *Ibid.*; Marcus, *op. cit.*

4. Marcus, *op. cit.*; Patricia Bauer, "The Abortion Debate No One Wants to Have," *Washington Post*, Oct. 18, 2005, p. A25; "Disability, Abortion and the Nature of a Tough Decision," letters to the editor, *Washington Post*, Oct. 22, 2005, p. A19.

5. Leon Kass, "A More Perfect Human," speech at the U.S. Holocaust Memorial Museum, March 17, 2005. Of course, "private reproductive choice" does worse than "coerce" the unborn child.

6. Joycelyn Elders, testimony before Senate Committee on Labor and Human Resources, May 23, 1990.

7. Justice Oliver Wendell Holmes's opinion for the Court in *Buck* v. *Bell* (1927). See also Paul Lombardo, "Three Generations, No Imbeciles: New Light on *Buck* v. *Bell*," *New York University Law Review*, vol. 30 (April 1985).

8.   At least in public. See Angela Franks, *Margaret Sanger's Eugenic Legacy* (McFarland & Co., 2005), p. 11.

9.   Sanger was a sponsor of Americans for Voluntary Sterilization, but both its and her view of what constituted a "voluntary" sterilization were elastic. See Ian Dowboggin, "'A Rational Coalition': Euthanasia, Eugenics, and Birth Control in America, 1940-1970," *Journal of Policy History*, Vol. 14, No. 3 (2002), pp. 238-39. See also Franks, *op. cit.*, pp. 187-88.

10.   David Tell, "Planned Un-Parenthood," *Weekly Standard*, Jan. 27, 2003; see generally Franks, *op. cit.*

11.   "The Control of Births," *The New Republic*, March 6, 1915, p. 114.

12.   "Letters to the Editor," *New York Times*, Feb. 28, 1969.

13.   Bentley Glass, "Science: Endless Horizons or Golden Age," *Science*, Vol. 171 (1971), p. 28.

14.   To be precise, the *Freakonomics* theory is *eucultural* rather than eugenic. The authors don't claim that genes destine certain unborn children to be criminals; poor upbringing, brought on by their unwantedness, does. Such distinctions probably have little to do with the *popularity* of the theory.

15.   See George Will, "It's Better to Exercise the Right to Live," *Augusta Chronicle*, April 14, 2005.

16.   Jim Holt, "Euthanasia for Babies?" *New York Times Magazine*, July 10, 2005.

17.   Bernard Nathanson, *The Hand of God* (Regnery, 1996), esp. pp. 129, 140-41.

Chapter 15

1.   Singer, *Practical Ethics*, 2nd Ed. (Cambridge: Cambridge University Press, 1993), pp. 170-1.

2.   Peter Singer, "The Sanctity of Life: Here Today, Gone Tomorrow," *Foreign Policy*, Sept./Oct. 2005.

3.   Singer, *Practical Ethics*, p. 182.

4.   *Ibid.*, p. 173.

5.   *Ibid.*, p. 183. Cf. Jim Holt, a popular writer on science and philosophy: "Like any sane person, Singer opposes the killing of healthy newborns, just as he opposes late-term abortions" (slate.msn.com/id/2000013/entry/1002123/). See also Krishna Guha, "Lunch with the FT: Meaty arguments," *Financial Times*, July 29, 2005.

6.   *Ibid.*, pp. 186, 190-91.

7.   Kathryn Federici Greenwood, "Dangerous Words" (interview with Singer), *Princeton Alumni Weekly*, Jan. 26, 2000. Singer's case-by-case

review would balance "the seriousness of the problems. . . against the age of the child," but on his professed principles the review should examine only whether the infant is aware of its own existence over time. If it isn't, and its parents would be happy to kill it, their happiness should be the decisive factor. For someone so proud to be provocative, he is eager to downplay the scope of his radicalism.

8.   Marvin Olasky, "Blue-State Philosopher," *World Magazine*, Nov. 27, 2004.

9.   Singer, *Practical Ethics*, pp. 353-9.

10. See Wesley Smith, *Culture of Death* (San Francisco: Encounter Books, 2000), pp. 59-60.

11. Michael Tooley, "Abortion and Infanticide," *Philosophy & Public Affairs*, Vol. 2, No. 1 (Autumn 1972), pp. 40, 50-51, and 37-65 general.

12. Mary Anne Warren, "On the Moral and Legal Status of Abortion," in T. A. Mappes and D. DeGrazia, eds., *Biomedical Ethics*, 4th Ed. (New York: McGraw Hill, 1996), pp. 434-440. Emphases in original.

13. Joseph Fletcher, *Humanhood* (Buffalo, New York: Prometheus Books, 1979), p. 144.

14. Jonathan Glover, *Causing Death and Saving Lives* (New York: Penguin Books, 1977), p. 158.

15. John Harris, "The Concept of the Person and the Value of Life," *Kennedy Institute of Ethics Journal*, Vol. 9, No. 4, pp. 293-308.

16. Jeffrey Reiman, *Critical Moral Liberalism* (Lanham, MD: Rowman and Littlefield, 1997), p. 203.

17. Singer, *Practical Ethics*, p. 344 n11.

18. Smith, *op. cit.*, pp. 54-5.

19. Steven Pinker, "Why They Kill Their Newborns," *New York Times Magazine*, Nov. 2, 1997.

20. Jim Holt, "Euthanasia for Babies?" *New York Times Magazine*, July 10, 2005.

21. Astrid Vraaking, "Medical end-of-life decisions made for neonates and infants in the Netherlands, 1995-2001," *The Lancet*, Vol. 365, April 9, 2005, pp. 1329-31. Veerle Provoost et al, "Medical end-of-life decisions in neonates and infants in Flanders," *The Lancet*, Vol. 365, April 9, 2005, pp. 1316-8, indicates that 7 percent of Belgian infants' deaths were caused by doctors' deliberate administration of lethal drugs, with an additional 21 percent caused by doctors' withholding medicine with the sole intent to hasten or cause death. The non-consent figure comes from Wesley Smith, "Now They Want to Euthanize Children," *Weekly Standard*, Sept. 13, 2004.

22. Peter Singer, "Pulling Back the Curtain on the Mercy Killing of Newborns," *Los Angeles Times*, March 11, 2005.

23. Disease, genetic defect, accident, and violence can of course block the development of this capacity in particular human beings, but these possibilities do not call its existence in those beings into question.

24. Anyone who is still worried about the specter of species chauvinism should rest easier at the thought that the members of an extraterrestrial non-human species that had a rational nature—including the immature and handicapped members—would also have rights on this account.

25. Singer, *Practical Ethics*, pp. 188, 190.

26. The same linkage holds true in reverse. A ban on partial-birth abortion makes it more likely that we will eventually ban other abortions, too. How should the person to whom these "slippery slope" arguments are addressed—the person who opposes partial-birth abortion and infanticide but supports legal abortion, at least sometimes—evaluate them? It will depend on how much he thinks legalized abortion increases the risk of legalized infanticide, how much he thinks a ban on partial-birth abortion increases the risk of abortion restrictions he would consider excessive, and how great an evil he thinks legalized infanticide or excessive restrictions on abortion would be. My own view is that legalized infanticide would be a great evil, while most restrictions on abortion would be no evil at all—would be, indeed, a great good.

27. Singer, "The Sanctity of Life."

28. Hoche quoted by Leon Kass, "A More Perfect Human," speech at the U.S. Holocaust Memorial Museum, March 17, 2005.

Chapter 16

1. David Shaw, "Can Women Reporters Write Objectively On Abortion Issue?" *Los Angeles Times*, July 3, 1990.

2. See, e.g., Linda Greenhouse, "A Telling Court Opinion," *New York Times*, July 1, 1992, p. A1; "How a Ruling on Abortion Took On a Life of Its Own," April 10, 1994, Section 4, p. 3.

3. The series ran from July 1 through July 4, 1990.

4. Richard Harwood, "When Readers Are Wrong," *Washington Post*, March 25, 1990, p. C6.

5. Richard Harwood, "A Weekend in April," *Washington Post*, May 6, 1990, attributing the observation to *Post* managing editor Len Downie.

6. Tony Case, "We're Biased," *Editor & Publisher*, Dec. 11, 1993, p. 11.

7. Daniel Okrent, "Is the New York Times a Liberal Newspaper?" *New York Times*, July 25, 2004, Section 4, p. 2.

8. Jonathan Chait, "Victim Politics," *The New Republic*, March 18, 2002.

9. Stanley Rothman and Amy Black, "Media and Business Elites: Still in Conflict?" *The Public Interest*, Spring 2001.

10. David Shaw, "Abortion Bias Seeps Into News," *Los Angeles Times*, July 1, 1990, p. A1.

11. See Chapter 4.

12. Cynthia Gorney, "Gambling with Abortion," *Harper's*, Nov. 2004.

13. David Savage, "Roe's Ruling," *Los Angeles Times*, Sept. 14, 2005.

14. Karen Tumulty, "Where the Real Action Is. . ." *Time*, Jan. 22, 2006.

15. Tara Parker-Pope, "What the New Abortion Legislation Means (and Doesn't Mean) for Women," *Wall Street Journal*, Oct. 28, 2003, p. D1.

16. Susan Milligan, "Senate OKs ban on a later-term form of abortion," *Boston Globe*, March 14, 2003; Bob Egelko, "California abortion rights threatened," *San Francisco Chronicle*, March 15, 2003. The *Miami Herald* also made the false claim, but in an editorial: "A flawed bill," June 6, 2003.

17. Douglas Johnson, memorandum for journalists, Feb. 1, 2003.

18. Kenneth Woodward, "What's in a Name?" *Notre Dame Journal of Law, Ethics & Public Policy*, 2005.

19. Don Wycliff, "Words of discontent about the abortion-debate terminology," *Chicago Tribune*, Nov. 6, 2003.

20. Helen Dewar, "Senate Votes to Override Gag Rule," *Washington Post*, Oct. 2, 1992, p. A1; Michael York, "Court Voids Gag Rule On Abortion," *Washington Post*, Nov. 4, 1992, p. A3; Felicity Barringer, "Untying the Gag," *New York Times*, Nov. 8, 1992, Sec. 4, p. 4;

21. Linda Greenhouse, "Votes to Spare," *New York Times*, Feb. 2, 1992, Section 4, p. 3.

22. "Censoring the Partial-Birth Abortion Basics," Media Research Center news release, Oct. 27, 2003.

23. Sidney Schanberg, "Assembly Blocks Abortion Reform in Sudden Switch," *New York Times*, April 18, 1969, p. 1; Bill Kovach, "Abortion Reform After Long Fight," *NYT*, April 12, 1970, p. E10; Linda Greenhouse, "Constitutional Question: Is There a Right to Abortion?" *New York Times Magazine*, Jan. 25, 1970, p. 88; "Respect for Privacy," editorial, *NYT*, Jan. 24, 1973.

24. Francis X. Clines, "Abortion Bill Advocate: Constance Eberhardt Cook," *NYT*, April 9, 1970, p. 46; David Dempsey, "Dr. Guttmacher Is the Evangelist of Birth Control," *New York Times Magazine*, Feb.

9, 1969; "Abortion Reform At Last," editorial, *NYT*, April 11, 1970, p. 29.

25. Robin Finn, "Choosing When to Be a Mother Hen," *NYT*, Aug. 5, 2005.

26. Patti Davis, "'God Has a Plan,' My Dad Always Said," *Newsweek*, June 21, 2004, p. 34; Claudia Kalb and Debra Rosenberg, "Nancy's Next Campaign," p. 38; Jonathan Alter, "Reagan's Last Political Gift," p. 45.

27. Evan Thomas and Eleanor Clift, "Battle for Bush's Soul," *Newsweek*, July 9, 2001, p. 28; Sharon Begley, "Cellular Divide," p. 22; Kenneth Woodward, "A Question of Life or Death," p. 31.

28. *World News Tonight*, ABC, March 18, 2005; *CBS Evening News*, March 31, 2005.

29. Brain-dead descriptions: Wolf Blitzer on CNN, March 18, 2005; Deepak Chopra on CNN, March 25, 2005; Dan Abrams on MSNBC, March 18, 2005; Vickie Chachere, "Schiavo guardian calls for definitive tests," Associated Press, Jan. 26, 2005; Lynn Sweet, "Lawmakers jump in where closest loved ones fear to tread," *Chicago Sun-Times*, March 24, 2005, p. 35; "Gov. Jeb Bush Doesn't Have the Last Word" (editorial), *San Jose Mercury News*, Sept. 27, 2004, p. 6B; Mike Thomas, "No Scripps, But It's a Great Place to Visit," *Orlando Sentinel*, Oct. 31, 2003, p. B1; Sheryl McCarthy, "However Hard, Terri Schiavo Has To Be Let Go," *Newsday*, Oct. 20, 2003, p. A24. Terminally ill: Carol Lin on CNN, March 26, 2005. John Schwartz, "New Openness in Deciding When and How to Die," *NYT*, March 21, 2005, p. A1, strongly implies terminal illness.

30. Wesley Smith, *Culture of Death* (Encounter Books, 2002), p. 100; Mike Wallace, "A Note on Dr. Kevorkian and Timothy McVeigh," *New York Review of Books*, July 5, 2001.

31. Michael Betzold, "The Selling of Doctor Death," *The New Republic*, May 26, 1997.

Chapter 17

1. Charles Krauthammer, "Abortion: The Debate is Over," *Washington Post*, Dec. 4, 1992, p. A31.

2. Michael Fletcher, "Bush the Conservative vs. Bush the Pragmatist," *Washington Post*, Oct. 9, 2005, p. A11.

3. I draw throughout from Karlyn Bowman's compilation of abortion polls, available at www.aei.org/publicopinion15, and additional polls available at pollingreport.com/abortion.htm.

4. Center for Gender Equality news release, Jan. 27, 1999.

5. Statement by David O'Steen, Nov. 4, 2004. That 40 percent included 15 percent who thought it should be legal in the second trimester, which in turn included 9 percent who thought it should be legal throughout pregnancy.

6. See John Westfall et al, "Abortion attitudes and practices of family and general practice physicians," *Journal of Family Practice*, July 1991; and "Views and Practices of Women's Health Care Providers on Medical Abortion," Kaiser Foundation Survey Snapshot, Sept. 2001, for evidence of significant moral qualms about abortion among doctors.

7. Rachel Fudge, "You Can't Do That on Television," *Utne Reader*, Sept.-Oct. 2005, pp. 43-46; Jennifer Lenhart, "The Last Taboo," *Soap Opera Digest & Weekly*, May 20, 2005.

8. Rebecca Raber, "Born Again," *Village Voice*, Nov. 15, 2005 (emphasis in original).

9. Fawn Vrazo, "Adoption ads spur wrangling," *Houston Chronicle*, March 21, 1992, p. A9; Maria McFadden, "The Choice that Pro-Choicers Aren't Pro," *National Review*, June 7, 1993; Jennifer Pozner, "Pro-Choice Not Networks' Choice," *Extra!* Sept./Oct. 2000; Jennifer Baumgardner, "The Pro-choice PR Problem," *The Nation*, March 5, 2001; Michelman, *With Liberty and Justice For All*, p. 161.

10. I'm using somewhat old data because media exit pollsters have stopped asking the question in useful form.

11. Debra Rosenberg, "Roe's Army Reloads," *Newsweek*, Aug. 8, 2005.

12. This discomfort gives an advantage to the side that can portray its opponents as the aggressor in any fight. Establishing which side is the aggressor thus becomes an important point of contention in debates surrounding abortion. Are Republicans being aggressive when they nominate a justice who might overrule *Roe*, for example, or are Democrats being aggressive when they raise the issue? Each side will want to blame the other for forcing a discussion of abortion.

13. Michael New, "Analyzing the Effects of State Legislation on the Incidence of Abortion During the 1990s," Report of the Heritage [Foundation] Center for Data Analysis, Jan. 21, 2004. See also his report, "Using Natural Experiments to Analyze the Impact of State Legislation on the Incidence of Abortion," issued by the same group, Jan. 23, 2006.

14. P.J. Huffstutter and Stephanie Simon, "States Step Up Fight on Abortion," *Los Angeles Times*, Jan. 22, 2006.

15. Alina Tugend, "Confronting Abortion Anew," *Los Angeles Times*, July 8, 2005, p. A28; Elizabeth Hayt, "Surprise, Mom: I'm Against Abortion," *New York Times*, March 30, 2003.

16. Susan Dominus, "The mysterious disappearance of young pro-choice women," *Glamour*, Aug. 2005, pp. 200-1.

17. Norma McCorvey with Gary Thomas, *Won by Love* (Thomas Nelson, 1998), excerpted at leaderu.com/common/roev.html; David Garrow, *Liberty and Sexuality*, p. 402; Douglas Wood, "Who is 'Jane Roe'?" CNN.com, Jan. 1998; Genevieve Kineke, "Roe No More," *Catholic Exchange*, Jan. 22, 2002. See also Naomi Wolf, "Our Bodies, Our Souls," *The New Republic*, Oct. 16, 1995, on the feminist reaction to McCorvey's switch.

Chapter 18

1. Kristen Day, "A Pro-Choice Party No More," *National Review Online*, Dec. 2, 2004.

2. Katha Pollitt, "Regressive Progressive?" *The Nation*, May 9, 2002.

3. Mark Shields, "The 'tolerant' Democrats," CNN.com, July 21, 2003.

4. Rob Moll, "Putting (Pro)Life into the Party" (interview with Kristen Day), *Christianity Today Online*, July 30, 2004.

5. The numbers understate how liberal, and pro-life, Kildee is. The National Right to Life Committee foolishly treated a vote for Bush's Medicare reform bill as a vote against euthanasia. If not for that decision, Kildee would have scored 100 percent. (Doyle would have, too, and McNulty would have scored 90 percent). If the ADA didn't count two abortion votes in its tally, Doyle would have scored 89 and Kildee and McNulty would have had perfect 100s.

6. John Leland, "Some Abortion Foes Forgo Politics for Quiet Talk," *New York Times*, Jan. 16. 2006, p. A1.

7. Jim Kessler, "The Demographics of Abortion," Third Way Issue Brief, p. 8.

8. Mark Roche, "Voting Our Conscience, Not Our Religion," *New York Times*, Oct. 11, 2004.

9. Glen Harold Stassen, "Pro-Life? Look at the fruits," *Sojourners* email newsletter, Oct. 13, 2004; Stassen and Gary Krane, "Why Abortion Rate Is Up In Bush Years," *Houston Chronicle*, Oct. 17, 2004.

10. He had taken no account of the unreliability of state governments' abortion statistics or of changes in their methods of collecting those statistics. (Most abortion researchers prefer to use other data sources.)

11. Sen. Hillary Clinton, speech to New York State Abortion Providers, Jan. 24, 2005; *Inside Politics*, May 26, 2005.

12. *Meet the Press*, Jan. 30, 2005; David Kirkpatrick, "Some Democrats Believe the Party Should Get Religion," *New York Times*, Nov. 17, 2004, p. A20; Nicholas Kristof, "Who Gets It? Hillary?" *NYT*, March 16, 2005, p. A23.

13. *Meet the Press*, May 22, 2005.
14. Lawrence Finer and Stanley Henshaw, "Estimates of U.S. Abortion Incidence in 2001 and 2002," Alan Guttmacher Institute paper, May 18, 2005; Randall O'Bannon, "California Seminary Prof. Pushes Unsubstantiated Claim that Abortions Increased under Bush," National Right to Life News, Nov. 2004, p. 14.
15. "The Biography of a Bad Statistic," Factcheck.org, May 25, 2005.
16. Jayson Whitehead, "I'm a Pro-Life Democrat" (interview with Kristen Day), *OldSpeak*, Sept. 24, 2004.
17. "The America we seek: a statement of pro-life principle and concern," *National Review*, March 25, 1996.
18. Jim Wallis, God's Politics (HarperCollins, 2005), p. 11; James Nuechterlein, "False Prophet," *Commentary*, June 2005.

Chapter 19

1. Stan Greenberg, James Carville, and Bob Shrum, "Politics After the Attack," Democracy Corps memo, Nov. 13, 2001; see also Howard Fineman, "Bush's Next Challenge," *Newsweek*, Dec. 31, 2001, p. 93.
2. Mark Gunderman, "Kerry delivers some specific ideas on campaign ride through state," *La Crosse Tribune*, July 4, 2004; Matea Gold, "Kerry Talking a Fine Line on Abortion," *Los Angeles Times*, July 26, 2004, p. A11; Joan Vennochi, "Can two Johns re-create a Jack?" *Boston Globe*, July 13, 2004; *World News Tonight*, July 22, 2004.
3. See, e.g., Kerry's votes on July 16, 1991, and Sept. 22, 1998.
4. Michelman, *With Liberty and Justice for All*, pp. 265-66.
5. Mary Curtius, "Antiabortion Groups Hope for Senate Support," *Los Angeles Times*, Dec. 26. 2004, p. A36.
6. Stan Greenberg with Matt Hogan, "Reclaiming the White Catholic Vote," Democracy Corps memo, March 29, 2005.
7. William Galston and Elaine Kamarck, "The Politics of Polarization," report for ThirdWay, October 2005, p. 61.
8. Debra Rosenberg, "Anxiety over Abortion," *Newsweek*, Dec. 20, 2004 (emphasis in original).
9. *Hardball*, July 25, 2005.
10. Adam Nagourney, "Democrats Weigh De-Emphasizing Abortion as an Issue," *New York Times*, Dec. 24, 2004.
11. Michael Lind, "The Only Way That Democrats Can Regain A Majority," Aug. 4, 2005, post at tpmcafe.com.
12. Susan Milligan, "Democrats eye softer image on abortion," *Boston Globe*, Dec. 19, 2004.
13. Fred Barnes, "When Harry Met *Roe*," *Weekly Standard*, Dec. 27, 2004.

14.   Thomas Fitzgerald, "Santorum a top target for Democrats," *Philadel-
      phia Inquirer*, March 30, 2005, p. B1.
15.   Sheryl Gay Stolberg and David Kirkpatrick, "Top Democrat Says
      He'll Vote No on Roberts," *New York Times*, Sept. 21, 2005, p. A1.
16.   Jill Lawrence, "Liberals respond to Dean's Rallying Cry," *USA Today*,
      March 13, 2003; *Meet the Press*, June 22, 2003.
17.   *Meet the Press*, Dec. 12, 2004; *Meet the Press*, May 22, 2005.
18.   *Hardball*, Oct. 31, 2005.
19.   See Patrick Healy, "Clinton Seeking Shared Ground Over Abor-
      tions," *New York Times*, Jan. 25, 2005; Greg Sargent, "Brand Hillary,"
      The Nation, June 6, 2005; E. R. Shipp, "Hillary Clinton's abortion
      stand shows compromise," *Milwaukee Journal-Sentinel*, Feb. 6, 2005;
      William Saletan, "Safe, Legal, and Never," *Slate*, Jan. 26, 2005;
      Michelle Cottle, "Moral Dilemma," *The New Republic Online*, Jan.
      28, 2005; Carl Cannon, "Why Not Hillary?" *Washington Monthly*,
      July/August 2005.
20.   Sen. Hillary Clinton, speech to New York State Abortion Providers,
      Jan. 24, 2005.
21.   Such as Margaret Atwood's *The Handmaid's Tale* (Houghton Mifflin,
      1986).
22.   Morton Kondracke, "Sen. Clinton Shows How Democrats Can Woo
      'Heartland,'" *Roll Call*, Feb. 1, 2005.
23.   Vice president Al Gore, speech to NARAL, Jan. 22, 1997.
24.   Hillary Clinton, speech to NARAL, Jan. 22, 1999.
25.   Matt Bai, "Democratic Moral Values?" *New York Times Magazine*,
      April 24, 2005, p. 25.

Chapter 20

1.   Michael Fletcher, "Bush the Conservative vs. Bush the Pragmatist,"
      Washington Post, Oct. 9, 2005, p. A11.
2.   Cass Sunstein, *Radicals in Robes: Why Extreme Right-Wing Courts
      Are Wrong for America* (Basic Books, 2005), Ch. 3, p. 105.
3.   Susan Dominus, "The mysterious disappearance of young pro-choice
      women," *Glamour*, Aug. 2005, p. 219.
4.   Stuart Taylor Jr., "What Does Bush Want From the Supreme Court?"
      National Journal, Nov. 22, 2004. See also Jeffrey Rosen, "Worst
      Choice," *The New Republic*, Feb. 24, 2003; Benjamin Wittes, "Let-
      ting Goe of *Roe*," *Atlantic Monthly*, Jan./Feb. 2005.
5.   Dan Balz, "Rep. Davis Warns of Backlash if Roe v. Wade is Over-
      turned," *Washington Post*, Nov. 17, 2005, p. A8; James Barnes and
      Peter Bell, "Political Insiders Poll," *National Journal*, Sept. 3, 2005, p.
      2627.

6. These mini-*Roes* make the scenario of pro-life political doom even
    less likely. State courts would have made it harder for pro-lifers to
    overreach.

7. Ron Harris, "Reasons abound for anti-abortion camp's lack of minori-
    ties," *St. Louis Post-Dispatch*, Jan. 29, 2006, p. A1.

8. In determining whether the law had sufficient deterrent effect, it
    would be important to remember that perfection is unattainable,
    there being lawbreaking under any legal regime.

9. Frederica Mathewes-Green, "Beyond 'It's a Baby,'" *National Review*,
    Dec. 31, 1997, p. 41.

10. The estimate can be found in the Alan Guttmacher Institute's "State
    Facts About Abortion" reports; I reached a similar conclusion in
    "Raw Numbers," *Human Life Review*, Fall 1999.

Index